DATE DUE

BRODART, CO.   Cat. No. 23-221-003

Global Civil Society?

John Keane, a leading political thinker, tracks the recent development of a powerful big idea – global civil society. Keane explores the jumble of contradictory forces currently nurturing or threatening its growth, and shows how talk of global civil society implies a political vision of a less violent world founded on legally sanctioned power-sharing arrangements among many different and intermingling forms of socio-economic life. Keane's reflections are pitted against the widespread feeling that the world is both too complex or too violent and crazy to deserve serious reflection. His account borrows from various scholarly disciplines, including political science and international relations, to challenge the normative silence and confusion within much of the contemporary literature on globalisation and global governance. Against fears of terrorism, rising tides of xenophobia, and loose talk of 'anti-globalisation', the defence of global civil society mounted here implies the need for new democratic ways of living – and for brand-new democratic thinking about such planetary matters as global markets, uncivil war, university life, and government with a global reach.

JOHN KEANE is founder of the Centre for the Study of Democracy and Professor of Politics at the University of Westminster. Born in Australia and educated at the universities of Adelaide, Toronto and Cambridge, he is a frequent contributor to radio programmes and newspapers and magazines around the world. Among his books are *The Media and Democracy* (1991), which has been translated into more than twenty-five languages; the prize-winning biography *Tom Paine: A Political Life* (1995); *Civil Society: Old Images, New Visions*, (1998); and a biography of power, *Václav Havel: A Political Tragedy in Six Acts* (1999). He was recently Karl Deutsch Professor of Political Science at the Wissenschaftszentrum Berlin and a Fellow of the influential London-based think-tank, the Institute for Public Policy Research. He is currently writing a full-scale history of democracy – the first for over a century.

Contemporary Political Theory

Series Editor
Ian Shapiro

Editorial Board
Russell Hardin Stephen Holmes Jeffrey Isaac
John Keane Elizabeth Kiss Susan Okin
Phillipe Van Parijs Philip Pettit

As the twenty-first century begins, major new political challenges have arisen at
the same time as some of the most enduring dilemmas of political association
remain unresolved. The collapse of communism and the end of the Cold War
reflect a victory for democratic and liberal values, yet in many of the Western
countries that nurtured those values there are severe problems of urban decay,
class and racial conflict, and failing political legitimacy. Enduring global injustice and inequality seem compounded by environmental problems, disease, the
oppression of women, racial, ethnic, and religious minorities and the relentless
growth of the world's population. In such circumstances, the need for creative
thinking about the fundamentals of human political association is manifest. This
new series in contemporary political theory is needed to foster such systematic
normative reflection.

The series proceeds in the belief that the time is ripe for a reassertion of the
importance of problem-driven political theory. It is concerned, that is, with works
that are motivated by the impulse to understand, think critically about, and address the problems in the world, rather than issues that are thrown up primarily
in academic debate. Books in the series may be interdisciplinary in character,
ranging over issues conventionally dealt with in philosophy, law, history and the
human sciences. The range of materials and the methods of proceeding should
be dictated by the problem at hand, not the conventional debates or disciplinary
divisions of academia.

Other books in the series

Ian Shapiro and Casiano Hacker-Cordón (eds.)
Democracy's Value

Ian Shapiro and Casiano Hacker-Cordón (eds.)
Democracy's Edges

Brooke A. Ackerly
Political Theory and Feminist Social Criticism

Clarissa Rile Hayward
De-Facing Power

John Kane
The Politics of Moral Capital

Ayelet Shachar
Multicultural Jurisdictions: Cultural Differences and Women's Rights

Global Civil Society?

John Keane
University of Westminster

9145949

PUBLISHED BY THE PRESS SYNDICATE OF THE UNIVERSITY OF CAMBRIDGE
The Pitt Building, Trumpington Street, Cambridge CB2 1RP, United Kingdom

CAMBRIDGE UNIVERSITY PRESS
The Edinburgh Building, Cambridge, CB2 2RU, UK
40 West 20th Street, New York, NY 10011-4211, USA
477 Williamstown Road, Port Melbourne, VIC 3207, Australia
Ruiz de Alarcón 13, 28014 Madrid, Spain
Dock House, The Waterfront, Cape Town 8001, South Africa

http://www.cambridge.org

First published 2003

Printed in the United Kingdom at the University Press, Cambridge

Typeface Plantin 10/12 pt   *System* LaTeX 2$_\varepsilon$ [TB]

A catalogue record for this book is available from the British Library

ISBN 0 521 81543 6 hardback
ISBN 0 521 89462 X paperback

For Jürgen Kocka

Nimmt die Welt wie sie ist, nicht wie sie sein sollte
(Take the world as it is, not as it ought to be)

(Old German proverb)

Contents

Preface

Big ideas, attempts at grasping the whole world in thought, are renowned for breeding discontent and raising future expectations. Big ideas are also well-known sources of fear and contempt among their opponents, who accuse them of oversimplified descriptions of the world, often suspecting them as well of serving as ideological alibis for power groups bent on dominating others. So controversy and opposition have been the fate of all modern versions of the big idea: the recent claim that history has ended in undisputed victory for liberal democracy and free markets, for instance, has fared no better in this respect than the earlier presumptions that socialism would win world victory, or that fascist dictatorship would purify nations and make them capable of super-human achievement.

Given this jumbled history of humbled big ideas, eyebrows may well cock at the large claim made in this slim book. Concerned with globalisation and its discontents, it puts forward the thesis that a big but modest idea with fresh potency – global civil society – is today on the rise. The book explores the historical origins of this planetary vision and analyses its present-day meanings and usages and future political potential. Not only does the argument suppose that periodic fascination with big ideas is a necessary condition of politically imagining a social order. The book also notes the unusual promiscuousness of the idea of global civil society – its remarkable ability to attract a wide variety of supporters in all four corners of the earth. It sees this promiscuity as a symptom of contemporary struggles to make sense of the growth spurt of globalisation now unfolding before our eyes. So attention is paid to the forces – turbocapitalism, global media, social movements, publicly funded universities and other governmental agencies – that are currently nurturing its growth. Violence, xenophobia, hunger, fatalism and other forces presently thwarting this new global vision are also foregrounded. Political distinctions and theoretical qualifications are made, including the point that global civil society – a neologism of the 1990s – is a big idea with a radical difference. When used by its friends as an ethical standard, I argue, it champions the political vision of a world founded on non-violent, legally sanctioned power-sharing arrangements among many different and interconnected forms of socio-economic life that are distinct from governmental institutions. The pluralist ideal of a global civil society openly challenges previous big ideas, all of which were held together by monistic presumptions of one sort or another. The whole image of a global civil society finds monism distasteful. To speak of a global civil society in empirical terms is to emphasise the fact that most people's lives today dangle on ten thousand different global strings. To speak of a global civil society in normative terms is to dismiss the big ideas of the past as wooden horses used by certain power groups to build unaccountable institutions wrapped in ideological deception – in the extreme case, by pushing victims down the dark alleyways of terror, cruelty and organised murder.

These reflections on global civil society may be seen as an experiment conducted in the laboratories of contemporary democratic thinking. Their findings are neither pessimistic nor optimistic, but they are definitely pitted against the widespread feeling that the world is going to the dogs: that it is both too complex or too violent and crazy to deserve serious reflection. The experiment draws upon a variety of scholarly disciplines, including political science, modern history, geography, anthropology, economics and international relations. The work is intended as a contribution to the field of applied political philosophy, as a small gift to those who are interested in the practical importance of ideas. The vision of a global civil society is presented as a challenge to the normative silence or confusion within much of the contemporary literature on globalisation and global governance. In opposition to mounting fears of terrorism, rising tides of bigotry and nationalism and loose talk of 'anti-globalisation', the defence of global civil society mounted here implies the need for a defence of democratic ways of life – and for brand-new democratic thinking about such matters as violence, global markets, and government with a global reach. The claims made in support of a global civil society try hard to be hard-nosed. They are not simple-minded defences of 'the West', or of 'liberalism', or of 'cosmopolitanism' or empire: they are something different, something new.

Some readers may be surprised to discover that the case presented here challenges those who are enamoured of the idea of a 'civil society', especially those purists (as I call them) who set aside the muck of markets, conflict and violence and treat this society as a pleasant and peaceful form of voluntary cooperation – as something of a recipe for heaven on earth. This book calls on these purists to move on in their thinking. It reminds them and others that the resurgence of the concept of civil society is among the most significant developments within the contemporary human sciences. This originally eighteenth-century ideal continues to gain ground both inside and outside of academia; and it now seems probable that it will dominate the intellectual agenda in the years to come. That is why this book sides with efforts to radicalise the language of civil society. Against the forces of parochialism and social injustice, hubris and cruelty, it tries to breathe new life into this old language by pushing for answers to the following types of questions: supposing that the 'real-world' relationship between civil societies and territorial state forms is not necessary but contingent, does it make sense to say that a borderless 'global civil society' is today emerging? If so, what does the term mean? What are its origins? Is it important to distinguish among its different – descriptive, strategic, normative – uses? Can radically different understandings of the term 'civil society' in regions with different histories – in the Indian subcontinent, no less than in Muslim societies and in China – be represented within the idea of a global civil society? Given that such a society is fundamentally important in providing 'nests' and livelihoods for millions of people, and in constraining the unaccountable and bellicose governmental and corporate powers that currently shadow the world, how can a global civil society – a basic precondition of the democratisation of the emerging global order – be politically and legally secured? From 'below', through non-governmental organisations (NGOs) and social action alone? Through the influence and war-fighting capacity of the world's dominant power, the United States? Via the United Nations, or perhaps through a variety of context-dependent social and political strategies? What roles can global civil society play in the process of global governance? Can this society perhaps help to redefine the *universal* entitlements and duties of the peoples of the world, across borders?

Hannah Arendt once observed that giving a stray dog a name greatly increases its chances of staying alive. So might it be that a clearly articulated vision of global civil society – calling upon its friends to unite against misery and unfreedom – is a significant first step in the political task of re-naming our world, of offering it hope by freshly defining its future?

London 1 August 2002   JOHN KEANE

Unfamiliar words

A new cosmology

All human orders, hunting and gathering societies included, have lived off shared images of the cosmos, world-views that served to plant the feet of their members firmly in space and time. Yet very few have fantasised the linking of the five oceans, six continents and peoples of our little blue planet wrapped in white vapour. Each of these world-views in the strict sense emerged only after the military defeats suffered by Islam, in early modern Europe. They included the forceful global acquisition of territory, resources and subjects in the name of empire; the efforts of Christendom to pick-a-back on imperial ventures for the purpose of bringing spiritual salvation to earth; and the will to unify the world through the totalitarian violence of fascism and Marxism–Leninism. Each of these globalising projects left indelible marks on the lives of the world's peoples, their institutions and ecosystems, but each also failed to accomplish its mission. In our times, against the backdrop of those failures, the image of ourselves as involved in another great human adventure, one carried out on a global scale, is again on the rise. A new world-view, radically different from any that has existed before, has been born and is currently enjoying a growth spurt: it is called global civil society.

These unfamiliar words 'global civil society' – a neologism of the 1990s – are fast becoming fashionable. They were born at the confluence of seven overlapping streams of concern among publicly-minded intellectuals at the end of the 1980s: the revival of the old language of civil society, especially in central–eastern Europe, after the military crushing of the Prague Spring; a heightening appreciation of the revolutionary effects of the new galaxy of satellite/computer-mediated communications (captured in Marshall McLuhan's famous neologism, 'the global village'); the new awareness, stimulated by the peace and ecological movements, of ourselves as members of a fragile and potentially self-destructive world system; the widespread perception that the implosion of Soviet-type communist systems implied a new global political order; the world-wide growth spurt of neo-liberal economics and market capitalist economies; the disillusionment with the broken and unfulfilled promises of post-colonial states; and the rising concern about the dangerous and misery-producing vacuums opened up by the collapse of empires and states and the outbreak of uncivil wars.[1] Fed by these developments, talk of global civil society has become popular among citizens' campaigners, bankers, diplomats, NGOs and politicians. World Bank documents welcome 'the opportunity to work with civil society'; the Asian Development Bank (ADB) similarly speaks of the need to 'strengthen cooperation with civil society'; and even the World Trade Organisation (WTO) declares its support for dialogue with the world's civil society institutions.[2] The phrase 'global civil society' becomes protean and promiscuous. It even peppers speeches of prominent figures like UN Secretary-General Kofi Annan, former US Secretary of State, Madeleine Albright, and Chancellor Schröder, sometimes to the point where the words themselves become as fickle as they are fashionable.

There is today much chatter about global civil society, but too little thinking about it. That is why the phrase 'global civil society' must be used with caution. Like all other vocabularies with a political edge, its meaning is neither self-evident nor automatically free of prejudice. So how can we best think about these words? Current usages are quite confused. There is general agreement that talk of global civil society is a response to rising concerns about the need for a new social and economic and political deal at the global level. And parallels are sometimes observed with the early modern European invention of the distinction between 'government' and 'civil society', which emerged during the period of questioning of the transcendental foundations of order, especially

[1] Among the earliest expressions of these concerns is the theory of a 'world civic culture' in Elise Boulding, *Building a Global Civic Culture. Education for an Interdependent World* (New York, 1988); the idea of 'global civilization' in the working paper by Richard Falk, 'Economic Dimensions of Global Civilization' (Global Civilization Project, Center for International Studies, Princeton University, 1990); the theory of the 'internationalisation' of civil society and the terms 'cosmopolitan civil society' and 'global' or 'transnational' civil society in John Keane, 'The Future of Civil Society', in Tatjana Sikosha, *The Internationalisation of Civil Society* (The Hague, 1989) and *The Media and Democracy* (Cambridge, 1991), pp. 135ff.; and Morten Ougaard, 'The Internationalisation of Civil Society' (Center for Udviklingsforskning, Copenhagen, June 1990). Among the first efforts to draw together this early work is Ronnie Lipschutz, 'Reconstructing World Politics: The Emergence of Global Civil Society', *Millennium*, 21:3 (1992), pp. 389–420.

[2] Each case is cited in Aziz Choudry, 'All this 'civil society' talk takes us nowhere', http://globalresearch.ca/articles/AZ1201A.html, p. xxi; cf. the call for 'a new international social covenant between markets, states and civil society', in Gerhard Schröder (ed.), *Progressive Governance for the XXI Century* (München, 2002), p. xxi; 'The United Nations: Partners in Civil Society', www.un.org/partners/civil_society/home.htm; Madeleine Albright, *Focus on the Issues. Strengthening Civil Society and the Rule of Law. Excerpts of Testimony, Speeches and Remarks by US Secretary of State Madeleine K. Albright* (Washington, DC, 2000).

of monarchic states claiming authority from God.[3] Beyond this elementary consensus, many discrepancies and disagreements are evident. Some writers see in the idea of global civil society a way of analysing the empirical contours of past, present or emergent social relationships at the world level. Others mainly view the concept in pragmatic terms, as a guide to formulating a political strategy; still others view it as a normative ideal. In practice, these different emphases often criss-cross and complement each other. Yet since they can and do also produce divergent types of claims, it is important to distinguish among them and, as far as possible, to avoid mixing them up and producing confusion.[4]

Analytic–descriptive usages of the term 'global civil society' selectively name key institutions, actors and events, examine their complex dynamics and – using theoretical distinctions, empirical research and informed judgements – attempt to draw some conclusions about their origins, current development patterns and (unintended) consequences. Within such analyses – the first and second sections of this book are an example – the concept of global civil society is used to probe either the past or the present, or both past and present simultaneously. The aim of such probes is not to recommend political strategies or to pass normative judgements on the world; they rather seek an explanatory understanding of the world's complex socio-political realities. The term global civil society also can be used as an aid to *strategic political calculation*. In this second approach, evident in this book's treatment of global social movements, the term serves as a campaigning criterion – to establish what must be done (or what must be avoided) in order to reach goals, like freedom and justice, whose desirability is more or less presumed. Strategic uses of the term are directly concerned with political questions. They concentrate upon institutional constraints and opportunities as well as the manoeuvres of power groups and movements – upon the (potential) political gains and losses of supporters and opponents that operate from within or outside the structures of global civil society. The normative concerns that inevitably attend such 'tactical' approaches are treated as a given; their

---

[3] Compare my 'Despotism and Democracy: The Origins and Development of the Distinction Between Civil Society and the State 1750–1850', in John Keane (ed.), *Civil Society and the State: New European Perspectives* (London and New York, 1988 [reprinted 1998] pp. 35–72 and Adam Seligman, 'Civil Society as Idea and Ideal', in Simone Chambers and Will Kymlicka (eds.), *Alternative Conceptions of Civil Society* (Princeton, 2002), pp. 13–33. In my view, Seligman's explanation of the rise of the ideal of a civil society suffers from the same weakness evident in Marxian accounts: their one-sided emphasis upon the growth of market economies and the corresponding search for a new ethical order in which individual interests could be reconciled with the public good.

[4] The importance of distinguishing among these different usages is analysed in more detail in my introduction to *Civil Society and the State: New European Perspectives* and *Civil Society: Old Images, New Visions* (Oxford and Stanford, 1998).

main preoccupation is with the calculation of the *means* of achieving or stabilising a global civil society. Finally – as evidenced by the final section of this book – the term global civil society can be wielded as a *normative ideal*. The ethic or big idea of a global civil society is said to be warranted and plausible and desirable, and on that basis it can be used in two complementary ways: as a *precautionary* concept that serves to issue warnings about the undesirable or unworkable consequences of practical efforts to weaken or abolish the institutions of global civil society, for instance through unilateral military intervention, or the imposition of martial law. Such precautionary usages of the norm are usually reinforced by its *advocacy* function: gentle or strong efforts to explain and highlight the reasons why a global civil society, ethically speaking, is a good thing.

Empirical contours

Given the versatility of the term, which is surely one of the reasons for its rising popularity, it follows that its different usages should not be conflated, as is typically done when the words global civil society are flung about in vague, simplistic or tendentious speech. This is the point at which empirically minded researchers arrive on the scene. They point out that the quest to map and measure the contours of global civil society is essential for clarifying its empirical scope and complexity, its strategic or political capacity and its normative potential. They call upon the facts to speak for themselves. They pursue (what appears to them, anyway) a straightforward empirical approach that supposes (as the American expression has it) that if something in the world walks like a duck and quacks like a duck, then it is a duck. The approach points to the sketchy data that are available, thanks to the path-breaking contributions of bodies like the Union of International Associations, the *Index on Civil Society* project supported by CIVICUS (World Alliance for Citizen Participation), a Ford Foundation-funded comparative study of civil society in twenty-two countries and other recent publications. These data-gathering efforts are seen to confirm the widespread impression that, during the twentieth century, the world witnessed a tectonic – perhaps two hundred-fold – increase in the number and variety of civil society organisations operating at the planetary level.[5] Today, in addition to many hundreds of thousands

---

[5] See www.ids.ac.uk; Helmut Anheier *et al.* (eds.) *Global Civil Society 2001* (Oxford, 2001); and the data covering the period 1909–7 presented in the Union of International Associations (ed.), *Yearbook of International Organizations*, 34th edn. (München, 1997–8), vol. 4, p. 559; compare René-Jean Dupuy (ed.), *Manuel sur les organisations internationals* (Dordrecht, 1998); Thomas Risse-Kappen (ed.), *Bringing Transnational Relations Back In. Non-State Actors, Domestic Structures and International Institutions* (Cambridge,

of small, medium and large firms doing business across borders – a trend that is dealt with shortly in this book – there are an estimated 5,000 world congresses held annually and some 50,000 non-governmental, not-for-profit organisations operating at the global level. The numbers of these international non-governmental organisations (INGOs) have grown rapidly in recent years; helped along by access to money and communications technology, many thousands have come into being since 1985. Nearly 90 per cent of them have been formed since 1970.[6] While a disproportionate number (over one-third) have their main offices in the European Union and Switzerland, these INGOs now operate in all four corners of the earth, including sub-Saharan Africa, where hundreds of main offices are now based. INGOs employ or use volunteer labour of several millions of people: one study estimates that in Germany, France, Spain, Japan, Brazil, Argentina, the United Kingdom and the Netherlands alone, INGOs employ over 110,000 full-time equivalent workers as well as many more full-time equivalent volunteers.[7] INGOs currently disburse more money than the United Nations (excluding the World Bank and the International Monetary Fund (IMF)); more than two-thirds of the European Union's relief aid is currently channelled through them; and in many parts of the world there is a strong trend towards the disbursement of governmental funds – currently totalling $US 7 billion per annum – more or less exclusively through INGOs.[8]

Empirical perspectives on global civil society have limitations. In spite of a growing body of data, the actual contours of global civil society remain elusive, for understandable reasons. Histories of the globalisation of civil society – studies of the rise of cross-border business, religion and sport, for instance – are in short supply.[9] Lots of activities within this society, for instance the travel patterns of individuals, the initiatives of grass-roots groups, the loose networks of organisations and the growth

---

1995); Jessica T. Matthews, 'Power Shift', *Foreign Affairs*, 76: 1 (January–February 1997), pp. 50–66; and the misleadingly titled, country-by-country study by Lester M. Salamon *et al.*, *Global Civil Society. Dimensions of the Non-Profit Sector* (Baltimore, 2001).

[6] See the country-by-country figures – covering only the numbers of secretariats of not-for-profit NGOs that operate transnationally – in Anheier *et al.* (eds.), *Global Civil Society*, table R19, pp. 283–6; cf. Michael Edwards, 'Herding Cats? Civil Society and Global Governance', *New Economy* (Summer 2002).

[7] See the figures drawn from The Johns Hopkins Comparative Non-Profit Sector Project (1999), originally published as Salamon *et al.*, *Global Civil Society*, summarised in Anheier *et al.* (eds.), *Global Civil Society*, table, R24, p. 302.

[8] OECD, *Geographical Distribution of Financial Aid to Developing Countries* (Paris, 1997); compare Anheier *et al.* (eds.), *Global Civil Society*, table R19, pp. 283–6.

[9] But on these topics see, for instance, Eric Hobsbawm, *The Age of Empire 1875–1914* (New York, 1989); Jack Beeching, *An Open Path. Christian Missionaries 1515–1914* (London, 1979); Joseph Maguire, *Global Sport. Identities, Societies, Civilizations* (Oxford, 1999); and Lincoln Allison, 'Sport and Civil Society', *Political Studies*, 46 (1998), pp. 709–6.

of public opinion across borders, are informally structured, and for that reason do not register (easily) as 'data'. Much of the data that is available is also highly imperfect.[10] It presents a picture of the actually existing global civil society that is no more than a torn-edged daguerrotype. Very little reliable empirical data from the past has survived intact, or was collected in the first place – which is not surprising, considering that the concept of global civil society itself had not even been invented. This present-day bias is compounded inadvertently by other forms of bias, for instance in favour of the clusters of northern hemisphere INGOs, whose visibility is greatest because they tend to be based there; data from elsewhere, for instance that related to protests in defence of aboriginal rights or civil liberties or ecological complexity, either go unnoticed or unnoted.

Much potentially usable data on global civil society is distorted by a form of conceptual nationalism. The fact is that most systems of national accounting provide few detailed statistics on either INGOs or social movements or the economic contributions and activities of corporations with a global reach. That is why, sadly, global statistical agencies usually rely on empirical data supplied on a country-by-country basis by individual governments and nationally based organisations. Only a few organisations, for instance some agencies within the United Nations, are experienced collectors of standardised data about global *flows* of people, goods, information and services.[11] Even then, despite stringent efforts to collect, process and disseminate statistics on a standardised basis, huge gaps remain. Statistics on the landscapes of global poverty well exemplify these problems of coverage, comparability and reliability: about one-third of the countries of the world have either no data or inadequate data on the incidence of poverty and malnourishment, and around one-half are similarly lacking information on rates of literacy among youth.[12] Researchers also disagree about which criteria – book translations, diasporas, links among global cities, the spread of the English language, telephone traffic, geographic locations of websites, the mobility patterns of corporate nomads – are the most pertinent for picturing the complex interdependencies of the emerging global society. In-depth, qualitative accounts of global summits, forums and other eye-catching events – like the global campaign against landmines and public protests against the G7 powers – are also rare. And – despite catchy titles that imply more than

---

[10] Some of the empirical problems are discussed in Helmut Anheier, 'Measuring Global Civil Society', in Anheier *et al.* (eds.), *Global Civil Society*, pp. 221–30.

[11] See the report of the OECD Development Cooperation Directorate, *Partnerships in Statistics for Development in the 21st Century* (Paris, 2001).

[12] See the UNDP's *Human Development Report 2000: Human Rights and Human Development* (New York, 2000); www.undp.org/hdr2000/english/book/back1.pdf.

they deliver[13] – studies of the intimate details of everyday life, especially research that concentrates on the socialising and civilising effects at the global level of matters like food consumption and television news-watching, are either non-existent or confined to comparative national surveys that neglect cross-border trends.

These empirical and technical barriers to mapping and measuring global civil society are compounded by a basic epistemological difficulty. Simply put, its actors are not mute, empirical bits and bytes of data. Linked to territories but not restricted to territory, caught up in a vast variety of overlapping and interlocking institutions and webs of group affiliations, these actors talk, think, interpret, question, negotiate, comply, innovate, resist. Their recalcitrance in the face of classification is a basic feature of global civil society, which is never a fixed entity, but always a temporary assembly, subject to reshuffling and reassembly. Static measures, like the numbers of INGOs registered within a country, fail to capture many of its qualities. Dynamism is a chronic feature of global civil society: not the dynamism of the restless sea (a naturalistic simile suggested by Victor Pérez-Diaz[14]), but a form of self-reflexive dynamism marked by innovation, conflict, compromise, consensus, as well as rising awareness of the syncretic architecture, the contingencies and dilemmas of global civil society itself. Beck's terse formulation is correct: the emergent global civil society is not only marked by '*non*-integration' and '*multiplicity without unity*', but its actors treat it as '*perceived* or *reflexive*'.[15] At each moment, the threads of this civil society are deliberately spun, dropped, taken up again, altered, displaced by others, interwoven with others, then deliberately re-spun, again and again. In this way, global civil society enables its participants – athletes, campaigners, musicians, religious believers, managers, aid-workers, teleworkers, medics, scientists, journalists, academics – not only to regard this society as *theirs* but also to see through global civil society by calling it (more impersonally) *this* world or *that* world. For this reason alone, those who speak of global civil society should not lose sight of its elusive, *idealtypisch* quality. The concept of global civil society has what Wittgenstein called 'blurred edges'. This does *not* mean – *pace* Anheier and others – that the term is uniquely imprecise or 'fuzzy' because of its youth.[16] Those who speak

---

[13] An example is Ronald Inglehart, 'Globalization and Postmodern Values', *The Washington Quarterly* (Winter 2000), pp. 215–28

[14] Victor M. Pérez-Diaz, *The Return of Civil Society. The Emergence of Democratic Spain* (Cambridge, MA and London, 1993), p. 62; compare my remarks on the self-reflexivity of actually existing civil societies in *Civil Society: Old Images* pp. 49 ff.

[15] Ulrich Beck, *What is Globalization?* (Cambridge, 2000), p. 10.

[16] Anheier, 'Measuring Global Civil Society', p. 224.

like that unfortunately bring discredit to the term which, like all concepts in the human sciences, is an ill-fitting term clumsily in search of an intelligent object that is always a subject on the run, striding unevenly in many different directions. Anheier is correct: 'Any measurement of global civil society will be simpler and less perfect than the richness, variety, and complexity of the concept it tries to measure.' But the converse of Anheier's rule must also be borne in mind: the conceptual theory of global civil society is infinitely 'purer' and much more abstract than the form and content of actually existing global civil society.

An ideal-type

So the principle is clear – theories without observations are bland, observations without theories are blind – even if the task of clarifying what we mean when we speak of a global civil society is difficult. For purposes of descriptive interpretation, or so this book argues, it is best to use the concept carefully as an ideal-type – as an intentionally produced mental construct or 'cognitive type'[17] that is very useful for heuristic and expository purposes, for naming and clarifying the myriad of elements of a complex social reality, even though it cannot be found in such 'pure' form anywhere within the social world itself. When the term global civil society is used in this way, as an ideal-type, it properly refers to *a dynamic non-governmental system of interconnected socio-economic institutions that straddle the whole earth, and that have complex effects that are felt in its four corners. Global civil society is neither a static object nor a* fait accompli. *It is an unfinished project that consists of sometimes thick, sometimes thinly stretched networks, pyramids and hub-and-spoke clusters of socio-economic institutions and actors who organise themselves across borders, with the deliberate aim of drawing the world together in new ways. These non-governmental institutions and actors tend to pluralise power and to problematise violence; consequently, their peaceful or 'civil' effects are felt everywhere, here and there, far and wide, to and from local areas, through wider regions, to the planetary level itself*.

We need to look carefully at the elements of this rather abstract definition. Considered together, *five* tightly coupled features of this global civil society mark it off as historically distinctive. To begin with, the term global civil society refers to *non-governmental* structures and activities. It comprises individuals, households, profit-seeking businesses, not-for-profit non-governmental organisations, coalitions, social movements and linguistic communities and cultural identities. It feeds upon the work of media celebrities and past or present public personalities – from Gandhi,

---

[17] Umberto Eco, *Kant and the Platypus. Essays on Language and Cognition* (London, 2000).

Bill Gates, Primo Levi and Martin Luther King to Bono and Aung San
Suu Kyi, Bishop Ximenes Belo, Naomi Klein and al-Waleed bin Talal. It
includes charities, think-tanks, prominent intellectuals (like Tu Wei-ming
and Abdolkarim Soroush), campaigning and lobby groups, citizens'
protests responsible for 'clusters of performances',[18] small and large
corporate firms, independent media, Internet groups and websites, employers' federations, trades unions, international commissions, parallel
summits and sporting organisations. It comprises bodies like Amnesty
International, Sony, Falun Gong, Christian Aid, al Jazeera, the Catholic
Relief Services, the Indigenous Peoples Bio-Diversity Network, FIFA,
Transparency International, Sufi networks like Qadiriyya and Naqsha-
bandiyya, the International Red Cross, the Global Coral Reef Monitoring Network, the Ford Foundation, Shack/Slum Dwellers International,
Women Living Under Muslim Laws, News Corporation International,
OpenDemocracy.net, and unnamed circles of Buddhist monks, dressed
in crimson robes, keeping the mind mindful. Considered together, these
institutions and actors constitute a vast, interconnected and multi-layered
non-governmental space that comprises many hundreds of thousands of
more-or-less self-directing ways of life. All of these forms of life have at
least one thing in common: across vast geographic distances and despite
barriers of time, they deliberately organise themselves and conduct their
cross-border social activities, business and politics outside the boundaries
of governmental structures.

Sometimes those who use and defend the term global civil society – the
World Passport initiative, for instance[19] – think of it in no other way than
as a synonym for an unbounded space of non-governmental institutions
and actors. This rather monistic understanding has the advantage of highlighting one of its principal qualities – that it is neither an appendage nor
a puppet of governmental power. Yet the price that is paid for this limited
definition is high: it enables the critics of the vision of global civil society
to accuse their opponents of careless blindness. These critics insist, with
some justification, that the term global civil society is too often used as a
residual or dustbin category that describes everything and nothing. The
term is used to refer to all those parts of life that are *not* the state; it seems
that it is a synonym for everything that exists outside of and beyond the
reach of the territorial state and other institutions of governance – that it

---

[18] Charles Tilly, 'From Interactions to Outcomes in Social Movements', in Marco Giugni
et al. (eds.), *How Social Movements Matter* (Minneapolis and London, 1999), p. 263.

[19] www.worldservice.org/docpass.htmil: 'The World Passport is . . . a meaningful symbol
and sometimes powerful tool for the implementation of the fundamental human right
of freedom of travel. By its very existence, it challenges the exclusive assumption of
sovereignty of the nation-state system.'

includes not only businesses and not-for-profit organisations and initiatives, but 'mafias, extremist networks of various kinds, and terrorists'.[20] The picture presented by the critics is overdrawn, even inaccurate, for global civil society, when carefully defined, is not a simple-minded *alter ego* of 'the state'. The truth is that in a descriptive sense global civil society is only *one* special set of 'non-state' institutions. Hunting and gathering societies and tribal orders, insofar as they have survived under modern conditions, comprise 'non-state' institutions, but it would be wrong to describe them as 'civil society' orders. The same point applies to mafias and mafia-dominated structures, which have *destructive* effects upon civil society institutions precisely because *mafiosi* rely upon kinship bonds, blood imagery, violence and intrigue to *dissolve* the boundaries between the governmental and civilian domains.[21] The same point can be put in another way: global civil society is indeed an extra-governmental space, but it is much more than that. It is defined by other qualities that beg us to see it with different eyes...

To say that global civil society is not merely a non-governmental phenomenon, for instance, is to confirm – this is its second feature – that it is also a form of *society*. Global civil society is a dynamic ensemble of more or less tightly interlinked *social* processes.[22] The quest to unlock its secrets cannot be pursued through the biological or mechanical sciences, for this emergent social order is neither an organism nor a mechanism. It is not a thing that grows according to the blind logic of dividing cells, untouched by human judgement and human will, by recursive reflection and self-generated learning; global civil society is also not a piece of machinery which can be assembled and re-assembled according to human design. The processes and methods through which it is produced and reproduced are unique.

So what does it mean then to speak of global civil *society*? The word 'society' is one of those household concepts that help us economise on lengthy and pedantic explanations – by hiding away or setting aside their complicated (sometimes self-contradictory) genealogy. The concept of society certainly has a complicated history, with two distinct and tensely related connotations. During the nineteenth and twentieth centuries,

---

[20] Barry Buzan, 'An English School Perspective on Global Civil Society', unpublished paper (Centre for the Study of Democracy, 17 January 2002), p. 1; cf. p. 3: 'In descriptive mode, civil society = non-state, and therefore includes mafias, pornography merchants, terrorists and a host of other dark side entities as well as the nicer side of civil society represented by humanitarian, animal welfare and humanitarian organizations.'

[21] Anton Blok, *Honour and Violence* (Oxford 2001), chapter 5.

[22] On the sociological concept of 'society', see Claus Offe, 'Is There, or Can There Be, a "European Society"?', in John Keane (ed.), *Civil Society: Berlin Perspectives* (London, 2004), forthcoming.

especially in the Atlantic region, the term came to be used as a signifier of a whole totality of interrelated processes and events, stretching from (and including) households to governmental institutions. This understanding of 'society' as a whole way of life, as a 'social organism, a holistic system of social relations, the social formation' (Lenin), can be thought of as a depoliticised, less normative version of the much older, early modern idea of a Civill Society, which referred to a well-governed, legally ordered whole way of life. Both usages of 'society' differ from a second, originally medieval meaning of the term: society as a particular fellowship or partnership of equals. St Augustine's description of the Church as the true 'society of the Father and the Son', identical neither with the City of Man nor with the City of God, pointed in this direction. 'Society' means sociable interaction at a distance from government and law. Vocational fellowships and commercial partnerships, the Dutch *matshappeij*, the German *Gesellschaft*, the English 'Societie of Saynt George' (1548) and the Anti-Slavery Society, or today's Society of Authors or the Society of Black Lawyers, all fall in this category. So do eighteenth-century references to the style-setting circles of the upper class, *le Monde*, or what the Germans called 'Die Sozietät', the same group described in Byron's *Don Juan*: 'Society is now one polished horde, Formed of two mighty tribes, the Bores and the Bored.'

We can say that global civil *society* means something quite different from these older usages, to which it is nevertheless genealogically related. It refers to a vast, sprawling non-governmental constellation of many institutionalised structures, associations and networks within which individual and group actors are interrelated and functionally interdependent. As a society of societies, it is 'bigger' and 'weightier' than any individual actor or organisation or combined sum of its thousands of constituent parts – most of whom, paradoxically, neither 'know' each other nor have any chance of ever meeting each other face-to-face. Global civil society is a highly complex ensemble of differently sized, overlapping forms of structured social action; like a Tolstoy novel, it is a vast scenario in which hundreds of thousands and millions of individual and group adventures unfold, sometimes harmoniously through cooperation and compromise, and sometimes conflictually. The key point is that General Motors plus Amnesty International plus the Ruckus Society plus DAWN (Development Alternatives With Women for a New Era) does not equal global civil society. Its social dynamics are more intricate, more dynamic, and more interesting than that.

Like all societies in the strict sense, it has a marked life or momentum or power of its own. Its institutions and rules have a definite durability, in that at least some of them can and do persist through long cycles of time. Global civil society, as we shall see in the coming pages, has much older roots. Most non-European civilisations have made contributions to it, and the effects upon our own times of early modern European developments – the ground-breaking pacifist tradition[23] and the growth spurt of globalisation during the half-century before the First World War – are easily observed. The institutions of present-day global civil society, like those of any functioning society, both predate the living and outlive the life-span of this society's individual members, every one of whom is shaped and carried along in life by the social customs and *traditions* of this global society. In various ways, the social actors of global civil society are both constrained and empowered by this society. These actors are enmeshed within codes of unwritten and written rules that both enable and restrict their action-in-the-world; they understand that many things are possible, but that not everything goes, that some things are desirable, and that some things are not possible, or that they are forbidden. Within global civil society – which is only one particular form of society – social actors' involvement in institutions obliges them to refrain from certain actions, as well as to observe certain *norms*, for instance those that define what counts as civility.

Civility – respect for others expressed as politeness towards and acceptance of strangers – is a third quality of this global society. Different civilisations entertain different notions of civility – they each make civil persons, as John Ruskin said – but because our world is comprised of intermingling civilisations that are not in any sense self-contained or 'pure',[24] global civil society is a space inhabited by various overlapping norms of *non-violent* politeness covering matters of indirection, self-restraint and face-saving. This society is a complex and multi-dimensional space of non-violence, even if it is not an irenic paradise on earth. On the outskirts of global civil society, and within its nooks and crannies, dastardly things go on, certainly. It provides convenient hideouts for gangsters, war criminals, arms traders and terrorists.[25] It contains pockets of *incivility* – geographic areas that coexist uneasily with 'safe' and highly 'civil' zones, dangerous areas like the Strasbourg district of Neuhof, with its crumbling buildings, walls splattered with graffiti and streets littered with car wrecks; the Los Angeles suburb of South Central, considered

---

[23] A good discussion of the long-term impact of the world's first peace movement, which appeared during the 1790s, as a reaction against the French wars, is Martin Ceadl, *The Origins of War Prevention. The British Peace Movement and International Relations, 1730–1854* (Oxford, 1996).

[24] Felipe Fernández-Armesto, *Millennium: A History of Our Last Thousand Years* (London, 1995), chapter 1 and *Civilizations* (London, 2000).

[25] See Mark Juergensmeyer, *Terror in the Mind of God. The Global Rise of Religious Violence* (Berkeley, 2000).

by many a 'no-go area' whose night streets are owned by black, Latino and Asian gangs; and whole cities like Ahmadabad in Gujarat, where in early 2002 many hundreds of people, mainly Muslims, were killed and wounded by semi-planned rioting, sabotage and ethnic cleansing, helped by local police with blind eyes. The spaces of freedom within global civil society also enable individuals and groups to network, in the form of criminal gangs that run world-wide industries. An example is the sale and sex trafficking of young girls and boys – an industry that is now contested by both governments (as in the 1996 Stockholm declaration of 122 countries against all forms of child sexual exploitation) and social campaign networks, like Plan International and End Child Prostitution, Pornography and Trafficking. These social initiatives specialise in repairing the torn fabric of global civil society. They organise against harmful prejudices (for instance, the belief that sleeping with a child can give protection against, or even cure HIV infection). They press political authorities to engage in legal and policing reforms which serve to restrict access to predator groups like tourists, businessmen and soldiers on overseas duty. These initiatives also dig away at the root causes of child prostitution: the enforced sale of children by families suffering pauperisation and the orphaning of children by the upheavals caused by war and the AIDS epidemic.[26]

In the wider schema of things, such initiatives provide the reminder – analysed in the third section of the book – that global civil society is marked by a strong and overriding tendency to both marginalise or avoid the use of violence and to take pleasure in violence. Its actors do not especially like mortars or tanks or nuclear weapons. They have an allergic – sometimes disgusted – reaction to images of gunmen firing rockets, or to supersonic fighter planes, or to tanks crashing mercilessly into people or buildings. The actors of global civil society, in their own and varied ways, admire the peaceful. Some do so after witnessing or suffering violence. Others believe that the peaceful right to have rights is fundamental to all human beings. Still others are disgusted by violence because of their belief in a peaceful and loving God, or their attempts to live the principle of Karma. All of them more or less observe the rule that non-violent respect for others overrides any considerations of their national identity or skin colour or religion or sex, or that murder and other forms of violence against others is undesirable, and should be minimised, or strictly prohibited. Thanks to such shared norms, the participants within this society are prone to exercise physical restraint, to mix non-violently with

[26] See www.ecpat.net/eng/index.asp; and Dennis Altman, *Global Sex* (Chicago and London, 2001).

others, 'foreigners' and 'strangers' included. Normatively speaking, the killing rituals of hunting and gathering orders, or tribal violence, or mafia thuggery tend to have no place within this society. Its extra-governmental institutions and forms of action are marked by a proclivity towards non-violence and respect for the principles of compromise, mutual respect, even power-sharing among different ways of life. The implication is clear: global civil society is not just any old collection of ways of life that have nothing in common but their non-identification with governing institutions. Factually speaking, this society encourages compromise and mutual respect. There is (to speak literally and metaphorically) plenty of room within its walls for people who believe in God, as well as for religious people for whom the idea of a creator God is anathema, as well as for people who feel only diffuse respect for the sacred, as well as for people who believe in nothing else except themselves. Insofar as these various actors have a more or less deep sensitivity towards violence and violence-prone institutions, they enable global civil society to be 'civil' in a double sense: it consists of non-governmental (or 'civilian') institutions that tend to have non-violent (or 'civil') effects.

Precisely because global civil society harbours many ways of life it means many different things to those who live their lives within its structures. This is its fourth quality: it contains both strong traces of *pluralism* – and *strong conflict potential*. Within its economic domains – as the second section of the book explains – this society sustains the livelihoods of many hundreds of millions of people. It is a dynamic source of technological innovation, capital investment, production, distribution and consumption stretched across vast distances. It is home to businesses of all shapes and sizes, ranging from the self-employed importer of goods produced on the other side of earth to retail companies like Sears Roebuck, whose annual sales of commodities produced in more than a hundred countries are comparable to the total annual income of the 100 million citizens of one state alone, Bangla Desh. None of this economic activity could take place unless the institutions of global civil society performed other, non-economic functions: like that of providing social 'homes' or 'nests' within which individuals and groups fashion and re-fashion their identities, familiarise and make sense of each other, find meanings in life, get their bearings through activities that cross borders, which are seen as bridges rather than as places where wars start or trouble begins.

The cross-border links and activities also help to draw boundaries between themselves and governmental power, for instance by pressuring and bouncing off territorial states and their sub-units, as well as regional and supranational government bodies. To speak (as some do) of a 'world order' or 'one world' or 'a global community' is misleading: the world is in fact sub-divided in two basic ways by the emergent global society. First, its civilian institutions place limits upon government. They guarantee power-sharing by ensuring that cross-border contests with governmental power become commonplace. Global civil society serves as a brake or potential check upon various forms of government, and especially absolutist political rule. *All* governmental institutions, from local councils through territorial states and regional and supranational institutions like the United Nations and the WTO, are now feeling the pinching effects of this civil society. Meanwhile – secondly – scuffles and skirmishes over the distribution of socio-economic power also regularly take place *within* global civil society itself. These contests typically become visible through media coverage, which attracts witnesses to both local and world-wide disputes concerning who gets what, when and how. In this way, global civil society functions as a monitoring and signalling platform, from which both local matters – mimicking the 'butterfly effect' that has been held responsible for fluctuations in whole weather patterns – can assume global importance, and global-level problems (like nuclear weapons, terrorism, the environment) are named, defined and problematised. A sense of 'the world' and 'humanity' as complex and vulnerable totalities consequently strengthens. Global civil society – contrary to its communitarian interpreters – does not resemble a 'global community'.[27] For its participants, rather, this society nurtures a culture of self-awareness about the hybridity and complexity of the world.

The heterogeneity of global civil society works against enforced unity. It throws into question presumptions about spontaneous sympathy and automatic consensus.[28] It heaps doubt upon claims (famously associated with Seneca) that all human beings are 'social animals',[29] or that they stand firm upon some bedrock of essential 'humanity'. This complex society is not a space wherein people naturally touch and feel good about the world. Certainly that happens. Dressed in the clothing of honest pilgrims, young people take time off, travel the world, odd-job, sleep rough, sleep around, wonder and marvel at the complexity and beauty of the world, just like a satisfied botanist observing and contemplating the extraordinary complexity of plant life. Others meanwhile dedicate their lives to charitable or volunteer work by putting their minds and hearts to work with others. They speak of compassion, and practise it. Yet despite all this, the world of global civil society can be tough, calculating

---

[27] Amitai Etzioni, Implications of the American Anti-Terrorism Coalition for Global Architectures, *European Journal of Political Theory*, vol. 1, no. 1 (July 2002), 9–30.

[28] Francis Fukuyama, *The Great Disruption. Human Nature and the Reconstitution of Social Order* (London, 1999), chapter 13.

[29] Seneca, *De Beneficiis* (Cambridge, MA and London, 1935), book 7, section 1.

and rough n tumble. It looks and feels expansive and polyarchic, full of horizontal push and pull, vertical conflict and compromise. Take a stroll through the heart of Riyadh, a city of astonishing contrasts between ancient social customs and ultra-modern norms: women shrouded in black *abayas* shop at Harvey Nichols inside a Norman Foster building, their eyes fully covered; the street corner McDonald's close five times a day for prayers; men crowd into mosques surrounded by giant neon signs advertising Sony. Global civil society – to use a term of psychoanalysis – is richly conflicted. That fact helps many participants within this society to know and to understand that it is neither self-reproducing nor spontaneously self-regulating. They are more or less reflexively aware of its *contingency*. They sense that its dynamic structures and rules and various identities – even supposedly 'ascriptive' primary groups like kinship ties – are not somehow naturally given, for all time; they see that they are subject to strenuous negotiation and modification, through complex processes – parallel summits, blockades, media events, for instance – whose consequences are often better understood after the fact, with hindsight. This shared sense of contingency defies presumptions about the 'natural sociability of humans'.[30] It also feeds social conflict, thus ensuring that global civil society stands precariously between the boundaries of orderly equilibrium and disorder at the edge of chaos.

The volume of this worldly self-awareness of the complexity of the world, should not be exaggerated. It is hard to estimate its extent, but probably only 5 per cent of the world's population has an acute awareness of the tightening interdependence of the world, its ecosystems, institutions and peoples. Perhaps another 25 per cent are moderately or dimly aware of this interdependence.[31] While most others have not (yet) thought over the matter, or don't much care, or are too cynical or self-preoccupied to open their eyes and ears, the aggregate numbers of those who are globally aware are weighty enough to spread awareness that global civil society exists; that it is a force to be reckoned with; that it both operates within, and resembles, a patchwork quilt of power relations. Global civil

---

[30] Buzan, 'An English School Perspective', p. 3.

[31] Data generated by recent World Values Surveys suggests that 'almost one-fifth of the baby boomers born after World War II see themselves as cosmopolitan citizens of the globe, identifying with their continent or the world as a whole, but this is true of only one in ten of the group brought up in the interwar years, and of even fewer of the prewar generation'; see Pippa Norris, 'Global Governance and Cosmopolitan Citizens', in Joseph S. Nye and John D. Donahue (eds.), *Governance in a Globalizing World* (Cambridge, MA and Washington, DC, 2000), p. 175. From a global civil society perspective, the concept of 'cosmopolitan citizens' is unfortunate, if only because awareness of the *interdependence* of the world is both more subtle and different than positive 'identification' with one's own 'continent' or 'the world'.

society is most definitely riddled with power relations.[32] Its social groups
and organisations and movements lobby states, bargain with international
organisations, pressure and bounce off other non-state bodies, invest in
new forms of production, champion different ways of life and engage in
charitable direct action in distant local communities, for instance through
'capacity-building' programmes that supply jobs, clean running water,
sporting facilities, hospitals and schools. In these various ways, the members of global civil society help to conserve or to alter the power relations
embedded in the chains of interaction linking the local, regional and planetary orders. Their cross-border links and networks help to define and
redefine who gets what, when, and how in the world. Of great importance
is the fact that these cross-border patterns have the power to stimulate
awareness among the world's inhabitants that mutual understanding of
different ways of life is a practical necessity, that we are being drawn into
the first genuinely bottom-up transnational order, a global civil society,
in which millions of people come to realise, in effect, that they are incarnations of world-wide webs of interdependence, whose complexity is
riddled with opportunity, as well as danger.

To say this is to note – this fifth point is obvious, but most crucial –
that global civil society is *global*. To speak of a *global* civil society is to
refer to politically framed and circumscribed social relations that stretch
across and underneath state boundaries and other governmental forms.
This 'macro-society' or 'society of interlocking societies' consists of a
myriad of social interactions stretched across vast geographic distances.
Global civil society is the most complex society in the history of the
human species. It comprises a multitude of different parts, which are
connected in a multitude of different ways. These diverse components
interact both serially and in parallel, and they produce effects that are
often both simultaneous and sequential. These effects, while normally
generated by local interactions and events, have emergent properties that
tend to be global. We are not exactly speaking here of a 'vast empire of
human society, as it is spread over the whole earth' (Wordsworth[33]) –
global civil society is neither a new form of empire nor encompassing of
the whole earth[34] – but it certainly is a special form of *unbounded* society
marked by constant feedback among its many components.

---

[32] On the concept of power and its wide variety of forms, see my *Václav Havel: A Political Tragedy in Six Acts* (London and New York, 1999).

[33] From William Wordsworth's Preface to the *Lyrical Ballads, with Other Poems* (2nd edn., London, 1800).

[34] Compare the claim that there is a spreading new form of empire – a 'global society of control' – ruled by global capital in Michael Hardt and Antonio Negri, *Empire* (Cambridge, MA and London, 2000), esp. pp. 325–50.

Global civil society can be likened – to draw for a moment upon ecological similes – to a vast, dynamic biosphere. It comprises a bewildering variety of interacting habitats and species: INGOs, voluntary groups, businesses, civic initiatives, social movements, protest organisations, whole nations, ethnic and linguistic clusters, pyramids and networks. To compare this society with a vast biosphere that stretches to every corner of the earth is to underscore both the great complexity of its linkages and (as we shall see) its vulnerability to internal and external interference. Just as nearly every part of the Earth, from the highest mountains to the deepest seas, supports life, so too global civil society is now found on virtually every part of the earth's surface. To be sure, everywhere it is tissue-thin – just like the natural biosphere, which resembles a paper wrapping that covers a sphere the size of a football – and its fringes, where ice and permafrost predominate, are virtually inhospitable. In the interior of the Antarctic, only restricted populations of bacteria and insects are to be found; and even on its coasts there are very few living inhabitants, among which are a handful of flowering plant species, as well as seals, whales, penguins and other birds. Global civil society is similarly subject to geographic limits: whole zones of the earth, parts of contemporary Afghanistan, Burma, Chechenya and Sierra Leone for instance, are 'no-go areas' for civil society actors and institutions, which can survive only by going underground, living in microniches, like the tens of millions of little invertebrates that run the biosphere.[35]

But in those areas of the earth where it does exist, global civil society comprises many biomes – whole areas (like North America and the European Union and parts of the Muslim world) characterised by specific animals and plants and climatic conditions. Each biome in turn comprises large numbers of living ecosystems made up of clusters of organisms living within a non-living physical environment of rocks, soil and climate. These ecosystems of global civil society – cities, business corridors and regions for instance – are interconnected. And they are more or less intricately balanced, through continuous flows and recycling of efforts among (as it were) populations of individuals of the same species, which thrive within communities (such as smaller cities) that are themselves embedded within non-living geographic contexts.

Biospheric similes are helpful in picturing the cross-border contours of global civil society, but they should not be overextended, if only because this society is not simply a *naturally occurring* phenomenon. Although it is embedded within a terrestrial biosphere – it is the first-ever planetary

---

[35] See Edward O. Wilson, 'The Little Things that Run the World', in Edward O. Wilson, *In Search of Nature* (Washington, DC, 1996), pp. 141–5.

order to understand itself as precarious, as *naturally* embedded – global civil society is *socially produced*. Its intricate social linkages stretched across vast distances are puzzling, indeed so difficult to grasp that new metaphors are urgently needed to help us to picture and understand them. Perhaps (to take an example) it is better to liken this society to the tens and hundreds of thousands of 'nested systems within nested systems' described in certain versions of complexity theory.[36] Certainly, this global society is both integrated and de-centred. It draws upon and is sustained by many different actually existing societies, whose members regularly interact and/or feel the effects of others' actions across political boundaries. These effects are not due to proximity alone; they are felt at great distances, usually by social actors who have no direct contact with one another, and who are otherwise fated to remain 'strangers' to one another.

The complexity and interdependence of the linkages is staggering, and striking as well is their combined effect, which is to 'socialise' actors in ways that 'thicken' or increase the density of social interactions across political borders. Consider one example: the luxuriant variety of languages spoken within global civil society. While today's 6,000 languages are rapidly disappearing, one by one, on average every two weeks, many of them still spawn pidgins (rudimentary languages concocted to facilitate communication among speakers of mutually unintelligible tongues) that sometimes mutate into Creoles (pidgins that have matured into the first language of a community). Meanwhile, global efforts to revive dying or dead languages, such as Ainu in Japan and Romansch in Switzerland, are underway. Strong resistance to extinction is also evident in the fact that the remaining top twenty languages that are today spoken by over 95 per cent of the world's population are deeply resilient; they are highly complex clusters of intermingling sub-languages and dialect families. None of them is 'pure' – 99 per cent of words in the *Oxford English Dictionary* are of foreign descent – and all of them are split into sub-varieties that are constantly subject to further hybridisation.[37] Or consider one other example: the rapidly increasing mobility of people across borders in recent decades, especially into and out of rich countries (nearly 90 million people enter Britain annually, for instance). The trend has many faces: it includes the influx of visitors, working migrants and their households, refugees and asylum seekers, all of whom have made many so-called 'national' societies both much more heterogeneous and other-regarding. Cultural minorities are no longer easily assimilated, partly because of the

---

[36] The vast literature includes David Bohm and F. David Peat, *Science, Order, and Creativity* (London, 2000) and John Briggs and F. David Peat, *Turbulent Mirror* (New York, 1990).
[37] John McWhorter, *The Power of Babel. A Natural History of Language* (London, 2002).

speed and volume of migration, but also because of their socially diverse origins and the ease with which they remain in contact with their society of origin. Many countries consequently contain whole categories of people who can be described as 'denizens' (Tomas Hammar), people who are foreign citizens enjoying permanent legal resident status, or as 'margizens', long-term immigrants who lack secure residence status: illegal workers, unauthorised family entrants, asylum seekers, refused asylum seekers who have not (yet) been deported, and temporary workers who are in fact permanently integrated into the workforce.[38]

Old habits

Defined in this way, as a vast, interconnected and multi-layered non-governmental space that comprises many hundreds of thousands of self-directing institutions and ways of life that generate global effects, the ideal-type concept of global civil society invites us to improve our understanding of the emerging planetary order. It calls on us to think more deeply about it, in the hope that we can strengthen our collective powers of guiding and transforming it. This clearly requires sharpening up our courage to confront the unknown and to imagine different futures.[39] And it most definitely obliges us to abandon some worn-out certainties and outdated prejudices. Let us dwell for a moment on what the new understanding of global civil society obliges us to give up.

The words 'global civil society' may be said to resemble signs that fix our thoughts on winding pathways that stretch not only in front of us, but also behind us. To utter the words 'global civil society', for instance, is to sup with the dead, with an early modern world in which, among the educated classes of Europe, 'world civil society' meant something quite different than what it means, or ought to mean, today. Just how different our times are can be seen by revisiting this older, exhausted meaning of 'world civil society'.

Consider the works of two influential authors of the eighteenth century: Emmerich de Vattel's *Le droit des gens* (1758) and Immanuel Kant's *Idee zu einer allgemeinen Geschichte in weltbürgerlicher Absicht* (1784) and *Zum ewigen Frieden* (1795).[40] These books stand at the end phase of a long

---

[38] Stephen Castles and Alistair Davidson, *Citizenship and Migration. Globalization and the Politics of Belonging* (Basingstoke, 2000).

[39] A stimulating example of such rethinking that is guided by the idea of a global civil society is Michael Edwards, *Future Positive. International Co-Operation in the 21st Century* (London, 2000).

[40] Emmerich de Vattel, *Le droit des gens, ou principes de la loi naturelle, appliqués à la conduite et aux affaires des nations et des souverains* (London, 1758); Immanuel Kant, *Idee*

cycle of European thinking that understands civil society (*societas civilis*) as the condition of living within an armed legal order that guarantees its subjects stable peace and good government. 'A State is more or less perfect according as it is more or less adapted to attain the end of civil society', wrote Vattel, for whom the distinction between state and civil society was literally *unthinkable*. A civil society is a special form of government. It 'consists in procuring for its citizens the necessities, the comforts, and the pleasures of life, and in general their happiness; and in securing to each the peaceful enjoyment of his property and a sure means of obtaining justice, and finally in defending the whole body against all external violence.'[41] Kant joined him in making it clear that civil society in this normative sense was not necessarily synonymous with the modern territorial state and its legal codes (*ius civile*). Their classically minded theory of civil society emphasised that war-mongering among states and what Kant called the 'unsocial sociability' of subjects could be cured by subordinating them within a cosmopolitan alliance of states that is overridden and protected by its own legal codes. Vattel insisted that states are obliged to respect and to protect what he called the universal society of the human race. 'When... men unite in civil society and form a separate State or Nation... their duties towards the rest of the human race remain unchanged.'[42] Kant went further. He envisaged a two-tiered 'law of world citizenship' [*ius cosmopoliticum*] which binds citizens and states into a higher republican commonwealth of states. This commonwealth, which resembles not a peace treaty [*pactum pacis*] but a league of peace [*foedus pacificum*], would put an end to violence forever by treating its subjects as citizens of a new law-governed political union. This union he called 'universal civil society' (*einer allgemein das Recht verwaltenden bürgerlichen Gesellschaft*).[43]

The invention of the distinction between government and civil society, and the subsequent birth of modern colonial empires, the rise of nationalism from the time of the French Revolution, and the trend towards a global system of complex governance, or cosmocracy – analysed below – arguably confounded this eighteenth-century vision of two-tiered global government, or a world civil society. Two centuries later, the concept

---

zu einer allgemeinen Geschichte in weltbürgerlicher Absicht, first published in the *Berlinische Monatsschrift* (Berlin), November 1784, pp. 385–411, and *Zum ewigen Frieden. Ein philosophischer Entwurf* (Königsberg, 1795). The emergence of the distinction between civil society and governmental/state institutions is examined in my 'Despotism and Democracy: The Origins and Development of the Distinction between State and Civil Society, 1750–1850', in John Keane (ed.), *Civil Society and the State: New European Perspectives* (London and New York, 1988 [reprinted 1998]).

[41] Vattel, 1758, chapter 1, section 6.   [42] *Ibid.*, book 1, introduction, section 11.

[43] Kant, *Idee zu einer allgemeinen Geschichte in weltbürgerlicher Absicht*, fifth thesis.

of 'international society', familiar in the early work of Philip Marshall Brown and the work of later scholars like Hedley Bull and Martin Wight, tried both to register this historical change and to preserve something of the old-fashioned meaning of *societas civilis*. The global system of interlocking territorial states was said not to resemble Hobbes' classic description of a lawless state of nature racked by deathly strivings after power over others. Territorial states were rather seen by Bull and others as socialised by the behaviour of other states. They were linked into 'the most comprehensive form of society on earth',[44] an increasingly global framework of mutually recognised, informal customs and formal rules – diplomatic protocol, embassy functions, multilateral treaties, and laws governing matters as diverse as trade and commerce, war crimes and the right of non-interference. These state-enforced customs and rules that limit sovereignty by respecting it came to be called international society, a strangely state-centred term that Hedley Bull considered to be a basic precondition of contemporary world order. International society, he wrote, 'exists when a group of states, conscious of certain common interests and common values, form a society in the sense that they conceive themselves to be bound by a common set of rules in their relations with one another, and share in the working of common institutions'.[45]

The terms 'world civil society' and 'international society' still have their champions,[46] but from the standpoint of the new concept of global civil society their 'governmentality' or state-centredness are today deeply problematic. Neither the classical term *societas civilis* nor the state-centric concept of 'international society' is capable of grasping the latter-day emergence of a *non-governmental* social sphere that is called global civil society. These words, 'global civil society' may well sound old-fashioned,

---

44 Martin Wight, *Power Politics*, eds. Hedley Bull and Carsten Holbraad (Leicester, 1978), p. 106; cf. Philip Marshall Brown, *International Society. Its Nature and Interests* (New York, 1928).

45 Hedley Bull, *The Anarchical Society. A Study of Order in World Politics*, 2nd edn. (New York, 1995 [1977]), p. 13; see also his 'The Importance of Grotius in the Study of International Relations', in Hedley Bull *et al.* (eds.), *Hugo Grotius and International Relations* (Oxford, 1990), pp. 64–93.

46 Examples include Ralf Dahrendorf's stimulating neo-Kantian defence of a universal civil society in *The Modern Social Conflict. An Essay on the Politics of Liberty* (London, 1988), p. 189: 'The next step towards a World Civil Society is the recognition of universal rights of all men and women by the creation of a body of international law.' Compare the systems-theoretical interpretation of 'world society' (*Weltgesellschaft*) in Niklas Luhmann, *Die Gesellschaft der Gesellschaft*, vol. 1 (Frankfurt am Main, 1998), pp. 148–71, and the argument that a 'mature anarchy' among states is a precondition of a strong 'international society', in Barry Buzan, *People, States and Fear. An Agenda for International Security Studies in the Post-Cold War Era* (New York and London, 1991), pp. 174–81.

but today they have an entirely new meaning and political significance. Sustained and deeper reflection on the subject – and a willingness to puncture old thinking habits – is definitely warranted. Some examples are especially pertinent in this book's attempt to define and to understand global civil society in fresh ways.

Levels?

Among the primary needs is to question the current habit among researchers of speaking of civil societies as 'national' phenomena and, thus, of supposing or implying that global civil society and domestic civil societies are binary opposites. Many are still tempted to think in (architectural) terms of two different 'levels' of civil society – the 'national' and the 'global' – as if *homo civilis* was a divided creature, strangely at odds with itself, rather like a figure in the prose of Kleist: a figure pulled simultaneously in two different directions, towards 'home' and away from 'home'. 'Global civil society', runs one version of this way of thinking, is 'a transnational domain in which people form relationships and develop elements of identity outside their role as a citizen of a particular state'. It 'represents a sphere that thus transcends the self-regarding character of the state system and can work in the service of a genuinely transnational, public interest'.[47] Note the strong presumption that politically defined territory remains the ultimate foundation of civil society institutions – as if 'the global' was an add-on extra, a homeless extra-territorial phenomenon. Note as well how such images of global civil society draw upon architectural metaphors of up and down, here and there. They imply that the world of civil societies is split into two levels – that 'domestic' civil society is 'self-regarding', whereas the other-regarding global civil society is 'above and beyond national, regional, or local societies', or 'above the national level'.[48] Exactly how the two 'levels' are related, or how 'citizens' climb up and down the ladders in between, is left unclear.

In fact – the exemplary case is that of Ireland, easily the most globalised country in the world, according to the Globalisation Index[49] – the language of 'domestic' and 'foreign' or 'the local' and 'the global', as well as the architectural simile of 'above and beyond', are downright misleading.

---

[47] Paul Wapner, 'The Normative Promise of Nonstate Actors: A Theoretical Account of Global Civil Society', in Paul Wapner and Lester Edwin J. Ruiz (eds.), *Principled World Politics. The Challenge of Normative International Relations* (Lanham, MD, 2000), p. 261.

[48] Helmut Anheier *et al.*, 'Introducing Global Civil Society', in Anheier *et al.* (eds.), *Global Civil Society*, pp. 4, 3.

[49] *Financial Times* (London), 9 January 2002.

Within the forces and processes that operate from within global civil society there is no clear line separating the 'national' from the 'global'; the two dimensions – the 'inside' and the 'outside' – constantly intersect and co-define each other. Take a simple example: jeans. This item of clothing is worn world-wide, and one might even say, with just a touch of exaggeration, that jeans are the prized uniform of millions of people who live, work and play within civil societies. As an item of clothing, everybody knows that it had local American origins, and that as an American commodity jeans have travelled well. They are today a relatively cheap and popular form of casual dress on every continent, in over a hundred countries. Yet this globalisation of jeans has not been synonymous with the homogenisation of meaningful ways of life. Jeans are not worn in identical ways with identical connotations – Marlboro Man on his ranch competes for attention with Thai youths on motorcycles and Lebanese young women, veiled and unveiled, relaxing together in esplanade cafés, all wearing jeans, in non-standard ways. All these figures are incarnations of world-wide cultural webs that are themselves bound up with latticed global networks of production – including raw and processed materials like copper from Namibia, cotton from Benin and Pakistan, zinc from Australia, thread from Northern Ireland and Hungary, synthetic dye from Germany, pumice from Turkey, polyester tape from France, and steel zips machined in Japan. This single example highlights the normal patterns of complexity in the globalisation of civil society. It drives home the point that the so-called domestic and the global – to draw upon similes from the field of physics – are marked by strong interactions of the kind that hold together the protons and neutrons inside an atomic nucleus; or, to switch to the language of complexity theory, the domestic and the global are normally linked together in complex, cross-border patterns of looped and re-looped circuitry. When it comes to understanding the dynamics of global civil society, there is no definable or decidable boundary between interiority and exteriority. The 'micro' and the 'meso' and the 'macro' dimensions of this society are both interconnected and co-determinant of each other. The tiniest and the largest operations and events are implicated in loops that produce feedback – ranging from system-simplifying and system-upsetting (or negative) forms through to feedback that is more positive, in that it produces effects that are disproportionate to their causes, so adding to the overall heterogeneity and dynamism of the components of the global social system.

To repeat: the use of ecological similes and themes drawn from complexity theory may be questionable, but they serve the basic purpose of identifying the urgent need to develop theoretical imagery for better imagining global civil society, as it is and as it might become. The rule of thumb, both in the past and in the present, is that the liveliest 'local' civil societies are those enjoying the strongest world-wide links. To speak of a global civil society is to highlight the intricate patterns of interdependence and co-dependence of its many different parts, their implication as nodal points within an open system of networks fuelled by feedback and feed-forward loops. It is important to see that just as within locally bounded societies larger social aggregates like trade unions often reinforce (rather than simply subsume) the power and status of smaller social units, like households, so the relationship between these more local civil society units and their more distant or globalising connectors is not a zero-sum relationship.

Instead of a single commodity like jeans, consider a whole country, such as contemporary Japan: its government officials once regarded civil society organisations as interlopers in affairs of state, and it is therefore unsurprising that in 1960, the density of its non-profit associations (11.1 associations per 100,000 people) was only one-third that of the United States (34.6). By the early 1990s, the density had reached a level of more than 80 per cent of that of the United States (29.2 per 100,000 people versus 35.2).[50] Many factors help to explain this transformation, but among the principal causes has been the country's internationalisation (the local term is *kokusai-ka*), beginning with the widespread public involvement of citizens in assisting refugees from Indochina during 1979, and greatly boosted by a series of conferences hosted by the United Nations during the 1990s and media events like World Cup 2002. The result has confirmed the interdependence of 'the national' and 'the international': faced with the growing *de facto* involvement of civil society organisations in shaping foreign policy, Japanese government officials were pressured into including representatives of these organisations in their policy deliberations (during the G-8 Summit held in Japan, the government even appointed a special 'Ambassador in Charge of Civil Society' [*shibiru sosaeti tantshibiru*]), while the shift from patron–client relations in the foreign policy sector of government towards a model of political negotiation with civil society actors has been replicated in various fields of domestic policy.[51]

---

[50] Yutaka Tsujinaka, 'Interest Group Structure and Regime Change in Japan', in I. M. Destler (ed.), *Maryland/Tsukubu Papers on US–Japan Relations* (College Park, MD, 1996), p. 57.

[51] Toshihiro Menju and Takaka Aoki, 'The Evolution of Japanese NGOs in the Asia Pacific Context', in Tadashi Yamamoto (ed.), *Emerging Civil Society in the Asia Pacific Community: Nongovernmental Underpinnings of the Emerging Asia Pacific Regional Community* (Singapore and Tokyo, 1995), pp. 143–6, and Tadashi Yamamoto, 'Emergence of Japan's Civil Society and Its Future Challenges', in Tadashi Yamamoto (ed.), *Deciding the Public Good: Governance and Civil Society in Japan* (Tokyo, 1999), pp. 99–103.

European towns

This point about the dynamic osmosis between the 'domestic' and 'global' dimensions of civil societies must be taken into account when trying to understand the genealogy of civil societies, for instance in the European region. In practice, the development of modern civil societies within the framework of European states and empires contained from the outset the seeds of their own trans-nationalisation and interpenetration. This trend can be seen even in the most local civil societies, whose roots are partly traceable to the revival of towns in Europe during the eleventh century. The urban revival not only nurtured long-distance trade that linked the Europes of the Mediterranean, the Atlantic and the Baltic; it also marked the beginning of the continent's rise to world eminence – and its contribution to the laying of the foundations of a global civil society.[52] Although the distribution of these European towns – unusual clumps of people engaged in many different tasks, living in houses close together, often joined wall to wall – was highly uneven, with the weakest patterns of urbanisation in Russia and the strongest in Holland, they were typically linked to each other in networks, or archipelagos stretching across vast distances. Wherever these urban archipelagos thrived, they functioned like magnets that attracted strangers fascinated by their well-lit complexity, their real or imagined freedom, or their higher wages.

Towns like Bruges, Genoa, Nuremberg and London resembled electric transformers. They constantly recharged life by adding not only motion but also tension to its elements. Town-dwellers seemed to be perpetually on the move. They travelled regularly to and fro among built-up areas and regularly spent only part of their lives there: during harvest-times, for instance, artisans and others typically abandoned their trades and houses for work in fields elsewhere. The constant rumble of wheeled carriages, the weekly or daily markets and the numerous trades added to the sense of motion across distance: town-dwellers encountered water-carriers, floor polishers, sawyers, porters and chair-carriers, pedlars, rabbit-skin merchants, wigmakers, barbers, cobblers and domestic servants. All these occupations in turn rubbed shoulders with members of the better sort: merchants, some of them very rich, masters, mercenaries, engineers, ships' captains, doctors, professors, painters and architects, all of whom knew what it meant to travel through time and space.

The winding, twisting layout of towns added to their appearance of geographic and social dynamism. Medieval Europe was one of only two

---

[52] The following section draws upon the documents assembled in John H. Mundy and Peter Riesenberg, *The Medieval Town* (Princeton, 1858) and Fernand Braudel, *Civilization and Capitalism. 15th–18th Century*, vol. 1 (London, 1981), chapter 8.

civilisations – the other was Islam – that fashioned large towns with an irregular maze of streets. What was different about the medieval and early modern European towns was their unparalleled freedom from the political authorities of the emerging territorial states. Local merchants, traders, craft guilds, manufacturers and bankers formed the backbone of a long-distance money economy endowed with the power to dictate the terms and conditions on which governments ruled. Seen in this way, urban markets were the cuckoo's egg laid in the little nests of the medieval towns. These nests were woven from various non-governmental institutions, which together with the markets helped to nurture something brand new: unbounded social space within which the absolutist state could be checked, criticised and generally held at arm's length from citizens.

Universal history

The birth of civil societies in this sense did not simply lay the foundations for 'strongly connected national civil societies living in a system of many states'.[53] Historically speaking, the institutions of civil society were never exclusively 'national' or constituted by their exclusive relationship to the nation-state. All hitherto-existing civil societies have been linked by some common threads, which is why global civil society has to be thought of as more than the simple sum of territorially based and defined civil societies. It rather comprises local, regional, state-ordered and supranational civil society institutions that are melded together in complex chains of interdependence. The birth of local civil societies heralded the dawn of what has been called universal history marked by the constant reciprocal interaction between local and far-distant events.[54] The neologism, global civil society, belatedly names this old tendency of local and regional civil societies to link up and to penetrate regions of the earth that had previously not known the ethics and structures of civil society in the modern European sense. But the neologism points as well to current developments that speed up the growth, and greatly 'thicken', the networks of transnational, non-governmental activities. Universal history so understood is *not* the clichéd story of the one-way spreading of a bundle of 'Western' ideals to the rest of the world, whose contribution is a non-history of non-contributions, or what Mamdani has called a 'history of absences'.[55]

---

[53] M. J. Peterson, 'Transnational Activity, International Society and World Politics', *Millennium*, 21:3 (1992), p. 388.

[54] Raymond Aron, 'The Dawn of Universal History', in Miriam Conant (ed.), *Politics and History. Selected Essays by Raymond Aron* (New York and London, 1978), pp. 212–33.

[55] Mahmood Mamdani, *Citizen and Subject: Contemporary Africa and the Legacy of Late Colonialism* (Princeton, 1996).

It is universal in a more complex and messier sense: the local and the beyond are interrelated recursively, through power-ridden processes of entangled pasts and presents. So, for instance, it can be said that the eighteenth-century vision of cosmopolitanism defended by Vattel, Kant and others was a child of local civil societies; and that that cosmopolitanism was the privilege of those whose lives were already anchored in local civil societies. This does not mean or imply that their vision of cosmopolitanism was superior. Seen from the perspective of universal history, it was just one among many other modernities. The other-regarding, outward-looking openness of these local civil societies – their glimpse of themselves as part of a wider, complex world, their capacity to see space and time not as part of the bare bones of the world, but as constructions – constantly tempted them to engage and transform that world. Their stocks of social skills, their capacities for commercial enterprise, technical innovation, freedom of communication, for learning languages and saving souls in independently minded churches: all these qualities fed the developing worldliness and laid the foundations for their later globalisation.

Think for a moment of the example of the colonising process triggered by the British Empire, which at its height governed nearly one-third of the world's population.[56] Unlike the Spanish colonies, which were the product of a species of absolute monarchy that charged into the world under the flags of evangelisation and military glory, the British Empire was driven not only by maritime-backed colonial power, but also non-state initiatives based at home. These were either for profit, as in the Virginia Company and the East India Company, which combined the capital of wealthy magnates with the navigational skills of freebooting maritime adventurers to form a joint-stock organisation that not only conquered India and laid the foundations of the Raj, but also provided the means by which people, commodities, animals, plants and ideas circulated to and from the east. The British Empire also spawned non-state initiatives driven by religious ends, evident in extensive Christian missionary activity and the emigration of dissenters: Puritans to New England, Quakers to Pennsylvania, Methodists to Australia and Presbyterians to Canada. These non-state or civil initiatives did not simply have one-way effects

---

[56] Two phases of the expansion of Europe are commonly distinguished. The first encompasses the European conquest of the Americas; it stretches from Columbus' first voyage in 1492 to the final defeat of the Spanish armies in South America during the 1830s. During the second phase, the net of European power was cast over Asia, Africa and the Pacific; it began in the 1730s, but crystallised only after the American Revolution, which signalled the end of European dominance in the Atlantic; see Anthony Pagden, *Lords of All the World. Ideologies of Empire in Spain, Britain and France c. 1500–c.1800* (New Haven and London, 1995).

upon the colonised; they rather established complex social and economic chains of interdependence that contained a large number of components that interacted simultaneously with a rich variety of effects that soon began to be felt in all four corners of the earth. Empire promoted independence at a distance; various factors of socio-economic life, previously unrelated, became involved with one another.

Conceptual imperialism?

With this example of empire, a critic of the idea of a global civil society might well at this point lodge the objection that the language of civil society speaks with a Western accent. The development of long-distance social relations, the critic might observe, certainly had the effect of spreading the norms and institutions that would later be named civil society in the modern sense.[57] Yet a cursory glance at the historical record shows that this diffusion of the institutions and language of civil society everywhere encountered resistance – sometimes (as in parts of the East African mainland, during the Christian missions of the 1840s[58]) armed hostility, followed by a fight to the death. It is therefore obvious, or so our critic might conclude, that 'civil society' is not just a geographically specific concept with pseudo-universal pretensions; it also has a strong elective affinity with 'the West', and even potentially plays the role of an agent of Western power and influence in the world.

Might talk of a *global* civil society indeed be a wooden horse of European domination? Are there indeed good reasons 'to send back the concept of civil society to where ... it properly belongs – the provincialism of European social philosophy'?[59] Given the *prima facie* evidence, the suspicion that the language of civil society is mixed up in the nasty businesses of hubris and blood has to be taken seriously, and certainly any contemporary use of the phrase needs to be highly sensitive to what is conceptually and politically at stake here. At a minimum – there are many other controversial issues, discussed later in this book, such as the difficulties facing practical efforts to develop the idea of civil society as a

---

[57] The mid-eighteenth-century transition from classical European usages of *societas civilis* (a well-governed political community) to the modern sense of civil society as legally secured spaces of non-violent social interaction is examined in my 'Despotism and Democracy: The Origins and Development of the Distinction Between Civil Society and the State 1750–1850', in John Keane (ed.), *Civil Society and the State: New European Perspectives* (London and New York, 1988 [reprinted 1998]), pp. 35–72.

[58] Philip D. Curtin, *The World and the West. The European Challenge and the Overseas Response in the Age of Empire* (Cambridge and New York, 2000), chapter 7.

[59] Partha Chatterjee, 'A Response to Taylor's "Modes of Civil Society" ', *Public Culture* 3:1 (Fall 1990), p. 120.

global *norm* – it should be remembered that the phrase global civil society has so far been used in this discussion as an ideal-type, for heuristic purposes. This means (as Max Weber first pointed out[60]) that it does not aim initially to manipulate or to dominate others, but rather seeks to name and to describe and to clarify and interpret the world, either past or present. In other words, it seeks to help us better understand the world in all its complexity by simplifying it, intellectually speaking. Whether and how well it manages to perform this task can be decided only by bringing it to bear on the empirical 'reality', whose dynamics it seeks to interpret and to explain. The Western origins of the concept and the possibility that it imposes alien values are thus at this stage irrelevant considerations. What is rather at stake is whether and how well the research questions and empirical findings elucidated by the concept of global civil society prove to be illuminating for others elsewhere in the world.

Illumination here presupposes and requires clean hands. For one of the bitter truths lurking within the contemporary popularity of the language of civil society is the fact that European talk of civil society originally presupposed and required the disempowerment or outright crushing of others elsewhere in the world. Those who today want to universalise this language, to utilise it for descriptive interpretations throughout the world, must face up to this fact. They must acknowledge candidly – in effect, ask others forgiveness for the bad consequences of – some embarrassing historical facts.

The stench of violence that once surrounded talk of 'civilised society', 'civilisation' and 'civility' is prime among these facts. The foundations of civil societies have often been soaked in blood. 'Civilised' worldliness typically developed hand in hand with profoundly 'uncivil' or barbaric forms of domination. Worldly civil societies could nowhere have developed or survived without the superior naval power, deep-rooted pugnacity and comparative immunity to disease that had earlier facilitated the rise of the West, from around 1500 onwards, often in violent, uncivilised form. Among its landmarks, which appear barbaric by today's standards of civility, are the ruthless aggression of Almeida and Albuquerque in the Indian Ocean, the destruction of the Amerindian civilisations of Peru and Mexico, and the generalised hostility towards peoples as diverse as Muslim traders in the Mediterranean basin and aboriginal hunters and gatherers in such countries as Australia and Canada.[61]

---

[60] Max Weber, ' "Objectivity" in Social Science and Social Policy', in Edward A. Shils and Henry A. Finch (eds.), *The Methodology of the Social Sciences* (New York, 1949), p. 90.

[61] William H. McNeill, *The Rise of the West. A History of the Human Community* (Chicago and London, 1963), chapter 11.

Towards the end of the eighteenth century, when the modern language of civil society was still young, those who favoured its institutions and norms were often prepared to wield violence against its enemies, both at home and abroad. Supposing that they were on the side of God, or the angels, they were prepared to traverse unknown frontiers into strange lands, full sail or mounted on horseback, armed with swords, pistols and cannon. They were prepared to stand by the distinction between the 'non-torturable' and 'torturable' classes (Graham Greene). Napoleon's well-known address to his troops just before setting off to conquer Egypt – 'Soldiers', he shouted, 'you are undertaking a conquest with incalculable consequences for civilisation' – was the battle-cry of civil society on the march. The willingness of British colonisers to heap vast quantities of violence onto the bodies of the aboriginal occupants of the lands that they wanted to seize also stands in this tradition.

As well, outer-lying areas of the British Empire were laboratories in which 'civilising' measures were tested on the colonisers themselves. Norfolk Island, originally occupied by British settlers from 1788 to 1814 and today famous for its peaceful and austere beauty, counts as an example. During the second quarter of the nineteenth century, it was transformed by the British authorities into a place of extreme punishment for male convicts who had re-offended in Van Diemen's Land or New South Wales. In the name of a 'civilised society', they were forced to labour from dawn to dusk, and to eat like animals without utensils. At the smallest hints of disobedience, they were fed only bread and water. Frequent lashings – 500 at a time – were commonplace; stubborn offenders were locked in cells where they could neither lie nor stand; and since death was naturally a merciful release from this island hell, prisoners commonly drew lots to decide who would kill whom – and so to decide who could leave the island for Sydney, where murder charges were heard.[62]

Big violence, little violence

Insofar as the civilising mission of the friends of civil society assumed such forms, it should come as no surprise that many early modern champions of civil society scorned others for their alleged inability to develop its institutions. This is another historical fact to be grasped by those who today speak positively of global civil society: in early modern usages, 'civil society' was typically contrasted with 'the Asiatic' region, in which, or so it was said, civil societies had manifestly failed to appear. 'Among the Hindus,

---

[62] See the various pieces of documented evidence in Suzanne Rickard (ed.), *George Barrington's Voyage to Botany Bay* (Leicester, 2001).

according to the Asiatic model', wrote James Mill with India in mind, 'the government was monarchical, and, with the usual exception of religion and its ministers, absolute. No idea of any system of rule, different from the will of a single person, appears to have entered the minds of them or their legislators.'[63] Marx and Engels, who were otherwise no friends of modern civil society (*bürgerliche Gesellschaft*), similarly observed that in the East the 'first basic condition of bourgeois acquisition is lacking: the security of the person and the property of the trader'.[64] And along parallel lines, Tocqueville noted that whereas in America the spirit of Christianity enabled the growth of a civil society and democratic institutions, the Muslim faith and manners had heaped materialism and fatalism onto its believers. The chronic decadence of Islam meant that 'the great violence of conquest' initially carried out by Europeans in countries like Algeria would need to be supplemented by 'smaller violences'. He considered that 'there have been few religions in the world as deadly to men as that of Mohammed', and he was sure that it was 'the principal cause of the decadence so visible today in the Muslim world'. Civil society was impossible in Muslim societies. Their pacification required a two-tier political order: a ruling group based on the principles of Christian civilisation, and a ruled group of natives who would continue to live by the laws of the *Qur'ān*.[65]

Friends of global civil society must today be encouraged to ask tough questions of such views. They would be wise to cultivate an allergic reaction to such claims, not only because in practice (in the extreme) they can have murderous consequences, but also because the early modern picture of the Muslim world that pre-existed Western colonisation typically blanked out its plurality of social institutions that had all the qualities – but not the name – of a certain religious form of civil society.[66] Here the theory of global civil society encounters a semantic problem: the name (*koinonia politike*; *societas civilis*; civil society) was of course a European invention, but the substance of civil association protected by law was

[63] James Mill, *The History of British India* (London, 1817), vol. 1, p. 122.

[64] Karl Marx and Frederick Engels, 'The Foreign Policy of Russian Czarism', in *The Russian Menace in Europe* (London, 1953), p. 40.

[65] See the letter to Gobineau in Alexis de Tocqueville, *Oeuvres complètes*, ed. J. P. Mayer (Paris, 1951–), vol. 9, p. 69; the unpublished letter to Lamoricière (5 April 1846), cited in André Jardin, *Tocqueville: A Biography* (New York, 1988), p. 318; and Pierre Michel, 'Démocratie et Barbarie', in *Un mythe romantique, les Barbares, 1789–1848* (Lyons, 1981), pp. 267–92. More generally, see the important essay of Bryan S. Turner, 'Orientalism and the Problem of Civil Society in Islam', in Asaf Hussain *et al.* (eds.), *Orientalism, Islam and Islamists* (Brattleboro, VT, 1984), pp. 23–42.

[66] The literature on this topic is vast, but see Ira M. Lapidus, *History of Islamic Societies* (Cambridge, 1988) and 'Muslim Cities and Islamic Societies', in Ira M. Lapidus (ed.), *Middle Eastern Cities: A Symposium on Ancient Islamic and Contemporary Middle Eastern Urbanism* (Berkeley, 1969), pp. 47–74.

common throughout the world of Muslim societies *before* European conquest. This point was noted by quite a few eighteenth-century European observers with clear eyes and an open mind. Jean-Jacques Rousseau (who admittedly favoured undivided, small republics) even complained that Muslims too strictly distinguished between the theological and political systems. 'Mahomet held very sane views, and linked his political system well together; and, as long as the form of his government continued under the caliphs who succeeded him, that government was indeed one, and so far good', he wrote. 'But the Arabs', he added, 'having grown prosperous, lettered, civilized, slack, and cowardly, were conquered by barbarians: the division between the two [theological and political] powers began again; and, although it is less apparent among the Mahometans than among the Christians, it none the less exists, especially in the sect of Ali, and there are States, such as Persia, where it is continually making itself felt'.[67]

Rousseau's observation stood the charge of Caesaro-papism against the Islamic world on its head. It suggested, and more recent observers have agreed, that the East – a slothful term that projects ignorance onto the profound complexity of the vast geographic and cultural area to which it refers – was not a sewer of slavishness, a world without private property ruled by Great Monarchs who treated their subjects as if they were mere households of women, children and slaves. The fragmentary evidence that survives instead suggests that these early civil societies most probably were pioneers in the field of contract law. These societies, for instance, were dotted with cities that functioned as cosmopolitan traffic nodes, entrepôts and facilitators of a vast proto-world system.[68] These societies also had the longest recorded history of private and civil law covering the protection of trade and property, whose predominant form was that of partnership.[69] These partnerships were not based on the familiar European employer–employee relation (which was widely regarded as a form of slavery) and they certainly did not give rise to class differences between owners and non-owners of property; property, production and trade were rather embedded in households, neighbourhood or confessional groupings, in which business partners, women and men alike, considered each other as 'owners', regardless of whether they contributed capital or labour to the partnership. Social ties were typically multiple, fluid, and dynamic – 'fuzzy' rather than monolithic, enumerated, and

[67] Jean-Jacques Rousseau, *The Social Contract*, in *The Social Contract and Discourses* (New York, 1913), book 4, chapter 8, p. 109.

[68] J. Abu-Lughod, *Before European Hegemony: The World System AD 1250–1350* (Cambridge, 1989).

[69] Mikhail Rostovtzeff, *Caravan Cities* (Oxford, 1932), pp. 8–9; Solomon Goitein, 'Commercial and Family Partnerships in the Countries of Medieval Islam', *Islamic Studies* 3 (1964), pp. 315–37, and his *Studies in Islamic History and Institutions* (Leiden, 1966), pp. 270–8.

homogeneous, like many of the later forms of colonial bonds.[70] The effect, among others, was to block the emergence of large-scale trading and manufacturing firms of the kind that first developed in Britain, France and the Netherlands, and the rise of absolutist forms of political rule as well. Seen in this way, the 'Oriental' despotic state much analysed and feared by European writers was an *effect* of foreign conquest and Western colonisation. Its *'grande violence'* (de Tocqueville) typically succeeded because the colonisers had at their disposal military and communications resources and long experience of the arts of absolutist rule.

The effect, in most cases, was to destroy or badly maim the complex of pre-existing social institutions and business partnerships, so creating vacuums that could be filled up by the *étatiste* institutions of the colonial powers and their comprador rulers (shahs, emirs, kings).[71] The new Turkey under Kemalist rule (1923–38) is a clear case in point: the nationalist state-building led by Mustafa Kemal (later crowned with the name of Atatürk, or 'Father of the Turks') eliminated the entire system of religious schools, with the *mekteps* and *medreses* compulsorily reorganised under the direction of the Ministry of Education. Secular codes of law based on Italian, Swiss and German precedents were rigorously applied in the fields of civil, criminal and commercial law. Materials printed in the Arabic and Persian languages were banned, and Turkish translations of the *Qur'ān*, anathema to orthodox Muslims, were encouraged and recited publicly. Religious titles and their use were abolished, and dervish lodges (*tekke*) and cells (*zaviye*) were closed. Western clothing was officially encouraged, and Sunday, rather than the Muslim Friday holiday, was declared the official day of rest. The old system of locating places in relation to public squares and places was countered by laws specifying that buildings and houses had to be numbered and all streets named, according to the European custom. The first Turkish beauty contests were staged; alcohol was legalised for Muslims; and civil marriages for all became compulsory. And, as if to crown all these 'secular' measures backed by threats of military violence from above, regal statues and majestic paintings of Kemal were placed in public places – so violating the old Muslim tradition of opposition to the inflated representation and deification of living things.[72]

[70] Sudipta Kaviraj, 'The Imaginary Institution of India', in Partha Chatterjee and Gyanendra Pandey (eds.), *Subaltern Studies*, VII (New Delhi, 1992), pp. 20–6.

[71] See Hannah Batatu, *The Old Social Classes and the Revolutionary Movements of Iraq* (Princeton, 1978); the claim that theories of oriental despotism sprang up as a foil for classical republicanism is well defended in Patricia Springborg, *Western Republicanism and the Oriental Prince* (Cambridge, 1992).

[72] See, for instance, Stanford J. Shaw and Ezel Kural Shaw, *History of the Ottoman Empire and Modern Turkey*, vol. 2 (Cambridge and London, 1977), esp. chapter 6; Andrew Davison, *Secularism and Revivalism in Turkey* (New Haven and London, 1998).

Travelling

A final introductory thought: it is significant, and profoundly ironical, that descriptive usages of the concept of global civil society have now spread to every continent of the globe. The birth and maturation of global civil society has been riddled with many ironies. We shall see later that its civil institutions can even be understood and defended as the condition of a healthy, publicly shared sense of irony, but for the moment here is among the strangest ironies of all: an originally European way of life, some of whose members set out brutally to colonise the world in the name of a civil society, helped lay the foundations for its own universal appeal and, with that, strengthened civil resistance to colonising forms of power and prejudice originally traceable to the European region. The revolts of the colonised in the name of a 'civilised society' against British imperial power in the eighteenth-century American colonies was the first-ever case in point of this unintended consequence. There have subsequently been many more and recent instances of these ironic, failed attempts to crush the willpower of a (potentially) self-governing civil society through armed state or imperial power that once prided itself on its own 'civilising mission'. Examples range from the gentle and prolonged resistance to imperial power by locally formed civil societies (as in Australia and New Zealand) to the volcanic upheavals against colonial and post-colonial power in contexts otherwise as different as Haiti, India, South Africa and Nigeria.

One important effect of such unintended developments is observable: the contemporary 'emigration' of the language of civil society, from its original birthplace in Europe to all four corners of the earth.[73] In recent years, the family of terms 'civil society' and 'global civil society' have proved to be good travellers. After making a first appearance in Japan and then developing vigorously in the European region, including its eastern fringes – the *New York Times* has reported that civil society is 'almost a mantra in Russian politics these days'[74] – the terms spread to the United States and Canada, and throughout central and South America. They have appeared as well throughout sub-Saharan Africa, Oceania, and all regions of Asia and the Muslim world.[75] This globalisation of the concept of civil society is one aspect of the emergent global civil society,

---

[73] See my *Civil Society and the State: Old Images and New Visions*, esp. pp. 32 ff.

[74] *New York Times*, June 22, 2000.

[75] The literature is vast and still growing rapidly. Among the best-known contributions are Sudipta Kaviraj and Sunil Khilnani (eds.), *Civil Society: History and Possibilities* (Cambridge and New York, 2001); Richard Augustus Norton (ed.), *Civil Society in the Middle East*, 2 vols. (Leiden, 1995); Chris Hann and Elizabeth Dunn (eds.), *Civil Society: Challenging Western Models* (New York, 1996); Tadashi Yamamoto (ed.) *Emerging Civil Society in the Asia Pacific Community: Nongovernmental Underpinnings of the Emerging Asia*

for it shows how civil society ideas and languages and institutions are spreading beyond their place of origin into new contexts, where they are in turn conceptualised or re-conceptualised in local contexts, from where the revisions, which are sometimes cast in very different terms, may and often do feed back into the original donor contexts.[76] Not only is talk of civil society now heard world-wide within circles of journalists, lawyers and academics. NGOs, business people, professionals, diplomats and politicians of various persuasions also like to speak the same language. Its popularity may well convince future historians to look back on this globalisation of the term and to judge that its global extension, which is without precedent, signalled the first step in the long-term emergence of common frameworks of social meaning against the tyranny of distance and the constrictions of state boundaries. Tomorrow's historians may well conclude that the spreading talk of civil society was not just talk. They may highlight the fact that something new was born in the world – the unprecedented (if unevenly distributed) growth of the sense within NGOs and publics at large that civilians live in one world, and that they have obligations to other civilians living beyond their borders, simply because they are civilians.

Proof positive of this trend is the reception by scholars and activists alike of the idea and ideal of civil society in the Indian sub-continent. In recent years, this reception has been driven by renewed interest in indigenous traditions of civility, widespread disappointment with the post-colonial state, market reforms, and the defence of civil and political rights against religious nationalism and authoritarian state policies. Three different versions of the case for civil society seem to predominate. The *traditionalist* approach criticises state violence and calls for 'humane governance' based upon strengthened indigenous traditions. The project of strengthening a civil society that is 'rooted in diversity yet cohering and holding together' must draw upon 'surviving traditions of togetherness, mutuality and resolution of differences and conflict'.[77] Others reject this traditionalist approach as nostalgia for traditions that harbour inequality and individual unfreedom – and produce instability within modern institutions. These critics prefer instead to walk the path originally trodden by Paine and Tocqueville, to reach a different understanding of civil society as a distinctively modern sphere of voluntary associations, some of

---

Pacific Regional Community (Singapore and Tokyo, 1995); John L. and Jean Comaroff (eds.), *Civil Society and the Political Imagination in Africa: Critical Perspectives* (Chicago and London, 1999); and John Keane (ed.), *Civil Society and the State: New European Perspectives*.

[76] Makoto Iokibe, 'Japan's Civil Society: An Historical Overview', in Tadashi Yamamoto (ed.), *Deciding the Public Good: Governance and Civil Society in Japan* (Tokyo, 1999).

[77] Rajni Kothari, *State Against Democracy: In Search of Humane Governance* (Delhi, 1988).

them of colonial origin, that stand as buffer zones between the individual and governmental institutions. Constitutional democracy in India is seen to require a *modern* civil society: a plurality of secular and inclusive institutions that enjoy considerable autonomy from state power.[78]

Some who are otherwise sympathetic to this *modernist* approach doubt its implied teleology: they point out that such 'civil–social' institutions are in short supply, that they are confined to well-to-do strata, and that this *lack* of modern civil associations in a society dominated by caste and religious ties is the key indicator of the post-colonial condition.[79] Still others – the *anthropological* approach – question this interpretation of post-colonialism. They seek to cut through the pre-colonial/post-colonial dualism by pointing to the ways in which castes and religious communities deserve to be included in any descriptive–analytical account of civil society. Randeria, for instance, denies that castes and religious communities are (or were ever) describable as traditional 'organic bonds of kinship', as standard accounts of the tradition/modernity divide have supposed.[80] She points out, persuasively, that the social groupings within pre-colonial India, castes included, were typically multiple, flexible and fluid, rather than rigid and exclusive in outlook. The Gujarat community of Mole-Salam Garasia Rajputs, which until recently assigned a Hindu and Muslim name to each one of its members, is an example of this dynamic heterogeneity, which evidently survived colonial conquest: in the 1911 census, nearly a quarter of a million Indians described themselves as 'Mohammedan Hindus'.[81]

Randeria acknowledges that colonial administration, which sought to map and control Indian society, was responsible for the refashioning of territorially defined castes into enumerated communities through bureaucratic definition: for the purposes of census classification and counting, employment in the colonial administration, and the allocation of seats in representative bodies, colonial administrators twisted social identities like religion and caste (*samaj*, or society, in Gujarat) into political

---

[78] André Béteille, *Civil Society and Its Institutions*, delivered as the first Fulbright Memorial Lecture (Calcutta, 1996), as well as his *Society and Politics in India* (London, 1991) and 'The Conflict of Norms and Values in Contemporary Indian Society', in Peter Berger (ed.), *The Limits of Social Cohesion: Conflict and Mediation in Plural Societies* (Boulder, Co. 1998), pp. 265–92.

[79] Partha Chatterjee, 'On Civil and Political Society in Post-Colonial Democracies', in Sudipta Kaviraj and Sunil Khilnani (eds.), *Civil Society. History and Possibilities* (Cambridge, 2001), pp. 165–78.

[80] Shalini Randeria, 'Geteilte Geschichte und verwobene Moderne', in Jörn Rüsen et al. (eds), *Zukunftsentwürfe. Ideen für eine Kultur der Veränderung* (Frankfurt am Main, 1999), pp. 87–96, and 'From Cohesion to Connectedness: Civil Society, Caste Solidarities and Legal Pluralism in Post-Colonial India', in Keane (ed.), *Civil Society: Berlin Perspectives*.

[81] S. T. Lokhandwala, 'Indian Islam: Composite Culture and Integration', *New Quest*, 50 (1985), pp. 87–101.

categories. Randeria also acknowledges that these bureaucratic classifica-
tions had profound political and social effects, so that by the early decades
of the twentieth century, caste organisations and communal parties were
mobilising to define and protect their interests on an India-wide basis. Yet
she goes on to point out – against politically loaded, nationalist claims on
behalf of a homogeneous Hindu majority – that, despite their ascriptive
qualities, most lower castes, including the so-called 'untouchable castes'
(scheduled castes, as the Indian constitution calls them), continue to be
largely self-governing local collectivities. They enjoy a measure of self-
conscious jurisdiction and authority over their members – a power that
is often jealously guarded against state intrusions. Castes are far from
being kinship groups with unalterable customs and procedures. Their as-
semblies (*panchayat*), comprising all the adult members of a local caste
unit (*paraganu*), are sites of deliberations about rules and the contestation of norms that are vital for maintaining the patterns of solidarity and
belonging – and for resisting unwanted state intervention in such matters
as the rules of marriage, divorce and re-marriage, the exchange of food
and care arrangements for children.

Randeria points out that the European language of civil society first
travelled to India during the nineteenth century. With the founding of
the colonial state, the civil sphere – often not named as such[82] – took
the form of spaces of social life either untampered with by colonial rulers
or established through the resistance to their power by colonial subjects
themselves. Randeria shows that the subsequent debates about civil society in India have come to interact with different European images of
civil society, so highlighting not only their travelling potential but also
the ways in which 'foreign' or 'imported' languages both resonate within
local contexts, and are often (heavily) refashioned as a result. They then
become subject to 're-export', back to the context from which they originally came, in consequence of which the language of civil society is both
pluralised and *globalised*. The impressive cooperation between the coalition called Narmada Bachao Andolan (formed in 1988) and INGOs like
Oxfam and The Environment Defense Fund in campaigns in support of

---

[82] A difficult but interesting and inescapable problem of interpretation arises here: the
possibility that some of the institutional practices of global civil society in various parts
of the world neither presently consider themselves participants within this society nor
use nor understand the language of civil society. Throughout this book, the problem is
treated as generously as possible, in that actors and institutions that more or less abide by
the rules of global civil society, outlined in this introduction, can legitimately be called by
that proper name. Just as we commonly distinguish between the terms in which people
describe themselves and how they are described by others, so global civil society is a
space containing many identities that go by other names – including identities that smell
sweet despite the fact that they are not called roses.

the right of people *not* to be displaced by dam construction in western India illustrates what Randeria has in mind. The profound theoretical implication of her point should not be missed: *multiple* and *multi-dimensional* and *entangled* languages of civil society now contribute to the definition of the world of global civil society. Contrary to Gellner and Hall and others, civil society is not a uniquely Western achievement.[83] Its forms appeared in a large number of different contexts – even in the so-called 'dark' continent of Africa, with its pre-colonial institutions like the Tswana *kgolta* and old traditions of 'invisible governance' articulated through local, socially shared styles, aspirations and secrets of individuals and groups.[84] Not only that: Western definitions of civil society are not universal in any simple sense. The plural understandings of civil society within the modern West – the term itself now grates, since modern European definitions of civil society are much messier and more divided than that – are to be seen as one *particular* approach, and not as a universal language that is thought to be synonymous with a world history that leads teleologically, smugly, triumphantly, to the silencing or annihilation of other, 'residual' definitions of social order.

---

[83] Ernest Gellner, *Conditions of Liberty. Civil Society and Its Rivals* (London, 1994); J. A. Hall (ed.), *Civil Society: Theory, History and Comparison* (Cambridge, 1995).

[84] See David Hecht and Maliqalim Simone, *Invisible Governance: The Art of African Micropolitics* (New York, 1994); Ali A. Mazrui, 'Globalisation and the Future of Islamic Civilisation' (Centre for the Study of Democracy, London, June 2000); and John L. and Jean Comaroff, 'Postcolonial Politics and Discourses of Democracy in Southern Africa: An Anthropological Reflection on African Political Modernities', *Journal of Anthropological Research*, 53:2 (1997), pp. 123–46.

Catalysts

Traditions: the call of God

Both the idea and the concrete dynamics of global civil society can be better grasped by dwelling for a moment upon its historical origins. Intellectual proponents and activist champions of the idea of a global civil society have a bad habit of supposing that its institutions were born yesterday. By disregarding traditions – the gift of the dead to the living – the fans of global civil society fail to spot the deep roots of this globalising civil society. These run deep and have an entangled and branched – rhizomatous – quality about them. The social ties bound up with these traditions that feed present-day global civil society can be clarified by examining two separate but overlapping examples – taken from the worlds of Islam and Europe, respectively. They are arbitrarily chosen, but each illustrates two points that are of fundamental interest: that global civil society was formed by the horizon-stretching effects of previous social formations; and that these world-defining effects made possible the 'action and re-action at a distance' effects that are an intrinsic feature of global civil society.

Religious civilisations certainly developed world-views and world-girdling institutions that feed the streams of social life that are today global. Consider the new world religion of Islam, which was born in the early seventh century AD, in a region of the Arabian desert blanketed with crescent-shaped dunes and spotted with palm-fringed oases and teeming market towns populated by wandering tribes of Arab pagans and Jewish and Christian traders and travellers. Within a century of the Prophet's death (632 AD), the call of the muezzin from the minaret – 'There is no god except God and Muhammed is the Apostle of God' – echoed in communities as far afield as Spain and China.[1] The lands that curved from Gibraltar around through North Africa and stretched eastwards to the Middle East and Persia were typically seen by Muslim scholars and

---

[1] Richard M. Eaton, *Essays on Islam and Indian History* (Oxford, 2001).

clerics as the gravitational centre of the human world. That perception is evident in the world map prepared in 1154 AD by Muhammed al-Idrisi, the Arab cartographer of the court of King Roger of Sicily: with south at the top, it places the Arabian peninsula at the top centre, with the diminutive European lands on the right.

This Muslim view of itself as the fulcrum of the world – in reality it was (and remains) divided against itself and contained a rich fare of different perspectives and tendencies – was nurtured by the remarkable capacity of Islamic society to accept and make use of technical innovations, like paper; cities such as Baghdad were famous for their fine-quality paper, which enabled the development of Arabic numerals, map-making and the impressive calligraphic copies of the *Qur'ān*. Early Islam was also driven by an ethical vision that was universalising in two related senses. The *Qur'ān* rejected the idea of a chosen people. Instead, it emphasised a strong sense of common human destiny. The monotheistic belief in Allah as Creator implied universalism. It required that human life be measured by standards larger than tribal standards, such as individual and group pride and vengeful, blood-feuding honour; the quest for goodness implied living up to the God-given standards of the world as a whole. The universalism of Islam naturally implied the need to 'disenchant' the world by ridding it of superstition and idolatry. The belief in Allah as Creator was also seen to demand moral purity and responsibility of the individual. Although the *Qur'ān* made no attempt to lay down a comprehensive system of morals – it did not pretend to be a know-all ideology – its emphasis on moral purity and responsibility implied the need for just social behaviour, as well as the need for a just political system that would curb the licence of the strong and extend generosity to the weak.

The understanding by Muslims that Islam was a higher synthesis of two distinct predecessors – Judaism and Christianity – proved in the long run to be a vital contribution to the precious political principle of toleration of different, potentially conflicting ways of life. Although Islam's firm commitment to monotheism ruled out sympathy for scepticism or outright disbelief, and although it supposed (according to a species of teleological metaphysics) that Judaism and Christianity had been superseded, Islam was undoubtedly a force for cosmopolitan pluralism. Muslims drew back from the bigoted view that the belief systems of Jews and Christians were somehow 'irrational' or just plain 'wrong'. They instead reasoned that the birth of Muhammad and the revelations of the *Qur'ān* perfected the earlier revelations embodied in Judaism and Christianity. Muhammad was seen to have set the seal on the words and deeds of earlier prophets sent by God; analogously, the *Qur'ān* was His final and most perfect revelation. So it can be said with hindsight that Islam was the first of the world's great religious civilisations to understand itself as one religion among others. There is evidence as well that, quite unlike Judaism or Christianity or any previous ancient pagan cult, Islam was responsible for the invention of the very idea and term of religion itself. 'Say: O Unbelievers!', begins one command. It continues: 'I shall not worship what you worship. You do not worship what I worship. I am not a worshiper of what you have worshiped and you are not worshipers of what I have worshiped. To you, your religion. To me, my religion.'[2]

Islam's universalising achievements were impressive in a second – geopolitical – sense. During the first century and a half after the birth of the Prophet, Muslim believers and armies advanced westward to north Africa and thence into Spain and France, and eastward into Byzantium, across Persia and into India and China. These Muslims considered themselves as messengers in the world. They thought in terms of the distinction between people who had already heeded the call of God and people who still awaited (or were denied) that call. The distinction took various forms. Some jurists and scholars contrasted the actually existing community of believers (*ummat ad-da'wah*) with the potentially universal community of humanity (*ummat al-istijabah*). Others quoted the two-fold appeal within the *Qur'ān*: 'O you Believers' (*ya ayyuha allatheena aamanu*) and 'O Mankind' (*ya ayyuha'n-naasu*). Still others distinguished between the House of Islam (*Dār al-Islām*) and the House of Unbelievers (*Dār al-Kufr*). And there were some proselytising Muslims who supposed that the world was sub-divided into the House of Islam (*Dār al-Islām*), those territories where the laws of Islam prevailed, and the rest of the world, called the House of War (*Dār al-Harb*). This latter division, which had no basis in the *Qur'ān*, was not seen to be static, for in time, so Muslim scholars and jurists supposed, Islam would prevail among the world's peoples, either by willing acceptance, or by spiritual fervour, or (in the face of violent resistances) by conquest. Note that in every case, jurists and scholars agreed that all of humanity, including those who lived in the House of Unbelievers, would either accept or (voluntarily) submit to Islam. Note as well Islam's lack of interest in the originally European project of dividing the world into nations or states. Islamic scholars instead supposed that since there is only one God, so there must be only one law on earth – and therefore only one religious duty, the struggle to serve God by effort or striving (*jihād*).

In practice, things turned out differently. Islam's universalism was thwarted, leaving many Muslims with a forward-looking memory that

---

[2] *Sū-rat* 109. On the path-breaking conception of religion in Islam, see W. Cantwell Smith, *The Meaning and End of Religion* (New York, 1964), pp. 58ff. and 75ff.

remains strong until today: a vivid awareness of Islam's splendid historical achievements combined with the refusal to accept the present-day world, which is felt to be an imposed burden. There were several reasons why Islam's universalising vision did not fully mature, including the elementary fact that, at its highpoint, some parts of the world were not 'discovered' by Islam, let alone drawn into the *Umma* through conquest. Until the nineteenth century, for instance, Muslims knew nothing of *terra australis* and its surrounding islands. The Europe – spelled *Urūba* – from which Islam had been militarily expelled had become rather ill-defined; and the southern Americas, conquered by the Spanish, Portuguese and British, among others, were off-limits. Moreover, when it came to dealing with the House of Unbelievers, Islam demonstrated a willingness to compromise with its opponents, one of which, Christianity, subsequently stopped it in its tracks. Consequently, the principle of *jihād*, the duty to struggle for God against His doubters and enemies, was rarely put unconditionally. Since victory over the world of non-believers was ultimately assured, others, including trade and traffic with the infidel, were encouraged. Figures like Ibn Maaja, al-Miqreezi, and Saa'id al-Andalussi excelled at the art of travel and, in fact, many Muslims considered travellers (*rahhaalah*) and traders (*tujjaar*) as engaged in forms of worship. The point was to change the world by using all means, including the stretching of one's perceptual horizons, so that all human beings, young and old, rich and poor, black and white, male and female, Christian and Jew, would come to regard Islam as *the* universal religion.

In practice, these precepts met with mixed success, especially from the time of the Crusades. Between the eleventh and fifteenth centuries, not only was Islam forced militarily to withdraw from certain territories, like Italy, Portugal and Spain, whose reconquest was in effect postponed from earthly to messianic time. Its vision of world unity also fragmented into many smaller regional or state units. Truces and peace agreements with infidels, across borders, became prolonged. The practice of extending the right of safe conduct (*amān*) of infidels to visit and pass through Muslim lands, extending this right even to whole communities (of traders and diplomats, for instance) to reside there indefinitely, became commonplace. There were also moves by certain jurists to recognise what was called the House of Truce or House of Covenant (*Dār al-Sulh* or *Dār al 'Ahd*). This was understood as a kind of intermediary zone comprising non-Muslim political units which were allowed to retain and enjoy their quasi-independent status and engage in political and commercial exchanges for the price of paying financial tributes and giving contractual recognition (*'ahd*) to Muslim suzerainty.

The path to 1914

The complex history of the interaction of the Christian and Islamic universes – the dialectics of their mutual admiration, their intercourse, mutual suspicion and military hostilities – need not detain us here.[3] It is important only to note that the rise of the Christian West out of the heartlands of the European region effectively blocked the Islamic quest for world supremacy. The appearance of the West on the world stage – the birth around 1500 of what Fernand Braudel famously called 'histoire globale' – was made possible by its superior naval power, deep-rooted pugnacity and comparative immunity to disease. Although it often triumphed by using uncivilised, violent means, this world-conquering power of the West became the saddle in which European versions of civil society institutions rode to the four corners of the earth, for the first time.[4] The West was not just synonymous with great voyages of discovery and the rise of capitalism and the territorial state. It gave birth as well to modern struggles for liberty of the press, written constitutions, religious toleration, new codes of 'civil' manners (often connected with sport), non-violent power-sharing, and talk of democracy and human rights, whose combined 'ethos' gradually spawned the growth of civil society institutions.

By the nineteenth century, the visible outlines of a robust global civil society were evident. During the half-century of events that unfolded prior to the outbreak of the First World War, it underwent a great growth spurt. Graham Wallas summarised this trend towards 'The Great Society'. 'During the last hundred years', he wrote in 1914, 'the external conditions of civilised life have been transformed by a . . . general change of social scale. Men find themselves working and thinking and feeling in relation to an environment, which, both in its world-wide extension and its intimate connection with all sides of human existence, is without precedent in the history of the world.'[5] During these years, the foundations of worldliness markedly strengthened. Today's global civil society rests on these foundations: it grows in old soil and – to switch to a favourite simile in the arsenal of modern conservatism – it would perish like an insect at the end of summer were it not for the worldly traditions of long-distance trade and commerce, travel and self-organisation that are now

---

[3] Among the reliable studies are Ira M. Lapidus, *A History of Islamic Societies* (Cambridge and New York, 1988), esp. part 3.

[4] See, for example, the studies of Kenneth Pomeranz and Steven Topik, *The World That Trade Created. Society, Culture, and the World Economy, 1400 to the Present* (London, 2002), and R. J. Barendse, *The Arabian Seas. The Indian Ocean World of the Seventeenth Century* (London, 2002).

[5] Graham Wallas, *The Great Society* (London, 1914), p. 3.

part of the world's inheritance. The new-fangled words 'global civil society' are sorcerous in this respect. Their recent invention might convince the uninitiated that a global civil society is a recent invention. The plain fact, however, is that quite a lot of what is characteristic of today's global civil society originated in the half-century before 1914, when the planet began to feel much more tightly knitted together by the threads of people, capital, commodities and ideas in motion.[6]

Lots of examples spring to mind. In this period, for the first time in human history, the globe was finally mapped adequately, thanks to cartographers armed with guns and expeditions like the race of Peary of the United States to the North Pole (1909) and Amundsen of Norway to the South Pole (1911).[7] This same period saw radical changes in the nature and scope of transportation and communication technologies, for instance the invention and diffusion of the telegraph, telephones and wireless communications. The first transatlantic cable was laid in 1866. During the same decade, the steamship connected masses of people and goods to the shores of the world's great oceans. The world's railway network expanded five times between 1875 and 1914 (from 200,000 km to over 1 million km), while available figures of the tonnage moved by merchant ships show a doubling in the same period. Travel by rail and steamship naturally became commonplace and – thanks to developments like the completion in 1904 of the Trans-Siberian Railway, which enabled passengers to travel between Paris and Vladivostok in a fortnight – the time of intercontinental and trans-continental journeys was reduced from months to weeks. Little wonder, then, that one-seventh of the world's population moved countries during this period. 36 million people alone left Europe between 1871 and 1915.[8] Meanwhile, the motorised car was made operational by Daimler and Benz during the 1880s, and there were even some signs that the new means of space- and time-conquering means of communication would become genuinely popular. The average number of letters sent annually by each adult inhabitant in Britain rose from two in 1815 to forty-two in the 1880s. Submarine and overland cabling

---

[6] The seminal account of this period is Eric Hobsbawm, *The Age of Empire 1875–1914* (New York, 1989); see also Roland Robertson, 'Mapping the Global Condition: Globalization as the Central Concept', in Mike Featherstone (ed.), *Global Culture* (London, 1993), pp. 15–30.

[7] A fascinating example, the mapping of Guyana, is analysed in D. Graham Burnett, *Masters of All They Surveyed. Exploration, Geography, and a British El Dorado* (Chicago, 2000). Note the contemporary remark of Max Weber in *Archiv für Sozialwissenschaft und Sozialpolitik*, 12:1 (1906), pp. 347–8: 'there is no new continent at our disposal.'

[8] Dudley Baines, *Emigration from Europe* (Cambridge and New York, 1995), p. 1; W. Arthur Lewis, *Growth and Fluctuations, 1870–1914* (London, 1978), p. 181; and Aron Segal and Linda Marston, 'World Voluntary Migration', *Migration World*, 17:1 (1989), pp. 36–41.

enabled telegraph messages to whizz around the world as never before. The telephone also spread rapidly so that by 1910 significant numbers of households in countries like the United States and Britain were proud owners and users, mainly for conversing at a distance with family and friends.

Another striking development during this period was the creation, for the first time, of a single global economy that stretched from its European homelands towards every remote atoll, desert plateau and jungle basin of the earth.[9] Measured in terms of gross national product (GNP), both the exports and imports of capital were considerably greater than today. The long-distance networks of trade and commerce grew especially tight among the more 'developed' countries; four-fifths of imports and exports of goods and foreign investments flowed *within* this bloc.[10] There were nevertheless modest increases in trade with Asia, Oceania and Africa; and webs of interdependence were spun over most of the rest of the world, transforming them into colonial or semi-colonial territories. The whole world consequently began to feel much smaller, thanks to long-distance trade in commodities entering markets in Europe. The new motor and electrical industries hungered after copper from Zambia, Zaire, Peru and Chile. Meat came from Uruguay, wheat from Australia, nitrates from Chile, rubber from the Congo and the Amazon basin, coffee from Brazil, and cigars and sugar from Cuba. A whole world clothed itself in cheap and hygienic cotton textiles developed originally in Manchester.

The dramatic expansion of long-distance commerce was flanked by the full-throated growth in the number and scope of cross-border, non-governmental, not-for-profit organisations. Their significance is some-times ignored by historians.[11] Or it is claimed that their influence was restricted to Christian missionary activity; or that the social and political impact of this part of the nascent global civil society was at first minimal, becoming significant for the first time only in the aftermath of the Second World War.[12]

These three approaches are misleading, for several reasons. Contrary to some secularist accounts of the pre-1914 period, Christian missionary

---

[9] Eric Hobsbawm, *The Age of Capital 1848–1875* (London, 1988), chapter 3.

[10] P. Bairoch, 'Geographical Structure and Trade Balance of European Foreign Trade from 1800 to 1970', *Journal of European Economic History*, 3 (1974), pp. 557–608.

[11] Eric Hobsbawm does so in his classic account of this period, *The Age of Empire*. Compare Harold K. Jacobson, *Networks of Interdependence. International Organizations and the Global Political System* (New York, 1984), esp. pp. 32–58 and John Boli and George M. Thomas (eds.), *Constructing World Culture* (Stanford, 1999).

[12] Hobsbawm, *The Age of Empire*; and, for example, David Armstrong *et al.*, *From Versailles to Maastricht: International Organisation in the Twentieth Century* (Basingstoke, 1996), pp. 5, 55, 85, 250.

activity reached record proportions. Championed by bodies bearing fearsome names like the Society for Converting and Civilizing the Indians, Franciscan Missionaries of the Divine Motherhood, and the Society for the Propagation of the Gospel in Foreign Parts, the numbers of translations of the Bible soared to nearly 120 different languages and dialects; the number of new missions, especially in Africa, also soared.[13] Although missionary adventures typically pick-a-backed on the industrial and military and naval might of imperial states, sheltering under the sword to save the soul, the missionaries were often at odds with the authorities in such colonies as Uganda, Nyasaland (Malawi) and Rhodesia (Zimbabwe and Zambia). They were not the only examples of 'civilising' initiatives. In fact – contrary to the standard account – during this period many scores of civic initiatives, not only religious endeavours, ensured that groups that later came to be called NGOs came to play a visible role in publicising social problems and grievances and fostering new forms of intergovernmental cooperation.

Examples spring readily from the pages of much-neglected histories and primary accounts of the period. Path-breaking negotiations took place on the need to grant a juridical status (international legal personality) to non-profit 'private' groups having an international purpose and permitting membership from different countries.[14] This period also saw the emergence, for the first time, of a new collective self-awareness among NGOs of their moral influence and power potential in trans-national settings. The decision in Brussels in 1910 to found the Union of International Associations at the World Congress of International Associations attended by 132 international associations and thirteen governments was one important symbol of this emergent self-reflexiveness.[15] Meanwhile, in various policy areas, civic initiatives and movements started lessons in the art of pressuring political power; they discovered that they could dig their fingers into the flesh of governments, and extract concessions, either in the form of intergovernmental agreements to cooperate in policy matters, or through new social policy measures.

Practically all of the important social reforms backed by governments before 1914 – in areas like intellectual property, narcotics trafficking,

---

[13] James Sibree, *A Register of Missionaries... from 1796 to 1923* (London, 1923); *Encyclopedia of Missions*, 2nd edn. (New York and London, 1904), appendix iv, pp. 838–9.

[14] See the *23 Annuaire de L'Institut de Droit International* (Brussels, 1910), p. 551 and Peter H. Rohn, *Relations Between the Council of Europe and International Non-Governmental Organizations* (Union of International Associations, 6 [Brussels, 1957]), pp. 17–19.

[15] See *1 Congrès Mondial des Associations Internationales 1910* (Brussels, 1911) and the publication of the Union of International Associations, *Union of International Associations 1910–1970* (Brussels, 1970), pp. 26–7.

labour conditions and prostitution – were due not to government initiative, but rather to the direct or indirect pressures exerted by voluntary, self-organising social initiatives.[16] The practice of government officials participating alongside civil society actors in international conferences became customary. It is even correct to speak of the emergence, for the first time in the modern world, of *traditions* of cross-border civil initiatives. Some of these initiatives aimed to establish a standardised global legal infrastructure. Networks of associations of statisticians and scientists, for instance, pressed for the creation of an International Bureau of Weights and Measures, which was formed in 1875 at the International Metric Conference, attended by scientists representing each member country.[17] Measures were also tabled in the field of intellectual property. At the Universal Exposition of 1878, a Literary Congress of authors, artists and jurists presided over by Victor Hugo agreed to form a body that came to be called (in 1886) the International Union for the Protection of Literary and Artistic Works.[18] Similar trends were evident in the field of transportation. During the 1880s, business groups, Life Saving Service officials, masters from the merchant marine and other groups convinced the British and American governments to convene an International Maritime Conference to examine proposals for enhancing assistance and salvage of life and property on the high seas. Various railway companies and governments meanwhile formed the International Railway Congress Association, which was reshaped into the fully intergovernmental Central Office for International Railway Transport, founded in 1890.[19]

The pre-1914 world also saw the emergence of a wide variety of public initiatives concerned to blow the whistle on state institutions and social injustices and other incivilities. The civil societies of the period bordering on the First World War, like their contemporary counterparts, were both outward-looking and capable of demanding better political protection and service from governments – even of building civil bridges towards the wider world. When the first Hague Peace Conference convened in 1899, for instance, scores of 'peace societies' travelled to lobby the official conference delegates. A petition signed by millions of women in

---

[16] Raymond Leslie Buell, *International Relations* (London, 1926), p. 271, n. 2, and Jacobson, *Networks of Interdependence*, pp. 50–1: 'By the middle of the nineteenth century there were three times as many INGOs as IGOs, and until 1940 INGOs were created at a more rapid pace than IGOs. On the eve of World War II there were thirteen times as many INGOs as IGOs.'

[17] See John A. Johnson, 'Scientific Organizations and the Development of International Law', *Proceedings of the American Society of International Law* (April 1960), pp. 206–7.

[18] Stephen P. Ladas, *The International Protection of Literary and Artistic Property* (New York, 1938), vol. 1, p. 73.

[19] Steve Charnovitz, 'Two Centuries of Participation: NGOs and International Governance', *Michigan Journal of International Law*, 18:183 (Winter 1997), p. 202.

eighteen countries was presented; deputations from members of stateless nations (Finns, Macedonians, Poles, Armenians) met with various delegates; and an unofficial newspaper covered the event, in defiance of the conference rules of secrecy. The event had all the qualities of a 'parallel' NGO forum designed to use an intergovernmental meeting as a platform for publicising grievances and lobbying for different government policies.[20] Events leading up to the Hague Opium Convention (held in 1912) and the struggles of reform societies, temperance groups and missionaries for the international prohibition of alcohol followed a similar course.[21]

Meanwhile, the rise of the cooperative and workers' movement represented a profound challenge to market domination within the actually existing civil societies. It put its finger on a central organising mechanism of these societies: commodity production and exchange. And it organised to counter the power of private capital by means of counter-institutions, like the cooperative and the trade union, which backed new public policies such as the abolition of child labour and night work by women, the reduction of working time, and improved conditions of employment, including the elimination of health hazards. Such demands sometimes stimulated the growth of trans-national organising, the first fruits of which included the International Federation of Tobacco Workers and the International Federation for the Observation of Sunday, both founded in 1876. 'Workers of all countries unite!' was not just a slogan from the quills of Marx and Engels. Through the international idea of 'socialism' – the new, blood-red word minimally meant opposition to 'wage slavery', in favour of the de-commodification of social and political life – and through its newly-formed party-political organs, the workers' movement organised across borders to confront particular employers, whole industries and (in the case of general strikes) the capitalist economies inside whole states. The movement, whose support was drawn overwhelmingly from Europeans and white emigrants or their descendants, attacked governments as well: sometimes to seek their overthrow, but mostly to secure

---

[20] Barbara W. Tuchman, *The Proud Tower: A Portrait of the World Before the War, 1890–1914* (London, 1975), p. 257; more generally, Peter J. Spiro, 'New Global Communities: Nongovernmental Organizations in International Decision-Making Institutions', *Washington Quarterly*, 18 (Winter 1995), pp. 45, 49; George Frederick W. Holls, *The Peace Conference at the Hague* (New York, 1900), p. 329; and James Brown Scott, *The Hague Peace Conferences of 1899 and 1907* (Baltimore, 1909), pp. 172–3.

[21] On the efforts of groups like the Anglo-Oriental Society for the Suppression of the Opium Trade (founded in 1874), see Peter D. Lowes, *The Genesis of International Narcotics Control* (Geneva, 1966) and Virginia Berridge and Griffith Edwards, *Opium and the People* (London, 1981); on the anti-alcohol movement, see F. S. L. Lyons, *Internationalism in Europe 1815–1914* (Leyden, 1963), pp. 266–7 and Ernest Gordon, *The Anti-Alcohol Movement in Europe* (New York, 1913).

their reform. Demands for the extension of the franchise were common-place, as were calls for new government social policies (like unemploy-ment insurance) and the hosting of official and unofficial conferences, which led to the establishment of bodies like the International Working Men's Association, the International Association for Labor Legislation, and the International Labour Organisation (ILO).

The century of violence

It is unimportant in this context to judge the effectiveness of these various civil society initiatives, which serve here merely as illustrations of how, out of old Europe, the rudiments of a global civil society developed. Naturally, these rudiments raised questions about the proper governing structures for a world that felt (and was) ever more tightly knitted together. The mid-nineteenth-century trend towards free trade and free competition – symbolised by the staging of splendid International Expositions[22] – was accompanied by two striking developments on the governance front. The infrastructure of governmental power constructed during this pre-1914 period was the first of these trends. Max Weber, always an astute ob-server of power relations, noted (in 1897) that the 'trade expansion by all civilised bourgeois-controlled nations' would soon lead to a world in which 'only power, naked power' would decide each state's aggregate share in the universal appropriation of the world's resources.[23] He was not wrong. This period indeed saw an unprecedented carve-up of the world's land and oceans by a clutch of imperialistic states: France, Italy, Germany, Portugal, Belgium, Holland, Japan, the United States and the world's most powerful political unit, Great Britain. Formal annexation often resulted. During the four decades before 1914, driven by states' search for new markets and political hegemony, a quarter of the earth's land was formally colonised or re-colonised.[24]

The thrust towards global imperialism – the word itself first became part of the vernacular of journalism and politics during the 1890s – came

---

[22] Hobsbawm, *The Age of Capital*, chapter 2.

[23] Max Weber, *Badische Landeszeitung* (16 December 1897), p. 1, cited in Wolfgang J. Mommsen, *Max Weber and German Politics 1890–1920* (Chicago and London, 1984), p. 77.

[24] Cf. Hobsbawm, *The Age of Empire*, p. 59: 'Britain increased its territories by some 4 million square miles, France by some 3.5 millions, Germany acquired more than 1 million, Belgium and Italy just under 1 million each. The USA acquired some 100,000, mainly from Spain, Japan something like the same amount from China, Russia and Korea. Portugal's ancient African colonies expanded by about 300,000 square miles; Spain, while a net loser (to the USA), still managed to pick up some stony territory in Morocco and the Western Sahara.'

wrapped in racialist and public rituals (like Britain's 'Empire Day', launched in 1902, mainly to win over captive audiences of flag-waving children), nationalist appeals and calls for trade protection. The 1887 British Merchandise Marks Acts, which required products to be stamped with their country of origin, plus loud German complaints about British trade-envy (*Handelsneid*), together signalled the onset of political and military rivalries. It was therefore unsurprising that this period saw the rapid proliferation of state-sponsored congresses and witnessed various attempts – ill-fated, it turned out – to champion new regulatory structures.[25] For almost a century after the Congress of Vienna, which stabilised the continental order that had been threatened by Napoleon's armies, the political elites of Europe had tried to keep peace and improve intergovernmental links by hosting face-to-face meetings. Between 1850 and 1913, more than 100 such congresses were held.[26] They were often convened by cosmopolitan-minded monarchs – by figures like Baron Pierre de Coubertin, the creator of the modern Olympics, who were keen to exercise political initiative by riding their favourite hobby-horses and indulging their sense of *noblesse oblige*. These congresses touched on matters ranging from submarine cables and fishing zones to the opium trade, unemployment and 'the Eastern question'. They were supplemented by the first state-sponsored international exhibitions and fairs, like the 1851 Great Exhibition, convened in London at the height of Britain's imperial confidence by Prince Albert.[27] Serviced by railway trips organised by the entrepreneur Thomas Cook, and housed in an ultra-modern palace of glass, the exhibition highlighted the political pride standing alongside Britain's manufacturing industries and the exotic products of its Empire; the exhibition even had room for the latest technical gadgets, like the bed that physically ejected its occupant in the morning (Queen Victoria was apparently much taken with the design) and the American device for playing the piano and the violin at the same time.

During the same period, comparatively few of the new regulatory structures – the International Penitentiary Commission, the International Maritime Bureau against the Slave Trade, the Permanent Court of Arbitration and the International Bureau for Information and Enquiries regarding Relief to Foreigners – were set up for the stated higher purposes of

---

[25] Michael Wallace and J. David Singer, 'Intergovernmental Organization in the Global System, 1815–1964', *International Organization*, 24 (Spring 1970), pp. 239–87.

[26] See the list of major congresses collated in Craig N. Murphy, *International Organization and Industrial Change. Global Governance since 1850* (Oxford, 1994), pp. 57–9; see also Norman L. Hill, *The Public International Conference: Its Functions, Organization and Procedure* (Stanford, 1929).

[27] Michael Leapman, *The World For a Shilling. How the Great Exhibition of 1851 shaped a Nation* (London, 2001).

bringing legal harmony, peace and good government to the world. Most aimed to facilitate the expansion of communications and commerce. Bodies like the International Central American Office, set up by Mexico and the United States for the purpose of politically integrating Nicaragua, El Salvador and Honduras, were crafted as regional bodies with strictly defined mandates. Others had broad, ultimately universal remits. Their numbers grew exponentially. The International Telegraph Union (ITU) and the International Commission for the Cape Spartel Light in Tangier, both established in 1865, were the first such intergovernmental organisations, nearly all of which were not organisations with a life of their own; member governments held them in tight rein, restricting them to the role of forums for the exchange of information and policy coordination.

Contemporary proposals for global governing structures and a 'planetary patriotism' (Alfred Zimmern) appeared after 1917 in a surprising variety of contexts. This 'new internationalism' (as Trentmann has pointed out[28]) was inspired by the successful efforts of experimental intergovernmental bodies like the Allied Maritime Transport Executive (AMTE), set up for the purpose of removing bottlenecks and regulating the flows of global shipping. The bold political thinking inspired by such regulatory structures seems in retrospect to be rather naïve. They did not properly address the harsh facts of disorderly financial markets (caused by 'speculation' and 'fashionable fraud'[29]), big-power military and diplomatic rivalries and – presaged by mass protests against immigration during the 1890s in countries like Australia and the United States – the strong popular resistance to cosmopolitan values in many of the countries with weight to throw around in the world. And yet – from the standpoint of a theory of global civil society – among the positive effects of this period was a vast increase in the intermingling of Western cultures with those of the rest of the world. Sometimes, the results were democratic, in that they planted the seeds of a positive, world-wide recognition, in circles where it mattered, of the 'hybridity' of all cultures. Nineteenth-century humanitarians, treading the pathways opened up by figures like the Reverend John Philip, superintendent of the London Missionary Society in South

---

[28] Frank Trentmann, 'The Local and the Global: New Internationalism and the Reconfiguration of National and Transnational Citizenship During and After World War One', unpublished paper (Toronto, November 2001). Trentmann cites a remarkably prescient speech by Alfred Zimmern, founder of the School of International Studies in Geneva: 'If we want to have a really efficient international government', said Zimmern, anticipating by nearly a century the perspective of global civil society, 'we must build it up from international voluntary societies, so that at every step voluntary associations watch over the work of the governments in those subjects in which they are dealing' (Trentmann, 2001, p. 7).

[29] Lionel Robbins, *The Great Depression* (London, 1934), p. 63.

Africa, framed their missions in a universal language of civility that implied civil liberties and legal protections for colonised peoples. Mahatma Gandhi (1869–1948), the bespectacled saint who dressed in loincloth and practised the art of *satyagraha* ('firmness in truth') against social injustice and political unfreedom, remains another enduring symbol of this trend. From a modest caste of traders and usurers who had until then not been members of the westernised Indian elite that helped administer the British colony, Gandhi travelled to England to study law. It is well known that his return home to practise law was short-lived; he moved to South Africa, where discrimination against the Indian minority by whites there led him to experiment with non-violent tactics of political opposition: these later became central to his role as spearhead of the Indian resistance to empire. Determined to live his life as a *vishvamānav*, a man who belonged to the universe, he was elected (in 1925) president of the Indian National Congress, involved himself in long campaigns of civil disobedience, including a 'fast unto death' (1932) protest against the government's treatment of 'untouchables'. He continued to press his credo: 'I do not want my house to be walled in on all sides and my windows to be stuffed. I want the cultures of all lands to be blown about my houses as freely as possible. But I refuse to be blown off my feet by any.'[30] For his pains, he was repeatedly arrested and imprisoned and publicly abused, often nick-named 'Mohammed Gandhi'; and soon after negotiating Indian autonomy, he was assassinated (at the end of January 1948) by a Hindu fundamentalist.

The murder proved that the spirit of civility symbolised by Gandhi was wreckable; it also served as an epitaph for what had already happened to the *belle époque* and its globalising civil society. By the early years of the twentieth century, the belief (popularised by writers like Norman Angell[31]) that the dynamic of integration was unstoppable – that it made war between highly developed industrial states impossible – began to be exposed as an opium dream. Something far grimmer than gunboat diplomacy lurked just around the corner: humanity's first-ever global war, followed by three extraordinary decades of violence. The First World War was a great setback for civil society and its cosmopolitan ideals. The carnage produced by the clash of men and steel – 8 million people died and 21 million were wounded – was finally halted in 1918.[32] Peace seemed at

---

[30] Cited in Bhikhu Parekh, *Gandhi. A Very Short Introduction* (Oxford, 2001), p. 42.
[31] Norman Angell's *The Great Illusion: A Study of the Relation of Military Power in Nations to their Economic and Social Advantage* (London, 1910) reveals the beginnings of a global literary culture during this period. It was translated into eighteen languages and it appeared immediately in fourteen countries.
[32] See Michael Howard, *The First World War* (Oxford, 2002).

first to promise a new beginning. As whole empires and dozens of monarchies collapsed, the first Czechoslovak president Thomas Masaryk spoke of the post-war world as 'a laboratory atop a vast graveyard'. Woodrow Wilson was in no doubt that the experiment had everything to do with making the world safe for civil liberties and political democracy. In fact, social confusion, disappointment and political resistance to civil society flourished everywhere. Under pressure from peasant radicals, unemployed workers, nationalist demagogues, fascist paramilitaries, bandits and Bolsheviks, the new civil society chains and networks snapped, as if history itself had turned nasty. Most of the civil society failures were linked in one way or another with the breakdown of governmental structures, which typically passed through a sequence of three phases: a *loss* of governmental power, followed by a power *vacuum* that soon encouraged the *takeover* of power by uncivil and anti-democratic forces. The pattern was not confined to Europe, and it was to last for most of the twentieth century. So, between 1900 and 1985, around fifty-two experiments in civilised, democratic power-sharing at the level of the territorial state ended disastrously, to be replaced by one of three types of regime: nationalist military dictatorship, with its roots in the *poder moderador* model of nineteenth-century Spain and Latin America; royal dictatorship, like Rumania under King Carol and inter-war Yugoslavia; and totalitarian regimes led by charismatic figures like Mussolini, Stalin and Hitler.

Seen from a civil society perspective, these were highly destructive developments. Following the First World War, cross-border social initiatives no doubt survived. Peace societies indeed flourished. The newly established League of Nations played the role of catalyst to many globalising initiatives, many of them fragmentary and embryonic.[33] Bodies like the International Chamber of Commerce (founded in 1920) held periodic congresses that were seen by contemporaries as a 'world parliament of business'.[34] The ILO, comprising employer and worker delegates approved by governments, played a key role in hosting conferences and drafting conventions for the regulation of labour rights and standards, in diverse areas like women's employment and disabled workers. The women's movement, driven by world-wide hopes of enfranchisement,

---

[33] Examples included the Foreign Policy Association, the Anglo-Oriental Society for the Suppression of the Opium Trade, the International League for the Rights of Man and Citizenship, and the International Missionary Council. Salvador de Madariaga, *The World's Design* (London, 1938) notes that 'a whole vegetation of international societies has sprung up, or has gathered round, the League – pacifist, feminist, juridical' (p. 275); a similar view of the League as a 'phenomenon of *international professional representation*' is developed in Georges Scelle, *Une crise de la societé des nations* (Paris, 1927), p. 142.

[34] Lyman Cromwell White, *International Non-Governmental Organizations* (Philadelphia, 1951), p. 20.

made its presence felt through organisations like the Women's International League for Peace and Freedom (WILPF).[35] And solidarity campaigns developed around events like the collapse of the Primo de Rivera dictatorship and the outbreak of civil war in Spain.

On the scale of twentieth-century developments, alas, these developments were exceptional. Especially during the years after 1930, the world spun out of control, careering towards bellicose forms of political division and outbreaks of social violence, in the shadows of such novel experiences as total war, aerial bombardment, concentration camps, genocide and the threat of nuclear annihilation. The barbarous trends directly violated what Thomas Hobbes famously called 'the mutual relation between Protection and Obedience'.[36] According to the Hobbesian axiom of *protego ergo obligo*, no form of political order can exist without the protection and obedience of its subjects. Once upon a time, in many core countries of the Atlantic region, exactly this kind of political contract was struck between the authorities and officials of states, on the one side, and the citizen-inhabitants of those territorially defined states on the other. The contract read like this: citizens agree to accept the universality and legitimacy of the compulsory navigation functions and policies of the ship of state on the condition that its sovereign powers will be used to keep out interlopers – to use armies and weapons and passports and identity cards and surveillance systems to define 'who belongs and who does not, who may come and go and who not'[37] – as well as to keep order and secure the economic well-being and cultural identities of those same passenger citizens. In return, the captains of the ship of state authorise and seek to enhance certain entitlements of citizens, including their civil and political freedoms to organise and act with and against each other peacefully within civil society.

This political contract was strongly presumed in the United States, France and other actually existing parliamentary democracies; elsewhere, especially after the First World War in countries like Poland, Germany and Yugoslavia, it served as something of a political utopia for scores of new and reforming states and their would-be citizens. Their dreams were to be thwarted. For many millions of people, the unwritten Hobbesian contract proved worthless, especially during the Second World War, which undoubtedly proved to be the nadir of the contemporary history of global civil society. That global war certainly strengthened the

[35] Catherine Foster, *Women for All Seasons: The Story of the Women's International League for Peace and Freedom* (Athens, GA and London, 1989).
[36] Thomas Hobbes, *Leviathan* (London, 1651), p. 396.
[37] John Torpey, *The Invention of the Passport. Surveillance, Citizenship and the State* (Cambridge, 2000), p. 13.

political contract in the handful of victorious states like Britain, the United States and Canada; as well, it encouraged post-colonial and 'liberation' struggles and, hence, the spread of the modern territorial state system throughout the rest of the world.[38] But the bloody global conflict also triggered exactly the opposite trend: the territorial state's violation of the contract – the long-term de-legitimation and de-universalisation of state sovereignty – because of the total mobilisation and sacrifice of untold millions by both victorious and vanquished states, who stood accused for the first time (in the Nuremberg and Tokyo tribunals) of committing not just war crimes, but the 'crime of war'.[39]

The sheer scale of violence against civilians undoubtedly reinforced the civilian mistrust of political authorities, especially in areas where the distinction between combatants and non-combatants was utterly annulled. It is little wonder that the ideal of a global civil society was born towards the end of the twentieth century, which proved to be the most murderous in recorded history. The estimated death toll of 187 million souls was the equivalent of more than one-tenth of the world's population in 1913.[40] It was a century of the break-up of empires and revolutions, and thus of the violent blurring of the boundaries between inter-state violence and violent conflicts ('civil wars') within states. It was also a century in which the burdens of war weighed ever more heavily on civilians who, like defenceless pawns on a chessboard of cruelty, increasingly became the targets of military calculations. During the 1914–18 war, civilians comprised only one-twentieth of the victims of war; during the 1939–45 war, that proportion rose to two-thirds; while these days perhaps nine-tenths of the victims of war are civilians.

For the friends of civil society, matters worsened during the nuclear age that began with the devastation of Hiroshima and Nagasaki. As nuclear-tipped sovereignty became a chilling fact, it brought the world together, but only by subjecting it to the permanent threat of mutually assured destruction, many times over. Nuclear weapons transformed the final Armageddon from fiction into factual possibility. The violent destruction of all states and civil societies (where they existed) was now thinkable.

---

[38] Bertrand Badie, *L'état importé: L'occidentalisation de l'ordre politique* (Paris, 1992).

[39] Jürgen Habermas, 'Kant's Idea of Perpetual Peace, with the Benefit of Two Hundred Years' Hindsight', in James Bohman and Matthias Lutz-Bachmann (eds.), *Perpetual Peace. Essays on Kant's Cosmopolitan Ideal* (Cambridge, MA and London, 1997), p. 126; see also his 'Bestialität und Humanität: Ein Krieg in der Grenze zwischen Recht und Moral', *Die Zeit*, 29 April 1999, and the important studies by Gary Jonathan Bass, *Stay the Hand of Vengeance. The Politics of War Crimes Tribunals* (Princeton and Oxford, 2000) and Geoffrey Robertson, *Crimes Against Humanity* (London, 2000).

[40] Eric Hobsbawm, 'War and Peace in the 20th Century', *London Review of Books*, 21 February 2002, pp. 16–18.

Many citizens around the world consequently came to feel unprotected. It was as if a few core political units – the United States, the Soviet Union, Britain and France – had dragged every one of the world's inhabitants into the realisation that a main clause of any political contract between states and their citizens – to guarantee the physical security of their citizens – was now impossible. Orwell's comments on the political significance of the atomic bombing of Hiroshima and Nagasaki accurately summarised this mood of disappointment and fear. 'The great age of democracy and of national self-determination was the age of the musket and the rifle', he wrote. The nuclear age was of a different – more depressing – order. 'Had the atomic bomb turned out to be something as cheap and easily manufactured as a bicycle or an alarm clock', he continued, 'it might well have plunged us back into barbarism, but it might, on the other hand, have meant the end of national sovereignty and of the highly-centralized police state'. Alas, the human species now stood in danger of either destroying itself with its own weapons or destroying democracy with a new form of servitude wrapped in a peace that was not really peace at all. 'Looking at the world as a whole', Orwell continued, 'the drift for many decades has been not towards anarchy but towards the reimposition of slavery... in a state which was at once *unconquerable* and in a permanent state of "cold war" with its neighbours'.[41]

Civil society purism

So how was it possible for a civil society with global parameters to be reborn under these conditions of near-total fear and violence? And what forces today drive the globalisation of civil society? Many present-day activists and some of their intellectual supporters have no doubts about the correct answer: global civil society, they insist, proves the power of autonomous moral choice and moral action. They point to opinion polls that indicate far stronger support for NGOs like the World-Wide Fund for Nature and Amnesty International than for governments, big business and media.[42] They point as well to path-breaking initiatives, like the Greenpeace International and Rainbow Warrior campaigns in the mid-1980s to force the French authorities in Tahiti to allow the docking of Greenpeace ships, and like the 1990s boycotts of rain-forest timber, organised globally by groups like Friends of the Earth. The same activists and sympathisers find additional evidence for their belief in the

---

[41] George Orwell, 'You and the Atom Bomb', *Tribune* 19 October 1945, reprinted in *Selections from Essays and Journalism: 1931–1949* (London, 1981), p. 715.
[42] *Financial Times* (London), 12 December 2000.

'model' organisations of global civil society: trans-national advocacy non-governmental organisations (TANGOs) like the World-Wide Fund for Nature (4.7 million members, operating in thirty-one countries, including twelve in the South); Friends of the Earth (1 million members, in fifty-six countries, twenty-three in the South); and one of the first such global organisations, Amnesty International. The brainchild in the early 1960s of a young English lawyer, Peter Benenson, who dreamed up its basic aims and improvised its first strategies, initially in the form of a newspaper appeal, 'The Forgotten Prisoners', Amnesty has played a pioneering role in working globally to publicise cases of torture and political repression against individuals and groups, no matter in which country or region of the earth they had suffered their misfortune. The Amnesty ideal originally supposed that publicity, including celebrity appearances and letter-writing campaigns, could harm the reputations of bullies and dictators and torturers – through patient but persistent actions that resembled the drip, drip, drip of water on a stone. Its campaigns revealed a firm belief in the importance of expert-based impartiality, the power of fact-finding, and independence from governments and parties. The campaigns also supposed that respect for good laws could have civilising effects: that it was possible to act *as if* viable bodies of global law already existed, that in addition it was possible to create human rights norms by quietly promoting (in partnership with institutions like the United Nations) new bodies of law, so gradually accumulating global standards of conduct that could tame the hubris of governmental power. The initiative evidently worked, for Amnesty grew into a world-wide, highly networked campaign with more than 1.1 million members, subscribers and regular donors operating in more than 150 countries and territories, including thousands of local chapters in more than eighty countries in Africa, the Americas, the Middle East, Europe and the Asian/Pacific region.[43]

Defenders of the ideal of a global civil society often point to such examples to bolster their claim that this society is the child of imagination and boldness – the offspring of men and women who have seen or sensed the world-transforming potential of not-for-profit, non-governmental action. These activists and their supporters see themselves as countering the 'space-like coldness of globalisation' (Peter Schneider) with the voices, laughter, hopes and tears of human faces. They draw inspiration from the big demonstrations and bold civic initiatives that became commonplace during the 1990s. For many of these activists (and for state surveillance

---

[43] Ann Marie Clark, *Diplomacy of Conscience: Amnesty International and Changing Human Rights Norms* (Princeton, 2001); www.amnesty.org.

organisations[44]) the protests surrounding the Seattle meeting of the WTO in December 1999 were highly significant. Not only did the protests bring the meeting to an undignified halt after more than 50,000 demonstrators mounted blockades and publicly criticised transnational corporations, 'corporate censorship'[45] and global consumerism in the streets. Not only, in addition, did the protests raise more specific global concerns, like the protection of rain-forests, job losses, the need for cheaper AIDS drugs, bans on genetically-modified (GM) food, and concerns about the destruction of biodiversity, symbolised by dying turtles trapped in commercial shrimp nets. The ultimate achievement of the Seattle protests, many activists maintain, was symbolic of something bigger: it signalled the birth of an 'anti-globalisation movement'.

The novelty and historical significance of the 'battle for Seattle' protests can be exaggerated, but there is no doubt that the street-level champions of global civil society have a point: protests of this kind are symptomatic of the rebirth of civic actions that tend to grow into social movements, on a global scale.[46] These movements should not be thought of as (coalescing into) one big world movement. There is in fact a wide variety of such movements, whose activists specialise in publicising their experiences and applying their campaigning skills in particular policy areas as diverse as sexual politics, trade rules, religiosity, corporate power, post-war reconstruction, clean water, education and human rights. The targets of these movements are equally variable: they take aim at a whole spectrum of opponents and potential allies, from local institutions that have global effects to global institutions that have local effects. The spectrum of political loyalties within these movements is also very broad, ranging from deep-green ecologists to Christian pacifists, social democrats, Muslim activists, Buddhist meditators and anarcho-syndicalists. Their participants, contrary to some prevailing stereotypes, are not all rich, middle-class, Northern kids. Activists from the South or 'Third World' – a living-dead, zombie

---

[44] See, for example, the report (# 2000/08) by the Canadian Security Intelligence Service, 'Anti-Globalization – A Spreading Phenomenon', www.csis-scrs.gc.ca/eng/miscdocs/200008e.html.

[45] Naomi Klein, *No Logo* (London, 2000).

[46] Among the first analyses of social movements operating at the planetary level were Alberto Melucci, *Nomads of the Present: Social Movements and Individual Needs in Contemporary Society*, eds. Paul Mier and John Keane (London and Philadelphia, 1989), and his *Challenging Codes: Collective Action in the Information Age* (Cambridge, 1996). See also Margaret E. Keck and Kathryn Sikkink, *Activists Beyond Borders: Advocacy Networks in International Politics* (Ithaca and London, 1998); Jackie Smith, 'Characteristics of the Modern Transnational Social Movement Sector', in Jackie Smith *et al.* (eds.), *Transnational Social Movements and Global Politics* (Syracuse, 1997), pp. 42–58; and Dieter Rucht, 'Social Movements Challenging Neo-liberal Globalization', in John Keane (ed.), *Civil Society: Berlin Perspectives* (London, 2004), forthcoming.

phrase that has become so ideologically loaded and descriptively un-helpful that it deserves to be banished from the language of global civil society – are in fact in the ascendancy. The inner architecture of these movements is also complex, and marked by a variable geometry. Most of their sympathisers and supporters are part-time. Full-time activists and professional workers are in a definite minority within the movements, which have no globally recognised Spokesperson or Leader or Secretariat, and for that reason do not speak in one voice, with one point of view.

It is true that *simulated* unity momentarily appears during organised public protests: for instance, in the trend-setting public rally of 80,000 people, in 1988 in Berlin, where the representatives of the World Bank and the IMF were convening[47]; in the Intercontinental Caravan 99, a tour through North America and Europe by nearly 400 activists, from Nepal, India, Mexico, Bangladesh and Brazil, campaigning on behalf of fisher-men and farmers threatened by the aggressive marketing of pesticides, GM seeds and neo-liberal policies; in the successful alliance between the Uganda Debt Network and the Jubilee 2000 debt relief campaign[48]; and in the remarkably self-disciplined and peaceful gathering of 500,000 protestors in Barcelona, during an EU summit in the spring of 2002. Such unity is *exceptional* and *mobilised*: it always rests upon months or even years of hard planning, preparatory meetings, seminars and teachings. And in every case it draws upon movements that have strongly decentralised, constantly evolving, kaleidoscopic structures.[49] The movements of global civil society comprise a clutter of intersecting forms: face-to-face encoun-ters, spider-web-like networks, pyramid-shaped organisations, hub-and-spoke structures, bridges and organisational chains, charismatic person-alities. Action takes place at multiple levels – from the micro-local through to the macro-global – and sometimes movement organisations create ver-tical alliances for the purpose of communication and synchronisation. The well-known nodal organisations of these movements – the Global Action Project, Earthwatch, WEED (World Economy, Ecology and De-velopment), Jubilee 2000 – display a remarkable awareness of the need for striking a balance between common and particular concerns by means of a variety of decentralised, non-hierarchical, yet coordinated initiatives. Using advanced means of communication – such as the reliance upon the

---

[47] Jurgen Gerhards, *Neue Kofliktlinien in der Mobilisierung offentlicher Meinung. Eine Fall analyse* (Opladen, 1993).
[48] Carole J. L. Collins *et al.*, 'Jubilee 2000: Citizen Action Across the North–South Divide', in Michael Edwards and John Gaventa (eds.), *Global Citizen Action* (Boulder, 2001), pp. 135–48.
[49] A good summary of these features is John Gaventa, 'Global Citizen Action: Lessons and Challenges', in Michael Edwards and John Gaventa (eds.), *Global Citizen Action* (Boulder, 2001), pp. 275–87.

Internet by the Mexican Zapatistas in their global campaign for human rights – these nodal organisations are typically in touch, on a horizontal and spreadeagled basis, with many other initiatives and groups, which are themselves in touch with other initiatives, groups and individuals. Sometimes, as in the global campaign against landmines, conscious efforts to build a 'network of networks' prove to be a vital condition of campaigning success.[50] Because the acephalous social movements of global civil society are marked by hyper-complexity, some organisations concentrate on the task of heightening the movements' self-conscious commitments to networked and coordinated pluralism. They specialise in spreading the medium, not just the message – by encouraging others to embrace the techniques of participatory research, sophisticated policy analysis and continuous organisational learning. The Peoples Global Action, founded in February 1998 in Geneva, seeks to function as 'a world-wide coordination of resistance against the global market, a new alliance of struggle and mutual support'[51]; it sees itself as a social catalyst for drawing together such diverse groups as the Ogoni people in Nigeria, the Frente Zapatista in Mexico and the Sem Terra, a Brazilian organisation of landless peasants. The Association for the Taxation of Financial Transactions for the Aid of Citizens (ATTAC) similarly understands itself as a global platform for pluralism in support of the taxation of stock market transactions.[52] And at the front-lines of action, some networked, semi-professional groups, like the Wombles and the Ruckus Society, operate facilities for training groups and individuals in the arts of non-violent direct action and civil disobedience.[53]

Although these various self-organising efforts do not (and cannot) overcome the heterogeneity of the movements, it is important to see that they have more in common than their variable architecture. These movements are marked by a cross-border mentality. It is highly misleading to call them 'anti-globalisation movements' because each assumes the form of links and chains of non-governmental solidarity and contestation spanning vast spaces stretching to the four corners of the earth. Their participants, most of whom are part-time sympathisers and not full-time activists, do not see their concerns as confined within a strictly bounded community or locality. They are convinced that toxic chemicals and human rights and debt

---

[50] Matthew J. O. Scott, 'Danger – Landmines! NGO–Government Collaboration in the Ottawa Process', in Michael Edwards and John Gaventa (eds.), *Global Citizen Action* (Boulder, 2001), pp. 135–48.

[51] See www.tao.ca/fire/gatheer/0049.html.

[52] See www.attac.org/indexen.htm, and Susan George, 'Another World is Possible', www.dissentmagazine.org/archive/wio1/geroge.shtml.

[53] See www.ruckus.org.

relief and compassion for those whose dignity has been violated know no borders. For them the world is one world. So they nurture their identities and publicise their concerns in 'translocalities',[54] as if they were global citizens. They think of themselves as building cross-border cooperation in a variety of ways among a variety of potential supporters around a variety of shared goals, including efforts to apply the emergency brake (as in anti-nuclear protest and debt relief) and to effect positive social changes in the lives of women and men, regardless of where they are living on the face of the earth. An enduring symbol of the energy and vision of these movements is the Fourth World Conference on Women, held in Beijing in 1995, and attended by almost 35,000 NGOs: in the name of inclusive forms of globalisation, movement activists take advantage of global communication networks, share technical and strategic information, coordinate parallel activities and plan joint actions, often by putting direct pressure on governmental institutions and corporate actors – and by risking tear gas, baton charges, bullets and criminal proceedings – under the halogen lamps of media publicity.

Within these global movements, including the media events that they generate, empirical claims, normative visions and strategic concerns tend to be mixed together by activists: even when 'globalisation' is slammed in the name of 'self-sufficiency' or *souverainisme* or returning to 'the local' (note the performative contradiction), the existing global civil society is reckoned a good thing. It is said to be in need of militant defence, for instance through actions staged at the feet of global institutions, before the eyes and ears of the world's media. These campaigners' calculations sometimes draw implicitly upon scholarly definitions of civil society. They start with a strongly voluntarist picture of civil society as a 'public ethical–political community' based on a common ethos. Or they understand civil society as 'an intermediate *associational* realm between state and family, populated by organisations enjoying some *autonomy* in relation to the state and formed *voluntarily* by members of society to protect their interests or values'.[55] Global civil society is seen as an autonomous social space within which individuals, groups and movements can effectively organise and manoeuvre on a world scale to undo and transform existing power relations, especially those of big business. This society is conceived as 'a certain kind of universalising community' marked by 'public opinion', cultural codes and narratives 'in a democratic

---

[54] See Arjun Appadurai, 'The Production of Locality', in Richard Fardon (ed.), *Counterworks: Managing the Diversity of Knowledge* (London, 1995), pp. 204–25.

[55] Jean Cohen and Andrew Arato, *Civil Society and Political Theory* (Cambridge, MA, 1992), p. 84; Gordon White, *Civil Society, Democratisation and Development* (Institute of Development Studies, Brighton, 1994), p. 6 (emphasis mine).

idiom' and 'interactional practices like civility, equality, criticism, and respect'.[56]

Some activist species of this purist theory of civil society tread in Gramsci's footsteps, often without knowing it. They define global civil society more narrowly, as the *non-economic* space of social interaction 'located *between* the family, the state, and the market and operating *beyond* the confines of national societies, polities, and economies'.[57] Scholarly advocates of such definitions tend to be more cautious. They hasten to add that while the concept has normative connotations, any attempt to 'operationalise' the concept is risky, essentially because the term itself is 'too contested'.[58] They give the impression that global civil society is a loosely-woven net which can be used to catch various fish – so long as the fishing is restricted to non-governmental, not-for-profit ponds. There is some disingenuity here, because the very definition that is proposed has an identifiable normative bias. It tacitly favours the view that global civil society, narrowly defined, is an untrammelled good because it harbours all kinds of 'citizens' groups, social movements, and individuals' who 'engage in dialogue, debate, confrontation, and negotiation with each other and with various governmental actors – international, national, and local – as well as the business world'.[59]

Other scholars, especially those with an eye trained on the concept's political potential, speak more openly of global civil society, with all its blurred self-images and ambiguities, as a dynamic zone of cross-border relations and activities that keep an arm's distance from states and

---

[56] Jeffrey C. Alexander, 'Introduction' to Jeffrey C. Alexander, *Real Civil Societies. Dilemmas of Institutionalization* (London, 1998), p. 7.

[57] See the editors' introduction to Helmut Anheier *et al.*, *Global Civil Society 2001* (Oxford, 2001), p. 17. The reliance upon Gramsci in some of the recent literature is sometimes explicit, for instance in Paul Harvey, *Rehabilitation in Complex Political Emergencies: Is Rebuilding Civil Society the Answer?*, IDS Working Paper, 60 (Brighton, 2000), p. 10, where an appeal is made 'for a more Gramscian view of civil society which acknowledges questions of power, sees civil society as a contested arena and acknowledges attempts by the state to penetrate and control civil society'. Such appeals to the dead spirit of Gramsci are astonishing in their naïveté (see my 'Introduction' to *Civil Society and the State: New European Perspectives* [London, 1998], esp. pp. 24–5). It does not occur to the neo-Gramscians and to assorted fellow travellers of Gramsci that their master's (rather inchoate) account of civil society was bound up with all sorts of communist presumptions: about the ability of the Party-led proletariat to dismantle the 'bourgeois state' and institute a new social order ('regulated society') in which 'civil society' would become merely a word from the bourgeois past. Gramsci's interest in civil society was wholly opportunistic. Its reverie of using civil society to abolish civil society supposed that modern societies are riven by a central class-contradiction and that there is a privileged subject capable of acting out the telos of history. None of this belongs within a sophisticated and democratic theory of civil society and its globalising potential.

[58] Helmut Anheier *et al.* (eds.), *Global Civil Society 2001* (Oxford, 2001), pp. 221–7.

[59] *Ibid.*, p. 4.

markets. Global civil society is a force for 'globalisation from below'. It is potentially the champion of 'widely shared world order values: minimising violence, maximising economic well-being, realising social and political justice, and upholding environmental quality'.[60] Other radical champions of global civil society are more fulsome still in their support for its political potential. These civil society purists speak, rather romantically, of global civil society as a realm of actual or potential freedom, as a 'third sector' opposed to the impersonal power of government and the greedy profiteering of the market (households typically disappear from the analysis at this point). 'Civil society participates alongside – not replaces – state and market institutions', write Naidoo and Tandon. Global civil society 'is the network of autonomous associations that rights-bearing and responsibility-laden citizens voluntarily create to address common problems, advance shared interests and promote collective aspirations'.[61] Another scholar repeats much the same point: 'Global civil society, like its domestic counterpart, is that domain in which people voluntarily associate to express themselves and pursue various noneconomic aims in common, and it is in the practice of such association that one can look for progressive political activity.'[62]

Sometimes large historical claims are made in defence of this allegedly 'non-economic' sector; in recent years, there have even been references to a 'global associational revolution that may prove to be as significant to the latter 20th century as the rise of the nation-state was to the latter 19th century'.[63] And sometimes civil society purism is taken to extremes, towards the call for revolution against capitalist domination, as in the intellectual neo-communism of Hardt and Negri's *Empire*.[64] It imagines – with the help of Marx and Foucault and some quick-fingered theoretical sorcery – that there is a deep continuity between today's global protests

---

[60] Richard Falk, *Predatory Globalization: A Critique* (Cambridge, 1999), p. 130.

[61] Kumi Naidoo and Rajesh Tandon, 'The Promise of Civil Society', in the Civicus publication *Civil Society at the Millennium* (West Hartford, CT, 1999), pp. 6–7. The more recent campaign writings of Kumi Naidoo develop less romantic and more sophisticated images of global civil society, which however continues to be understood as the space wedged between global market forces and various forms of government; see for example his 'The New Civic Globalism', *The Nation*, 8 May, 2000, pp. 34–6.

[62] Paul Wapner, 'The Normative Promise of Nonstate Actors: A Theoretical Account of Global Civil Society', in Paul Wapner and Lester Edwin J. Ruiz (eds.), *Principled World Politics. The Challenge of Normative International Relations* (Lanham, MD, 2000), pp. 261–2.

[63] See the classic essay by Lester Salamon, 'The Rise of the Nonprofit Sector: A Global Associational Revolution', *Foreign Affairs*, 73:4 (1994).

[64] Michael Hardt and Antonio Negri, *Empire* (Cambridge, MA and London, 2000), esp. pp. xiii–xv, 25, 312–13, 326–9, 406–13; and Michael Hardt, 'The Withering of Civil Society', *Social Text*, 45 (1995), pp. 27–44.

and the communist revolutions of 1917 and 1949, the anti-fascist struggles of the 1930s and 1940s, and all the liberation struggles from the
1960s to 1989. A new political subject, a revolutionary giant variously
called 'an insurgent multitude', 'the global People', or 'a new proletariat',
is today stirring. It shakes the foundations of the world order, the new
'empire' dominated by the singular logic of commodity production and
exchange and the manipulative government of the bio-social realm ('the
production of subjectivity') in globalised form. Today's world empire effectively destroys civil society, or so they claim. 'In the postmodernization
of the global economy, the creation of wealth tends ever more toward what
we will call biopolitical production, the production of social life itself, in
which the economic, the political, and the cultural increasingly overlap
and invest one another.' Yet the disappearance of civil societies in modern
form – the melding of the boundaries between government and society,
the national and the global – produces generalised resistance to the imperial machine. Hardt and Negri call it global civil society. 'Civil society
is absorbed in the state, but the consequence of this is an explosion of
the elements that were previously coordinated and mediated in civil society. Resistances are no longer marginal but active in the center of a
society that opens up in networks; the individual points are singularized
in a thousand plateaus.' This global civil society is undoubtedly a force
for 'autonomously constructing a counter-Empire, an alternative political organization of global flows and exchanges'. But, according to Hardt
and Negri, global civil society is not an end-in-itself. It is a transient,
evanescent phenomenon. It is haunted by the spectre of communism: a
future social order unmarked by the division between government and
civil society, an order in which the 'irrepressible lightness and joy of being
communist' – living hard by the revolutionary values of love, cooperation,
simplicity and innocence – will triumph, this time on a global scale.

Turbocapitalism

Such purist images reduce actually existing global civil society to campaign strategies harnessed to the normative ideal of citizens' autonomy
at the global level. That in turn creates (in some quarters) the unfortunate impression that global civil society is a (potentially) unified subject,
a 'third force',[65] something like a world proletariat in civvies, the universal object–subject that can snap its chains and translate the idea of a

---

[65] The temptation to see global civil society in this way is evident in the introduction to
Ann M. Florini (ed.), *The Third Force. The Rise of Transnational Civil Society* (Tokyo and
Washington, DC, 2000), pp. 1–15.

'World Alliance for Citizen Participation'[66] into reality – therewith righting the world's wrongs. Although many things can be said for and against these conceptions, it is worth noting at this point their Gramscian bias. This draws a thick line between (bad) business backed by government and (good) voluntary associations. 'We are people, not a market, and our world is not for sale', the purists say, and this leads them to understate the *overdetermined* character of global civil society. 'Solidarity and compassion for the fate and well-being of others, including unknown, distant others, a sense of personal responsibility and reliance on one's own initiative to do the right thing; the impulse toward altruistic giving and sharing; the refusal of inequality, violence, and oppression'[67] are undoubtedly significant, even indispensable motives in the globalisation of civil society. But one-sided emphasis on the free civic choices of men and women has the effect of obscuring other planetary forces that currently constrain and enable their actions.

Among the principal energisers of global civil society are market forces, or what is here called 'turbocapitalism'.[68] To understand how and why this is so, and to understand what the term 'turbocapitalism' means, we need briefly to turn our attention back to the system of Keynesian welfare state capitalism (as it was called) that predominated in the West following the end of the Second World War. For some three decades thereafter, market capitalist economies like the United States, Sweden, Japan, the Federal Republic of Germany and Britain moved in the direction of government-regulated capitalism. In terms of the production of goods and services, firms, plants and whole industries were very much national phenomena; facilitated by international trade of raw materials and foodstuffs, production was primarily organised *within* territorially bound national economies or parts of them. Markets were *embedded* in webs of government.[69]

---

[66] Rajesh Tandon, 'Civil Society Moves Ahead', *Civicus. 1999 Annual Report* (Washington, DC, 1999), p. 5.

[67] Miguel Darcey de Oliveira and Rajesh Tandon, 'An Emerging Global Civil Society', in their *Citizens: Strengthening Global Civil Society* (Washington, DC, 1994), pp. 2–3. Similar views are defended in David Korten, *Getting to the 21st Century: Voluntary Action and the Global Agenda* (West Hartford, CT, 1990), and in Jürgen Habermas, 'Civil Society and the Political Public Sphere', in *Between Facts and Norms* (Cambridge, MA, 1996), chapter 8. The chief theoretical limitations of the (neo-)Gramscian approach are analysed in John Keane, *Civil Society: Old Images, New Visions*, (Oxford and Stanford, 1998), pp. 15–19.

[68] The term 'turbocapitalism' is drawn from Edward Luttwak, *Turbo-Capitalism. Winners and Losers in the Global Economy* (New York, 1999). It will be seen that my substantive account of the impact of the process differs considerably from that of Luttwak.

[69] Robert Boyer and J. Rogers Hollingsworth (eds.), *Contemporary Capitalism: The Embeddedness of Institutions* (Cambridge, 1997), and Eric Hobsbawm, 'The Development of the World Economy', *Cambridge Journal of Economics*, 3 (1979), p. 313.

So, for example, during the era of Keynesian welfare state capitalism private investment was subject to various governmental restrictions. Whole areas of investment considered 'strategic' to the overall economy, like airlines, railways and iron and steel, were effectively shielded from market forces, either by nationalisation or by a plethora of rules and regulations, like subsidies, tax breaks or matching funds. Hospitals, schools, welfare provision and other forms of social policy were also commonly run as de-commodified institutions. Geopolitically speaking, Keynesian welfare state capitalism was also subject to two kinds of political limits. Whole geographic areas of the earth, principally the socialist bloc dominated by Soviet-type regimes, were effectively no-go zones for private capitalism. Meanwhile, within the Western bloc, international trade and investment was subject to a plethora of state-enforced rules and intergovernmental regulations.[70] Especially from the time of the Bretton Woods agreement (1944), three major institutions helped to ensure that international finance and trade rotated around the American economy (which had emerged from total war, unscathed) and its currency. The International Monetary Fund (IMF), which set rules for currencies and world payments, functioned to encourage international monetary cooperation among states. The International Bank for Reconstruction and Development (IBRD, later renamed the World Bank) aimed to promote capital investment, initially in Europe and later in less developed economies. And the General Agreement on Tariffs and Trade (GATT) fought to overcome the previous 'beggar-thy-neighbour' protectionism by promoting free trade through devices such as the reduction of tariff barriers monitored by ongoing multilateral negotiations, like the Kennedy Round during the 1960s and the Tokyo Round in the 1970s.

In the era of turbocapitalism, by contrast, pressure builds up within civil society for the radical transformation of the regulatory regime operated by territorial states. Taking advantage of the new galaxy of digital communications, market institutions and market actors develop an allergic reaction to meddling state regulations, especially those which are perceived to have cramping and egalitarian social effects. Markets tend to become *disembedded*: they wriggle out of social obligations and break free of territorially based government controls. Wherever the turbocapitalist economy gains the upper hand, it thrives upon lighter regulations of capital flows, the deregulation of labour markets and welfare cutbacks. Turbocapitalism is a species of private enterprise driven by the desire for

---

[70] According to one method of counting, there were around eighty IGOs in 1945. Twenty-eight were formed in the five years starting in 1950 and ending in 1954, thirty in the five years that ended in 1959, and thirty-three in the next five years. By 1980, there were an estimated 621 IGOs. See Jacobson, *Networks of Interdependence*, p. 38.

emancipation from social custom, territorial state interference, taxation restrictions, trade union intransigence and all other external restrictions upon the free movement of capital in search of profit. Turbocapitalism kicks against the so-called 'law' (formulated by the nineteenth-century economist Adolph Wagner[71]) of the expanding public sector. Its advocates push for a new global regulatory regime – for deregulation, or lighter and more flexible regulation, on a global scale.[72]

In recent decades, the world has begun to dance to such tunes. Business is no longer exclusively 'homespun' (to use Keynes's famous term). The transnational operations of some 300 pace-setting firms in industries such as banking, accountancy, automobiles, airlines, communications and armaments – their combined assets make up roughly a quarter of the world's productive assets[73] – no longer function as production and delivery operations for national headquarters. Bursting the bounds of time and space, language and custom, they instead function as complex global flows, or integrated networks of staff, money, information, raw materials, components and products. The same trend is evident in smaller firms. One global register at the end of the 1970s listed more than 9,000 firms having operations outside their own home countries; together, these firms had more than 34,000 smaller subsidiaries scattered throughout the world. By 1997, there were some 53,000 trans-national corporations with 450,000 foreign subsidiaries operating world-wide. They spanned the world's principal economic regions in virtually every sector, from finance, raw materials and agriculture to manufacturing and services, including fields like 'telesales' (which in Europe alone employs a million-and-a-half teleworkers, connected electronically to the outside world). Selling goods and services to the value of some US$9.5 trillion, these trans-national enterprises accounted for 70 per cent of world trade and around 20 per cent of the world's overall production.[74]

Admittedly, the degree to which turbocapitalist firms operate globally, like border-busting juggernauts, should not be exaggerated. Turbocapitalism not only produces strong pressures for re-regulation on a global scale; it also has a marked geographic bias. Its home base lies within the OECD countries, and the capital, technology and trade flows

---

[71] Adolph Wagner, *Die Ordnung des österreichischen Staatshaushalts* (Vienna, 1863).

[72] Miles Kahler, *International Institutions and the Political Economy of Integration* (Washington, DC, 1995), esp. chapter 2.

[73] Richard J. Barnet and John Cavanagh, *Global Dreams. Imperial Corporations and the New World Order* (New York and London, 1995), p. 15.

[74] Some relevant data are usefully summarised in the United Nations Commission on Transnational Corporations, *Transnational Corporations in World Development: A Re-Examination* (New York, 1978), p. 211, and in David Held and Anthony McGrew (eds.), *The Global Transformations Reader* (Oxford, 2000), p. 25.

that it effects tend to be concentrated, for the time being, *within* (rather than among) the European, Asian-Pacific and NAFTA/Latin American regions.[75] Yet, wherever the turbocapitalist economy gains the upper hand, it has definite globalising effects. It leads to sharp increases in profit-driven joint ventures and co-production, licensing and sub-contracting agreements among local, regional and global firms. The trade negotiations that began at the global and regional levels during the 1980s and 1990s serve as an index of this spread of a new – more aggressive, genuinely border-busting – form of capitalism to the four corners of the earth. Regional measures such as the North American Free Trade Agreement (NAFTA) have complemented efforts to remove barriers to investment at the global level, notably through the 'trade-related investment measures' (TRIMs) section of the WTO and the proposed – highly controversial – Multilateral Agreement on Investments (MAI) arrangements that would effectively remove all remaining restrictions on investment.

So what (if anything) is new about this system of turbocapitalism? How (if at all) does it contribute to the current growth spurt of global civil society? The most obvious fact to be noted is that for the first time ever modern capitalist firms have unlimited grazing rights. Helped along by trade and investment liberalisation and radical improvements in transportation and communication technologies, they can do business anywhere in the world. The exceptions – North Korea, southern Sudan, Burma – prove the rule, especially since the collapse of the Soviet Empire and the beginning of the Chinese experiment with state-engineered market reforms. The old joke that socialism was that historical phase linking capitalism with capitalism needs to be amended. It turns out that Soviet-style socialism, which was a reaction against the last great growth spurt of globalisation, was a brief interregnum stretching between state-organised capitalism and today's global capitalism. The light-hearted joke contains a cruel truth: turbocapitalism both contributes to and thrives upon the compression of time and space, to the point where the world begins to resemble one giant marketplace, in which anything – nature, people, their tools and products, even their tastes and libidinal desires – can potentially be treated as commodities for sale on a global scale. Some economists describe this trend in terms of the historic development of *global commodity chains*: geographically dispersed yet transactionally linked sequences of functions, in which each phase adds market value to the overall worldwide process of producing goods or services.[76]

---

[75] Paul Hirst and Graeme Thompson, *Globalization in Question* (Oxford, 1999).

[76] Most notably Gary Gereffi, 'Global Commodity Chains: New Forms of Coordination and Control among Nations and Firms in International Industries', *Competition and Change*, 1 (1996), pp. 427–39, and Gary Gereffi and Miguel Korzeniewicz (eds.), *Commodity Chains and Global Capitalism* (Westport, CT, 1994), esp. chapter 5.

The chains of commodity production and exchange that currently straddle the earth are of course only trends, albeit deep-rooted ones. It is important to grasp as well that they are highly complex and unevenly developed. The contrasts with the past are clearer than the differences in the present. When Adam Smith famously analysed the 'division of labour' within the emerging civil societies of the Atlantic region, his references to the specialisation of workers within different parts of the production process had no specific geographic connotations. He could suppose that industries and services of all kinds enjoyed a 'natural protection' from foreign protection, thanks to the vagaries of geographical distance. That supposition continued to be plausible even during the vigorous growth spurt of global economic integration before the First World War, and until the 1970s, when *shallow integration* – arm's length *trade* in raw materials, goods and services among independent firms and through international movements of capital – was the norm.[77] Shallow integration is arguably what Marx and Engels – the first great critics of globalisation – had in mind in their stirring summary of the worldly thrust of mid-nineteenth-century capitalism. 'The need of a constantly expanding market for its products chases the bourgeoisie over the entire surface of the globe. It must nestle everywhere, settle everywhere, establish connections every-where', they wrote, adding that the owners of capital had become the agents of cosmopolitanism. 'The bourgeoisie has, through its exploita-tion of the world market, given a cosmopolitan character to production and consumption in every country. To the great chagrin of reactionaries, it has drawn from under the feet of industry the national ground on which it stood. All old-established national industries have been destroyed or are daily being destroyed. They are dislodged by new industries, whose introduction becomes a life and death question for all civilised nations, by industries that no longer work up indigenous raw material, but raw ma-terial drawn from the remotest zones; industries whose products are con-sumed, not only at home, but in every quarter of the globe. In place of the old wants, satisfied by the production of the country, we find new wants, requiring for their satisfaction the products of distant lands and climes. In place of the old local and national seclusion and self-sufficiency, we have intercourse in every direction, universal inter-dependence of nations.'[78]

The system of turbocapitalism differs from this picture drawn by Marx and Engels, especially because it draws everybody and everything within

---

[77] The useful distinction between 'shallow integration' and 'deep integration' is drawn from Peter Dicken, *Global Shift. Transforming the World Economy*, 3rd edn. (London, 2000), p. 5.

[78] Marx and Engels 1888, drawn from http://csf.Colorado.EDU/psn/marx/Archive/1848-CM/.

its wake into processes of *deep integration*, which extend from visible and invisible trading to the *production* of goods and services by means of globally connected commodity chains organised by trans-national corporations. These processes of deep integration, to repeat, are highly complex and uneven. Rather than seeing them as a finished outcome, they are better described as a constellation of interrelated *processes* that are very unevenly distributed in time and space. Turbocapitalism has unleashed *globalising* forces, but this has not yet resulted in a fully *globalised* world economy in which the lives and livelihoods of every person and patch of the earth are bound to and functionally integrated with all others. Turbocapitalism does not lead to a 'global marketplace', let alone a 'global village'. It has a variety of different effects, ranging from very weak or non-existent forms of integration to very strong or full integration.

At one end of the continuum stand whole peoples and regions who are routinely ignored by the dynamics of turbocapitalism. According to one estimate, in 1913 the countries in the bottom fifth of income per person received around 25 per cent of the world's stock of foreign capital, much the same as the countries in the richest fifth. By 1997, the poorest fifth's share was down to under 5 per cent, compared with 36 per cent for the richest fifth.[79] Capital investment is today mainly a rich–rich affair. For instance, many parts of sub-Saharan Africa, where despite flourishing global trends foreign direct investment (FDI) actually *declined* during the 1990s and today accounts for only some 1.4 per cent of investment world-wide,[80] fall into this category; these areas, victims of a form of capitalist 'legal apartheid' (a term coined by the Peruvian economist, Hernando de Soto[81]) suffer the consequences of 'dead capital' reinforced by the organised neglect by turbocapitalist investors. This is the world in which millions know in their bellies that there is only one thing worse than participating in the global system of turbocapitalism: being left out of the turbocapitalist system. So, for better or worse, people flee self-sufficient or violence-wrecked social nests in an effort to raise their standards of living by becoming interdependent in much larger markets. This is the sprawling, mostly illegal urban world of the Turkish *gekecondus*, the Haitian *bidonvilles*, the *barong-barongs* of the Philippines, Brazil's *favelas*, the swelling jumble of ramshackle houses and sweatshops on the outskirts of Beijing.

---

[79] Matthew Bishop, 'Capitalism and its Troubles', *The Economist* (London), 18 May 2002, p. 25
[80] *Trade and Human Rights: A Free Press, Development and Globalisation*, document prepared by the International Federation of Journalists (Brussels, 2000), p. 1.
[81] Hernando de Soto, *The Mystery of Capital: Why Capitalism Triumphs in the West and Fails Everywhere Else* (London, 2000), p. 237.

Elsewhere, moving across the continuum, straightforward exchange across vast distances between wealthy core and poorer peripheral areas – for instance, the exporting of granite mined in Zimbabwe to the kitchens and bathrooms of western Europe – is the norm. Then, towards the other end of the continuum, turbocapitalism slices through territorial and time barriers by bringing about highly complex, kaleidoscopic forms of market integration involving the fragmentation of production processes and their geographical relocation and functional reintegration on a global scale. And then, finally, there are some sectors of economic life – like the twenty-four-hour financial speculation conducted in cities like New York, London and Tokyo – in which the whole earth is literally a playground for turbocapital. In a stirring film from the 1960s, Phileas Fogg, the imperturbable English gentleman, attempted to win a bet by circumnavigating the globe in eighty days. By contrast, in the most globalised sectors of the world economy, money today flies around the world in eighty seconds, or less. Revolutionary advancements in information technology, combined with policies to lift barriers to investment, enable private capital to travel across borders at a pace that is baffling for government regulators and decisionmakers in every walk of life. Within this fully turbocapitalist sector, the volume of daily international foreign exchange transactions has grown from around US$500 billion in 1989 to over US$1.5 trillion in 1997. The figures have subsequently continued to rise, in no small measure because virtually all of it (around 98 per cent) is for speculation or short-term investment, rather than related directly to actual trade or FDI.[82] Instability is naturally inherent in these massive cross-border transfers of unregulated speculative capital. The flights of short-term capital at lightning speed from Mexico in late 1994, Thailand, Malaysia, Indonesia and South Korea in late 1997, from Russia and Brazil in 1998, from Turkey in November 2000, and from Argentina in 2002, were not mere accidents. They rather revealed that the field of global finance resembles a financial casino, in which nervous investors withdraw their money or move it elsewhere in the world, all with a tap of a computer key.

Also new, and equally striking, is the way in which firms exercise their freedom to set up offices, plants and subsidiaries wherever costs are lowest and safe to invest. They do so in accordance with what can be called the 'Low Cost and Safety Principle'. The first outlines of this principle were already at work from the early 1970s, when labour-intensive processes like sewing and assembling electronic goods began to be farmed

---

[82] Martin Khor, *The Economic Crisis in East Asia: Causes, Effect, Lessons* (Third World Network, 1998), p. 2.

out to parts of Asia, the Caribbean, and the Mexico–US border region; the workforces, comprising mainly poorly paid women workers, were effectively in the business of assembling imported inputs for export back to the countries in which the materials originated. This new international division of labour, as it was called by some economists at the time, anticipated the era of turbocapitalism and its *globalising* effects. By compressing time and space within the internal production operations of firms, it differed in one critical respect from the old capitalist practice of extracting raw materials from distant sources. That practice, noted Hegel, was already common to early-nineteenth-century civil societies, but in fact its roots run much deeper. The beginnings of a world economy were evident in the 'long sixteenth century' (1450–1640), a period in which the short-distance, local trade of basic commodities within and among medieval market towns began to be supplemented by long-distance trade in rare items and luxury goods, fine cloths and spices for instance, extracted from distant parts of the world for local elite consumption.[83]

Turbocapitalism no doubt sustains, in more developed form, this older *internationalisation* of production. But, uniquely, it does more than this: it *globalises* production by radically compressing time and space barriers to the movement of labour power and managerial expertise, raw materials and technologies of production, components and finished commodities. In recent years, the Low Cost and Safety Principle has been applied more intensively to overcome barriers of time and the tyranny of distance, so that global firms transfer sophisticated state-of-the-art production methods to countries where wages are extremely low. A number of poorer countries, Mexico and India and China among them, are consequently now equipped with the infrastructural means of housing any service or industrial operation – whether airline ticket and holiday telephone sales or capital-intensive, high-tech production of commodities like computers and automobiles. Sometimes the output from these high-tech operations is consumed locally. Coca-Cola, among the leading symbols of turbocapitalist enterprise, had no bottling plants in China in 1979; less than two decades later it had set up eighteen plants producing (in 1996) some 3 billion Cokes for that huge domestic market. Other transnational firms circulate both their materials and finished products globally, like the Caterpillar plant in Toronto that draws together components from other Caterpillar factories scattered around the world – transmissions from the

---

[83] See the important studies by Immanuel Wallerstein, *The Capitalist World Economy* (Cambridge, 1979) and Fernand Braudel, *Civilization and Capitalism, 15th–18th Centuries*, 3 vols. (London, 1984).

United States, axles from Belgium, winches from Brazil, engines from Japan – and then assembles them for export as a finished product to many countries, including the ones that produced the components in the first place.

The Low Cost and Safety Principle radically alters the shape of trade and investment within global civil society. For a start, transactions are no longer housed exclusively within or between territorial states. Not only do global commodity chains become the norm. Trade and investment *within* firms becomes commonplace. Estimates are that about a third of world trade is now taken up by trade between one part of a global firm and its other affiliates, and the proportion is growing. Such 'self-trading' is in effect an extreme form of border-breaking economic globalisation. It is strongly evident in the operations of General Electric, which like many other firms operating across the Mexican–US border ships machinery components to its own subsidiary in Nuevo Laredo. Intra-firm trading of this kind is oiled by so-called 'transfer pricing'. This is the practice whereby firms avoid taxes by setting prices in such a way that registered losses are maximised in countries where tax rates are high and, conversely, registered profits are highest in countries where taxes are low, or (as in 'tax haven' countries) where no taxes are paid at all.

The avoidance of company taxes paid to states is a definite new line on the contours of global civil society. So too is the formation of a *global labour pool*. When businesses develop globally interconnected chains of investment, resources and finished products and services workers based in richer countries like Germany and France are effectively forced to compete with workers living in places – China, Singapore, Taiwan, South Korea – where wages are low and social entitlements of workers are either poorly protected or non-existent. The figures on this new development are telling: in 1975, the top dozen exporters of goods were almost all rich capitalist countries with relatively small wage differentials. The highest average hourly wage was in Sweden (US$7.18); the lowest was in Japan (US$3), a differential of just under two-and-a-half times. By 1996, driven by the forces of turbocapitalism, a global labour pool had developed, with a corresponding dramatic widening of wage differences. The highest average hourly wages were found in Germany (US$31.87) and the lowest in China (US$0.31) – a pay differential of more than a hundred times.[84]

---

[84] Sarah Anderson and John Cavanagh, *Field Guide to the Global Economy* (New York, 2000), p. 30. The striking differences are of course compounded by much longer hours of work (sometimes up to 80 hours per week) and poorly protected working conditions in the low-wage sectors of the global economy.

Markets and civil society

The striking social discrepancies produced by market processes within global civil society have led some observers –Yoshikazu Sakamoto, for instance[85] – to question whether market forces with such destructive consequences properly belong within the category of global civil society. His question is important, and needs to be addressed, if only because it exemplifies the strong tendency within the existing academic literature on global civil society to draw upon the originally Gramscian distinction between civil society (the realm of non-profit, non-governmental organisations, in which humans are treated as ends-in-themselves) and the market (the sphere of profit-making and profit-taking commodity production and exchange, in which humans are treated as mere means).

In responding to Sakamoto, it is important from the outset to distinguish carefully, as has been done earlier in this book,[86] the different possible usages – empirical interpretation, strategic calculation, normative judgement – of the idea of civil society. Sakamoto's points are powerful, but they arguably conflate these differences, so much so that his understandably strong dislike of the socially *negative* (disruptive or outright destructive) effects of market forces within actually existing civil societies move him to banish the market altogether from the concept of global civil society. The reasoning secretly draws upon the distinction between 'is' and 'ought' in order to defend the latter against the former. The term global civil society is cleansed of the muck of markets. It is thereby turned into a normative utopia. Normatively speaking, it becomes a 'pure' concept – synonymous with 'equity, equality and public welfare', an unadulterated 'good', like a sparkling coveted diamond that all would want to prize, especially if offered it on a soft velvet cushion of fine words. Sakamoto's normative reasoning is tempting – who but curmudgeons, ideologists and crooks could be ethically opposed to civil society in his sense? – but it should be refused, for three reasons.

Normatively speaking, it implies that global civil society could in future survive without money or monetary exchanges – rather as nineteenth-century and early-twentieth-century communists naïvely imagined that

---

[85] Yoshikazu Sakamoto, 'An Alternative to Global Marketization', in Jan Nederveen Pieterse (ed.), *Global Futures: Shaping Globalization* (London and New York, 2000), pp. 98–116.

[86] See also Keane, *Civil Society: Old Images, New Visions*, pp. 36ff. and John Keane (ed.), *Civil Society and the State: New European Perspectives* (London and New York 1988 [reprinted 1998]), introduction. The infelicities of the (neo-Gramscian) distinction between market and civil society are discussed in my *Democracy and Civil Society* (London 1998 [1988]), esp. chapters 3 and 4. See also John O'Neill, *The Market: Ethics, Knowledge and Politics* (New York, 1998).

future communist society would be bound together by such attributes as love, hard work and mutuality. Both make the mistake of supposing that goods and services could be supplied in complex ways to complex societies by some non-market invisible hand, which in reality would turn out to be the whip hand of dis-organisation, hunger and chaos. The friends of global civil society must face up to this point. They must see that, in spite of all their well-known weaknesses, markets are a necessary organising principle of all durable civil societies, past and present, and that that rule will certainly apply in future to global civil society – supposing that it will enjoy such fate. This 'no market, no civil society' rule applies because economies driven by commodity production and exchange have two great advantages: under social conditions with many different preferences and values that are far too complex to be calculable by a central plan for resource allocation, market economies minimise collective losses. Market forces tend to guarantee that factors of production that fail to perform according to current standards of efficiency are continuously and often swiftly eliminated, and then forced to find alternative and more productive uses. In matters of resource allocation, market forces ensure that 'uncompetitive' factors of production go to the wall. Markets operate according to Abraham Lincoln's maxim that those who need a helping hand should look no further than the lower end of their right arm. In this way, markets invite the victims of competition to blame themselves – and to survive by adapting to new standards of efficiency.

In matters of strategy, the purist concept of a post-capitalist global civil society fares no better. If the aim is to strengthen global civil society by displacing market forces, then anything related to the market – money, jobs, workers, trade unions – cannot by definition be useful in struggles to achieve that civilising goal. The defence of global civil society resembles a physics of proportionate relationships. It must be thought of as a struggle to repair the damage done to it by capitalism and, ultimately, a struggle to 'push back' all things capitalist, perhaps even to rid the world of it. Otherwise, the chosen means – the *commodification* of social relations – would corrupt and potentially overpower the envisaged end: the *humanisation* of social relations. So it comes to seem (quite unrealistically) that global civil society will be possible only if people topple King Money by behaving themselves and acting as good people, as citizens rather than as market actors. Trade unions, corporate philanthropy, small businesses, advanced technologies supplied by local and multinational firms: none of this (it is supposed) could or should play a part in the struggle to expand and thicken the cross-border social networks that comprise global civil society.

Ultimately, the type of approach adopted by Sakamoto is scuppered by a bundle of strong empirical objections. We have seen that descriptive interpretations of global civil society, attempts to describe and explain its contours, should not be confused with normative judgements and strategic calculations. Descriptive interpretations begin where actuality itself begins. The point is elementary, but important, for whether we like it or not the division between market and civil society does not exist; the dualism wielded by Sakamoto is a phantom, a bad abstraction. Production – as Marx famously emphasised – is always the appropriation of nature within and through a determinate form of society.

Within market settings, those who go about their business and do their work chronically draw upon *endogenous* sources of sociability. Their activities are always embedded within civil society interactions that are lubricated by norms like punctuality, trust, honesty, reliability, group commitment and non-violence.[87] In the most productive sectors of global civil society, the need for lively and flexible civil society institutions is especially imperative, and publicly recognised. Norm-based exchanges and informal, decentralised and 'flat' socio-economic organisations – *a networking civil society* – become ever more important as the production and distribution of goods and services becomes more complex and computerised. In effect, this heightened co-dependence of contemporary markets upon other civil society institutions confirms an old rule: that markets are always and everywhere *human creations embedded in social and political relations*.

Today, we tend to overlook this point. We are inclined to take markets for granted, to see them as *naturally* occurring, as if they somehow spring like mushrooms out of the soil of 'society' or 'competition' or the 'natural'

---

[87] The tension within the systems-theoretical understanding of civil society proposed by Jeffrey C. Alexander (see his 'Introduction' to Jeffrey C. Alexander (ed.), *Real Civil Societies. Dilemmas of Institutionalization*, London, 1998) is instructive on this point. It insists upon the need to grasp the difference between the contemporary sub-systems of civil society (organised by public opinion, democracy, civility) and the 'instrumental, self-oriented individualism institutionalised in capitalist market life' (Alexander, 'Introduction', p. 8). The spatial metaphor coded into this approach leads to the conclusion that the relationship between civil society and the market is best analysed in terms of 'facilitating inputs, destructive intrusions, and civil repairs' (Alexander, 'Introduction', p. 8). A few lines later, drawing upon Marx's thesis of the socialisation of production at the point of production – a thesis that supposed that markets are the central organising principle of modern civil societies – Alexander virtually abandons this approach. He admits of the possibility that capitalist market life 'supplies the civil sphere with facilities like independence, self-control, rationality, equality, self-realization, cooperation, and trust' (p. 8). On the ground of 'realism' alone – the same ground on which Alexander stakes out his case – the analysis logically requires the abandonment of the civil society/market economy dualism. 'Realism' also demands a revision of his heavily normative picture of civil society, as this book explains at length. Parallel doubts about the purism of Alexander's image of civil society are raised in Victor Pérez-Diaz, 'The Public Sphere and a European Civil Society', in Pérez-Diaz, *The Return of Civil Society: The Emergence of Democratic Spain* (Cambridge, MA and London, 1993), pp. 211–38.

selfishness of people. This perception was not always taken for granted. Once upon a time, markets were seen to be delicate human creations – as inventions generated by wilful acts of power exercised by social and political agents. Consider the simple but fundamental example of free trade across borders. Although today the principle of free trade is presumed to be a vital and necessary rule of commodity production and exchange, there were times when the extension of market processes across borders had to be fought for by *social* agents. Look at the nineteenth-century European struggle for free trade. It opened in full force, between 1838 and 1846, with the campaigns of the Anti-Corn Law League against the British corn tariff. The League's efforts soon spread across the Channel. In 1846, the Belgian Association for Commercial Liberty and the Free Trade Association in France were founded; the International Association for Customs Reform, set up in 1856, worked for the creation of an International Union that published current tariff schedules for the benefit of businesses; and during the 1860s, so-called 'Cobden clubs' sprang up throughout Europe in support of freer trade.[88]

Such episodes in the history of modern markets imply another rule: that practical attempts to 'disembed' markets are doomed to failure. Efforts to abstract and insulate markets against all the social processes of civil society – to rid them of solidarity, language, laughter, friendship, free expression, family life, sociability, so that they strictly obey the accountants' and underwriters' criteria of minimum risk and coldly calculated profit and loss – may be an attractive fantasy in the minds of turbocapitalist ideologues. They are in reality neither the normal nor the sustainable case. Every known market, Karl Polanyi famously pointed out in *Origins of Our Time* (1945), is a particular form of *socially mediated* interaction centred on money, production, exchange and consumption. Three different, but related conclusions follow from this point: that markets are an intrinsic *empirical* feature, a functionally intertwined prerequisite, of the social relations of actually existing global civil society; that global civil society as we know and now experience it could not survive for more than a few days without the market forces unleashed by turbocapitalism; and that the market forces of turbocapitalism could themselves not survive for a day without *other* civil society institutions, like households, charities, community associations and linguistically shared social norms like friendship, trust and cooperation.

This unbreakable dependence of turbocapitalist markets upon other civil society institutions highlights the way in which labour is a 'fictitious'

---

[88] A history of these developments is found in Norman Maccord, *The Anti-Corn Law League, 1838–1846* (London, 1958).

commodity.[89] While labour is organised as a commodity in the markets of the turbocapitalist economy, it is not produced for sale. Labour is in fact just another name for a type of social activity that is ultimately not detachable from *six* other (overlapping), variously combined types of civil society institutions: *non-market forms of production* within households, voluntary and charitable groups and other 'parallel economy' activities; forms of *recreation*, in which people spend at least some of their disposable time in such activities as sport, travel, tourism and hobbies and the (often overlapping) organisations of the *arts and entertainment*, including galleries, cinemas, music and dance clubs, theatres, pubs, restaurants and cafés. Civil society institutions also encompass the *cultivation of intimacy* through friendships and household spaces of cooperation, sexual experimentation, procreation and the social nurturing of infants and adults; non-governmental *communications media*, such as newspapers and magazines, bookshops, internet cafés, television studios and community radio stations; and, finally, institutions for the definition and nurturing of the *sacred*, including cemeteries, places of religious worship, monuments and sites of historical importance. Given these various types of non-market social organisation, it is easy to see that both global civil society and its more local and regional counterparts can have a variable social ecology. It can be more or less pluralistic, more or less religious, more or less market-dominated. But – short of sociocide, the nervous breakdown of the social – this global society can never be transformed into one giant capitalist market, into something like a shopping mall stretched from one end of the earth to the other.

Some examples of the 'no civil society, no market' rule – one each from the local, regional, and global levels – should help to make this fundamental point clearer. One evening, enter a local taverna in the Pláka district of Athens. Amid its old houses and narrow, winding streets straggling up the slopes of the Acropolis, the taverna is both a business and a social experiment in warming the heart of the night. Most definitely, it is people before money. Guests must of course pay, or arrange credit. Otherwise words will fly like daggers, and the police may be called to

---

[89] Karl Polanyi, *Origins of Our Time* (London, 1945), pp. 78–9: 'To allow the market mechanism to be sole director of the fate of human beings and their natural environment, indeed, even of the amount and use of purchasing power, would result in the demolition of society. For the alleged commodity "labour power" cannot be shoved about, used indiscriminately, or even left unused, without affecting also the human individual who happens to be the bearer of this particular commodity. In disposing of a man's labour power the system would, incidentally, dispose of the physical, psychological, and moral entity called "man" attached to that tag. Robbed of the protective covering of cultural institutions, human beings would perish from the effects of social exposure; they would die as the victims of acute social dislocation through vice, perversion, crime, and starvation.'

settle the matter. Only good friends of the owner and local unfortunates are entitled to free meals. Yet the experience of the taverna is not purely and simply a business. Its owners and clients know no distinction between market and civil society. Under dimmed lights, Singapore fans rotating overhead, many pairs of eyes converge; they look without looking. There is the buzz of richly gestured conversation, waiters darting here and there, smells of grilling meat, garlic, warm bread. In one corner sits the owner, smoking a cigarette, looking bored, stroking the bridge of his nose, drinking coffee with iridescent bubbles. Nearby, a savvy barmaid chats up the cashier, seated at a flickering monitor, recording costs and earnings. Guests chatter, smile, conduct private quarrels, look vacant, flirt, smoke, inhale smoke, clink glasses, rub tired faces, clap hands to the lilting bouzouki. Tables are cleared, tables are filled, tables are soiled; the cycle seems endless. There are moments of hush, then yelps of laughter, followed by sounds of crashing cutlery, talk of Greece in Europe, and of the end of the drachma. Near midnight, tired chefs wearing white hats and aprons appear, looking triumphant. When ready, guests pay, at their leisure. They are then thanked and wished good evening, in accordance with the rule that money is buried in social custom.

A different example: embedded market transactions at the level of a region. It has been pointed out by economists and geographers that business firms tend to cluster geographically, in towns and cities that form part of a wider region. They form regionally-structured, socially embedded 'untraded interdependencies'.[90] Examples of such thriving regions include Seoul–Inchon, southern California, Singapore, the M4 corridor, and the conurbations of Stuttgart, Tokyo, Paris-Sud and Milan. The recently created Special Economic Zones (SEZs), open coastal cities and priority development areas in China, also count as striking examples. Like bees to a hive, firms swarm around such places not simply because it is profitable (thanks to reduced transaction costs), but because their own profitability *requires* the cultivation of densely textured socio-cultural ties ('untraded interdependencies') that come with agglomeration. Business dictates social bonding and social innovation. Profitability requires firms to embed themselves within the socio-cultural ties of the regional civil society; by so doing, of course, they increase its textural density. In this

---

[90] See M. Storper, *The Regional World: Territorial Development in a Global Economy* (New York, 1997); the various contributions to A. Amin and N. Thrift (eds.), *Globalization, Institutions and Regional Development in Europe* (Oxford, 1994); Meric S. Gertler and David A. Wolfe, 'Local Social Knowledge Management', unpublished paper (Brussels, 2002); Gernot Grabher, 'Rediscovering the Social in the Economics of Interfirm Relations', in Gernot Grabher (ed.), *The Embedded Firm* (London and New York, 1993), pp. 1–31; and Philip Cooke and Kevin Morgan, *The Associational Economy. Firms, Regions and Innovation* (Oxford, 1998).

way, the regional civil society becomes the hive and propolis of business activity. Firms find that face-to-face interaction with clients, customers and competitors is easier. They find as well that their chosen patch contains social spaces for gathering business information, monitoring and maintaining patterns of trust, establishing common rules of business behaviour, and socialising with others: in places like clubs, bars, cinemas, theatres, sports venues and restaurants. And the regional civil society acts as a 'technopole' or 'technology district'.[91] It enables firms to enhance their capacity for technical innovation: they can better develop, test, mimic and track innovations, find new gaps in the market and react more quickly to changing patterns of demand.

To find examples of socially embedded market activity at the global level seems most difficult, at first sight. Many observers warn that 'global capital' is socially rootless. It is often presented as a money-hungry juggernaut ruthlessly breaking down political borders and smashing through walls of social restraint embodied in local communities and other institutions. 'Cold-blooded, truly arm's-length and therefore purely contractual relations exemplify the entire spirit of turbo-capitalism', writes Luttwak.[92] In a similar vein, Soros describes the global capitalist system as 'a gigantic circulatory system sucking capital into the centre and pushing it out into the periphery'. Like former American President Ronald Reagan, who liked to speak of 'the magic of the marketplace', its protagonists suffer from excessive belief in profit-making through market mechanisms. Their dogmatic 'market fundamentalism' supposes that its dominant value, which in reality is no value at all, is 'the pursuit of money'. What sets global capitalism apart from its earlier versions is 'the intensification of the profit motive and its penetration into areas that were previously governed by other considerations...It is no exaggeration to say that money rules people's lives to a greater extent than ever before.'[93]

These descriptions of global business alert us to its novelty. They correctly capture something of its swashbuckling, buccaneering, time-and-distance-conquering tendencies – as well as its indulgence of excess

---

[91] The terms are developed, respectively, in Manuel Castells and P. Hall, *Technopoles of the World: The Making of 21st Century Industrial Complexes* (London, 1994) and M. Storper, 'The Limits to Globalization: Technology Districts and International Trade', *Economic Geography*, 68 (1992), pp. 60–93.

[92] Luttwak, *Turbo-Capitalism*, p. 43.

[93] George Soros, *The Crisis of Global Capitalism* (London, 1998), pp. 126, 114, 102, 115–16 and 112–13: 'there is a unifying principle in the global capitalist system . . . That principle is money. Talking about market principles would confuse the issue, because money can be amassed in other ways than by competition. There can be no dispute that in the end it all boils down to profits and wealth measured in terms of money.' See also his *On Globalization* (New York, 2002).

volatility, irrational exuberance and speculative collapses. Some have re-turned to the language of Marx. 'Accumulate, accumulate! This is Moses and the Prophets!', write Hardt and Negri. 'There is nothing, no "naked life", no external standpoint... nothing escapes money. Production and reproduction are dressed in monetary clothing.'[94] Such descriptions of turbocapitalism also pose a normative problem: they pinpoint the need to deal politically with the chronic tendency of commodity production and exchange to pick the locks of civil society and to roam freely through its rooms, like a thief in the night. Turbocapitalism is extraordinarily good at production, but it fails miserably at distribution. 'As long as capital-ism remains triumphant', Soros writes, 'the pursuit of money overrides all other social considerations... The development of a global economy has not been matched by the development of a global society.'[95] These various points are salutary, but arguably they exaggerate the degree to which turbocapitalism has become disembedded – broken free from – the emerging global civil society, including its local civil society habitats. Once again, we return to the central point: no business, global business included, can properly function as business unless it draws freely upon, and nurtures, the non-market environment of civil society in which it is more or less embedded, or seeks to embed itself.

Many examples at the level of global commodity chains spring to mind. All of them underscore two related points: that the artificial distinction between 'the market' and 'global civil society' is unwarranted because turbocapitalism both nurtures *and* disorders the structures of global civil society within which it operates. It is important to grasp these positive and negative dynamics, which most certainly cannot be grasped through the kind of static binary opposite defended by Sakamoto and others.

On the positive side, turbocapitalist firms, aided by the local and re-gional networks of smaller firms with which they do business, have defi-nite civilising effects on the global civil society in which they are embed-ded. Their corporate negotiations are an obvious case in point. Senior company executives who try to do business in foreign contexts know from experience that they cannot 'wheel and deal' or act like pirates on the open seas.[96] If they are serious about establishing business links, say, with South Korean firms, then they know that there are certain so-cial rules that have to be followed. Making the right connections at the

---

[94] Robert J. Shiller, *Irrational Exuberance* (Princeton, 2000); Hardt and Negri, *Empire*, p. 32.

[95] Soros, *The Crisis of Global Capitalism*, p. 102.

[96] See the remarks of Sergey Frank, a senior partner within the world-wide, German-based human resource consulting group, Kienbaum Consultants International GmbH, in 'Think Confucian while Bargaining', *Financial Times* (London), 30 October 2001.

outset, for instance with the polite help of an ambassador or the president of the chamber of commerce, is vital. So too is a bilingual business card and an interpreter. Cold-calling business contacts is most unwise. So too is impatience. Crass calculations and pushiness are to be avoided. The golden rule is: establish a good social relationship with one's potential partner. Informal socialising, before and after business hours, is a basic good, not just an add-on luxury item. Face-to-face interaction is much appreciated. So too is the observance of protocol. Dealings will typically be group-based. Quick recognition of the team's vertical system of ranking participants by age and gender is a must. Try to understand something of the proud sense of history and the local traditions of people working together. Expect tough negotiations and tiring last-minute renegotiations, or pull-outs. Never attach blame to others in public. Understand that disagreement and annoyance are likely to be hidden behind courteous smiles. Expect bad news to be communicated with polite or non-committal words, or through changes of subject, or encounters with low-level negotiators. Observe another golden rule: nobody should lose face.

Business firms operating within global civil society preserve or nurture its social codes in other ways. For instance, they show some signs of strengthening its social bonds through the old practice of corporate giving, which nearly doubled (to US$385 billion) during the 1990s.[97] The foundation set up by Bill and Melinda Gates, the Global Fund for Children's Vaccines, talks in terms of the need globally to revive the principle of corporate *noblesse oblige* by 'public-ising' the private sector. The US-based Varsavsky Foundation, which donated funds to create a national educational Internet portal in Argentina, champions 'venture philanthropy', whose motto is a new version of an old proverb: 'while you do your neighbours a favour if you teach them how to fish, you do them a much bigger favour if you teach them how to run a fish farm.'[98] Senior executives in Volkswagen AG also speak confidently about their social duties. 'Civil society [*Zivilgesellschaft*] is no fair-weather word', they say. 'Civil society activities are for Volkswagen bound up with corporate social responsibility. Employers' responsibilities are not mere altruism or charity... Especially under conditions of globalisation, civil society has a right to know and to judge the contribution of employers to wealth

[97] Francie Ostrower, *Why the Wealthy Give. The Culture of Elite Philanthropy* (Princeton, 1995); and Frances Pinter, 'Funding Global Civil Society Organisations', in Anheier *et al.* (eds.), *Global Civil Society 2001*, pp. 195–217.
[98] Martin Varsavsky, 'How to Build a Dream', in the special Davos edition of *Newsweek* (December 2000–February 2001), p. 86.

creation, guarantees of mobility, technical progress and job creation.'[99] And Shell, whose performance in Nigeria raised an international out-cry, now parades under the banner of the 'triple bottom line': economic superiority, environmental soundness and social responsibility.

Caution should certainly be exercised when analysing corporate so-cial responsibility, if only because global corporations today enter our living rooms aglow with public-image or 'pro-social' advertising. Many firms, backed up by high-flying, well-paid 'ethics officers', present the world with their 'we too are citizens-of-the-world' credo and do their best to distract their (potential) critics from saying that these firms em-ploy eight-year-olds in sweatshops or brazenly trample upon the environ-ment. Some global corporate executives are even prepared to roll up their sleeves and mix with their opponents – as was evident at the 2002 World Economic Forum held in New York City, where market researchers from PricewaterhouseCoopers reportedly trolled hotel lobbies looking for op-portunities to 'dialogue', and where business people, often claiming to be Trojan Horses, sometimes talked like NGO activists; and where Irish rock star Bono chatted with Microsoft's Bill Gates before the launch of a 'corporate citizenship' statement signed by the chief executives and board directors of global companies like Anglo American, Siemens, Coca-Cola and McDonald's.[100] Sometimes, keeping their social distance, global cor-porations instead try to sharpen their street credibility by directly em-ploying public relations firms like Burson-Marsteller, the world's largest, whose corporate clients have included: the Three Mile Island nuclear plant, which suffered a partial meltdown in 1979; Union Carbide after the Bhopal gas leak resulted in the deaths of up to 15,000 people in India; British Petroleum after the sinking of the Torrey Canyon oil tanker in 1967; and whose clients today include big tobacco companies and the European biotechnology industry.[101]

Turbocapitalist firms often dissemble, but there is no doubt that they contribute in other ways to the cultivation of world-wide social rela-tions. Aside from the 'untraded interdependencies' discussed above, they

---

[99] From remarks presented to a Bundestag-sponsored congress by the general manager of Volkswagen AG, Reinhold Kopp, 'Die Bedeutung des bürgerschaftlichen Engage-ments für eine Europäische Zivilgesellschaft – Impulse, Blockaden, Herausforderungen' (Berlin, 30 October 2001).

[100] See the report in the *Financial Times* (London), 4 February 2002, and Naomi Klein, 'Masochistic Capitalists', *Guardian* (London), 15 February 2002.

[101] *Guardian* (London), 8 January 2001, p. 6. Burson-Marsteller's clients have also included states: it was employed by the Nigerian government to discredit reports of genocide during the Biafran war, the Argentinian junta after the disappearance of 35,000 civilians, the Indonesian government after the massacres in East Timor, and rulers in need of an improved image, like the Saudi monarchy and the late Romanian president Nicolae Ceauşescu.

also generate (for some people) income, goods and services, and jobs (50 per cent of the world's manufacturing jobs are now located outside the OECD region, a twelve-fold increase in four decades[102]). As well, these firms produce some measure of 'social capital' by training local employees in such skills as self-organisation, punctuality and forward-looking initiative. The use of 'industrial' theatre groups to train and motivate staff by South African companies serves as an unconventional illustration of the point: blue-chip mining companies such as Harmony Goldmines (the sixth largest gold producer in the world) and AngloGold have contracted creative theatrical companies like Bluemoon and Jumping Dust (the name comes from the Afrikaans word for dynamite) to use live performance as a dynamic tool of communication.[103] Drawing upon techniques pioneered by the Brazilian director Augusto Boal, the industrial theatre companies begin by researching the company's problems by spending time in meetings with workers, supervisors and managers. They then write a script which is rehearsed and revised by the actors in front of the employees. In this way, the employees are encouraged to become 'spect-actors' (as they are called) by stepping in and assuming the roles that are being rehearsed. They are taught the arts of better communication with others, teasing out problems, building teams, rehearsing how things within the company might be different, and easing in changes – all within a highly multilingual context, in which literacy levels remain low but in which there are strong traditions of participation in the arts, and of teaching through storytelling, song and dance.

Turbocapitalist firms are also regularly in the business of cultivating social meanings through consumption. Here we encounter the vexed issue of how to understand the relationship between exchange value and prestige value, between turbocapitalist firms and consumer advertising – and whether (and in which senses) this advertising promotes 'globalised' patterns of consumption. It is obvious that particularly in the field of consumer retailing, through posters and billboards and commercial radio and television, firms engage local cultures for the purpose of constructing convincing worlds of more or less shared symbols, ideas and values. Consumer retailing by trans-national conglomerates is an especially apt, if politically controversial example of how markets are embedded in civil society institutions. Neo-Gramscian distinctions between struggles in the realm of 'civil society' for meaningful authenticity (for instance, in the idioms of food, dress, language, music and dance), and money-centred

---

[102] United Nations Development Programme, *Globalization and Liberalization* (New York, 1998).
[103] See www.bluemoon.co.za and www.learningtheatre.co.za.

conflicts over wealth and income in 'the economy' are obsolete. They do not make sense in the field of globalised advertising and consumption. To the extent that global civil society is shaped by global advertising, prestige values do battle with exchange values: conflicts about the generation of wealth and income within 'the economy' simultaneously become disputes about symbolic meanings.[104]

The lavish claims made for and against turbocapitalist consumer culture are a case in point. According to the Golden Arches Theory of Conflict Prevention, no two bordering countries that both have a McDonald's have ever gone to war. According to the opposite Americanisation of the World Theory, world-wide advertising and marketing strategies necessarily produce a bland, trivialised, homogenised – American shopping mall – consumer culture that is imperialist. Both theories are implausible. There is no doubt that the world is linked together by taste chains, but (as one would expect in matters to do with pockets and palates) they operate in highly complex ways. Some taste chains – like the global marketing of Australian and New Zealand wine[105] – prove the power of relatively powerless local economies in the turbocapitalist system. Other taste chains bear the traces of once-dominant economies: football and male fashion, although originally invented in Britain, today have global influence, despite the fact that that country is no longer the leader in either fashion or football. Present-day attempts to globalise taste chains sometimes backfire. The retailing of food products like Coke and Pepsi and American television programmes to the villages of south-east Asia and central America and to cities like Shanghai, Sydney, Johannesburg and Cairo, for instance, stirs up trouble within global civil society. If anything, these retailing strategies have had the effect of *accentuating* local cultural diversity within global civil society. This is partly because profit-seeking, turbocapitalist retailers themselves see the need to tailor their products to local conditions and tastes. It is also partly because (as Marshall Sahlins has wittily pointed out[106]) the local consumers display vigorous powers of reinterpreting and 'overstanding' these commodities, of giving them new

---

[104] See Aihwa Ong, *Flexible Citizenship: The Cultural Logics of Transnationality* (Durham, 1999).

[105] Kym Anderson, *The Globalization (and Regionalization) of Wine*, Centre for International Economic Studies Discussion Paper, 0125 (University of Adelaide, June 2001).

[106] Marshall Sahlins, *Waiting for Foucault and Other Aphorisms* (Charlottesville and Cambridge, 1999), p. 34: 'Why are well-meaning Westerners so concerned that the opening of a Colonel Sanders in Beijing means the end of Chinese culture? A fatal Americanization. But we have had Chinese restaurants in America for over a century, and it hasn't made us Chinese. On the contrary, we obliged the Chinese to invent chop suey. What could be more American than that? French fries?' See also his 'Cosmologies of Capitalism: The Trans-Pacific Sector of "The World System" ', in *Culture in Practice. Selected Essays* (New York, 2000), pp. 415–69.

and different meanings. Kellogg's tried to convince Indians to start the day with Corn Flakes and Sugar Puffs, but they recoiled at the thought, preferring traditional hot parathas or idlis. Kentucky Fried Chicken swaggered into India, convinced that it would win the country over to the 'KFC experience' and, humbled by vegetarians and lovers of tandoori chicken, was reduced to just one branch, a heavily vegetarian one at that. Pizza Hut and Dominos – which offers toppings such as 'Peppy Paneer' and 'Chicken Chettinad' (a topping that mimics a traditional southern dish) – suffered a similar fate. And McDonald's, the world's largest user of beef – it has some 30,000 franchised restaurants in 120 countries – knows what it means to think globally and act locally: in the Indian context, there is no beef or pork in its products, its mayonnaise is made without eggs, and its popular McVeggie Burger and McAloo Tikki Burger (a spicy potato concoction) are cooked in different parts of the kitchen, so as to avoid the slightest contamination that would lead to plummeting sales.

Turbocapitalist firms are not only caught up in the business of cultivating and negotiating social meanings. Their operations are also generally antipathetic to violence and, for that reason, they contribute to the civility upon which global civil society feeds. It is true that some companies, in certain contexts, have bad records of colluding with the violence of political or gun-toting authorities hell-bent on destroying their opponents and civil society itself – as they did in South Africa before the revolution against apartheid, or as they continue to do widely in the global small arms industry. There are even global businesses, like the diamond and cocaine trades, that operate through murderous networks of guerrilla armies and armed thugs. Yet – the qualification is important – most businesses that operate globally share a common, long-term interest in the eradication of violence. Their chief executive officers, for instance, do not like working within the shadows of knee-capping, abduction, or murder; they shudder at stories of corporate executives who have been forced to sit tied up on a concrete floor with hoods on, or being bundled into vans and forced to run blindfold across muddy fields, at gunpoint. Some businesses (like Wellington Underwriters and Kroll Associates) even specialise in making money from insuring against risk, or from providing a global kidnap security service.[107] In general, the conduct of business, which requires the freedom to calculate risk over time, prudently and without interruption, is made difficult or impossible when violence threatens, which is why investment is chronically low, or non-existent, in zones of uncivil war, like Sierra Leone, Angola, southern Sudan and parts of the former Yugoslavia.

[107] 'The Global Executive's Nightmare', *Financial Times* (London), 25 May 2001.

Finally, on the positive side, acknowledgement must be made of the contributions of global business to the 'thickening' of communications networks that enable the operation of the non-profit organisations and networks of global civil society. Under modern conditions, states rather than global businesses have usually been the inventors or initial applicators of new technologies of transport and communication. While this rule holds true, say, for the World Wide Web and geostationary satellites, subsequent new investments in these and other communications technologies are typically market-driven: private investment goes where the returns are high, and high they can be in the field of communications technologies. The commercial introduction of technologies like software systems, wide-bodied jet aircraft, fibre optics, superfreighters and containerisation (which enables safe transhipment from one type of transport to another), has several cumulative – revolutionary – effects. Through privately owned and leased networks, organisations large and small can now operate over vast geographical distances, thanks to the growth of country-to-country links, regional hub-and-spoke networks, and global telecommunications services.[108] There is a sharp reduction of both the operating costs and the time it takes both information and things and people to move from one part of the world to another. The friction of distance is greatly reduced.

Market inequalities

While the growth of market-driven communications within global civil society 'shrinks' the world, such time–space contraction is extremely uneven. Shaped like a slim octopus with the globe half in its clutches, influential cities, together with powerful national economies and globe-straddling firms, are drawn together, as if they are part of the same body; but while certain places and people become the head and eyes and tentacles of global civil society, whole geographic areas and whole peoples, many millions of them, are left out and left behind, in the spaces between the slim tentacles of communication.

Such gaps between the communication rich and the communication poor remind us that there are limits to the various ways in which turbocapitalism nurtures the precious social interdependencies of the emerging global civil society. Those who praise turbocapitalism as a force for 'one world' sadly tell half the story of turbocapitalism, which otherwise operates as a contradictory and disruptive force within global civil society.

---

[108] J. V. Langdale, 'The Geography of International Business Telecommunications: The Role of Leased Networks', *Annals of the Association of American Geographers*, 79 (1989), pp. 501–22.

Those who presently champion 'anti-capitalism' may be naïve in their analyses and short on viable solutions, but they have put their fingers on the key point: that commodified economies, left to their own devices, produce great social inequalities and, thus, tend to destroy the structures of civil society within which they are embedded, and upon which they depend for their reproduction. An obvious example is the way in which the business units of global civil society exercise what C. B. Macpherson once called 'extractive power' over their workers and other dependents, for instance through day-to-day hiring and firing practices, and their ability to pay ruinously low, take-it-or-leave-it wages.[109]

Turbocapitalist businesses also have at their disposal the power to weaken or ruin others' lives by deciding to invest here and not there, or instead by moving their investments from here to there, thus ensuring that our world is full of overworked and unemployed people and marked by extraordinary deprivation and staggering inequality.[110] The profit-hungry, speculative thrust of capital markets is a closely related, especially worrying example. High-risk, 'hot money' speculations produced a series of contagious financial crises in the summer of 1931, bringing to an end the last long cycle of economic globalisation. Similar worries about the boom–bust volatility of the turbocapitalist economy are today developing, fuelled by concern about stock exchange upsets, debt crises, corrupt banking and the general unease caused by such phenomena as the 'Asian flu', the Mexican 'tequila effect', and the ruinous collapse of the Argentinian economy. Such phenomena breed suspicion and nervousness. Many worry that our world's financial system, run as it is by organisations like the International Monetary Fund (IMF) and the World Bank, is deeply prone to collapse because it contains a basic instability: this system, in which (by agreement) the sum of trade deficits must equal the surpluses, is targeted at countries with trade deficits. When one country – Mexico or Thailand, say – reduces its deficit, as normally happens after it falls into crisis for local reasons, then another deficit soon appears elsewhere in the system. Of course, the United States acts as the deficit-of-last-resort within the system, thus prompting many to ask: For how much longer will the world have an appetite for America's equities and bonds? Can the richest sector of the turbocapitalist economy continue to borrow indefinitely from the rest of the world?

There are other problems. Pressured by turbocapitalism, global civil society, which otherwise displays a strong tendency towards polyarchy,

---

[109] C. B. Macpherson, *Democratic Theory. Essays in Retrieval* (Oxford, 1973).
[110] Amartya Sen, 'Work and Rights', *International Labour Review*, 139:2 (2000), pp. 119–28.

naturally cradles new property relations. It contains staggering discrepancies in wealth and income distribution. The economies of giant firms like Ford and Philip Morris exceed the gross domestic products (GDPs) of countries like Norway and New Zealand. Meanwhile, a small elite of winners, the 'transnational managerial class'[111] – corporate executives, peripatetic lawyers, rock-stars, jet-age nomads living in penthouse apartments in choice locations, like the Upper East Side of Manhattan, and holidaying in Tuscan palazzos, secluded spots in Mustique and Irish castles – monopolises more than its share of wealth and income. The combined wealth of the world's richest 200 billionaires reached an astonishing US$1.1 trillion in 1999 – the year in which the combined incomes of 582 million people living in the least developed countries was US$146 billion, or less than a dollar a day.[112] According to some estimates, based on Gini coefficient data, the gap between the poorest and wealthiest fifths of the world's population has risen from 1:30 in 1960, to 1:60 in 1990, to 1:74 in 1997; the annual income of 358 billionaires is now equivalent to that of the poorest 45 per cent of the world's population, that is, nearly 3 billion people.[113] For the time being, and in the absence of powerful redistributive mechanisms, this billionaire bourgeoisie exercises power globally over a mass of survivors or losers of varying affluence or poverty.

Not surprisingly, turbocapitalism strengthens the hand of market domination over the non-profit institutions of civil society, which tend to be pushed and pulled, twisted and torn into bodies that obey the rules of accumulation and profit maximisation. Given the virulence of these commodification imperatives, those who conclude that global civil society is 'first and foremost, a product of the rise of a newly globalised, neo-liberal form of capitalism'[114] can be forgiven for confusing trend and outcome. Global civil society is constantly under market pressures. Some NGOs formerly dependent on government funding, like the Seattle-based employment and rehabilitation service agency Pioneer Human Services, opt for self-financing through their own for-profit business enterprises.[115] Market forces also produce great inequalities among INGOs – Greenpeace, with a US$100 million annual budget, and the World Wildlife

---

[111] Robert Cox, 'Social Forces, States, and World Orders: Beyond International Relations Theory', in Robert O. Keohane (ed.), *Neorealism and its Critics* (New York, 1986), pp. 204–54.

[112] Michael Hirsh, 'Protesting Plutocracy', in the special Davos edition of *Newsweek* (December 2000–February 2001), p. 79.

[113] Data cited in Dieter Rucht, 'Social Movements Challenging Neo-Liberal Globalization', in John Keane (ed.), *Civil Society: Berlin Perspectives* (London, 2004).

[114] See the introduction to John L. and Jean Comaroff (eds.), *Civil Society and the Political Imagination in Africa: Critical Perspectives* (Chicago and London, 1999), p. 7.

[115] www.pioneerhumanserv.com.

Fund, with US$170 million, are wealthier than the UN Environment Programme (UNEP) and most other state-level governments they deal with[116] – while in some sectors it is as if the emerging global civil society is merely the appendage of the turbocapitalist economy. Some NGOs – business NGOs or BINGOs – even explicitly model themselves on business enterprises by developing commercial departments, head-hunters, media sections and private fund-raising and investment strategies. The neat division between the corporate and NGO worlds consequently dissolves.

[116] Timothy Shaw, 'Overview – Global/Local: States, Companies and Civil Societies at the End of the Twentieth Century', in Kendall Stiles (ed.), *Global Institutions and Local Empowerment. Competing Theoretical Perspectives* (New York, 2000), p. 14.

Cosmocracy

A court society?

Although turbocapitalism is arguably the force that most strongly energises the non-governmental sector from within, global civil society is not simply its child. To repeat: global civil society is overdetermined by various forces. It is a 'syndrome'[1] of processes and activities which have multiple origins and multiple dynamics, some of them (like the recent collapse and discrediting of communism) more conjunctural than deepseated. Together, these forces ensure that global civil society is not a single, unified domain, and that it will not be turned into something that resembles a combined factory, warehouse and shopping mall retailing consumer products on a global scale – let's say, a version of Disney's 'Its a Small World After All' or Naomi Klein's 'international rule of the brands'.[2] Global civil society is not simply reducible to the logic of commodity production and exchange, which helps to explain both its semantic promiscuity and its normative appeal to an astonishing variety of conflicting social interests, ranging from groups clustered around the World Bank to broad-minded Muslims defending their faith and radical ecological groups pressing for sustainable development.

If the institutions of global civil society are not merely the products of civic initiatives and market forces then is there a third force at work in nurturing and shaping it? It can be argued that global civil society is also the by-product of governmental or intergovernmental action or inaction. Contrary to those for whom global civil society is driven by a single social logic, like voluntary action or turbocapitalism, it is important to see the ways in which many global NGOs and actors are both framed and enabled by – and sometimes heavily dependent upon, in matters of funding and influence – governmental organisations of various

---

[1] The idea that globalising processes can be analysed as a multi-dimensional 'syndrome' is developed in James H. Mittelman, *The Globalisation Syndrome: Transformation and Resistance* (Princeton, 2000).
[2] Naomi Klein, *No Logo* (London, 2000).

kinds.[3] In fields like telecommunications and air, land and sea traffic, political bodies such as the International Postal Union (IPU) and the World Intellectual Property Organisation (WIPO), most of them resting formally on agreements to which states are signatories, exercise formidable regulatory powers that enable many parts of global civil society to keep moving, at a quickening pace. Governmental agencies, much more than corporate philanthropy, also currently play a major, positive-sum role in protecting, funding and nurturing non-profit organisations in every part of the earth where there is a lively civil society.[4] Included in this category are civil organisations that operate on the margins of the governmental institutions that license them in the first place. Examples include a body like the International Committee of the Red Cross which, although non-governmental, is mandated under the Geneva Convention and is linked to states through the organisation of the International Federation of Red Cross and Red Crescent Societies; similarly, the International Association of Religious Freedom, a forum for interreligious dialogue, has accredited NGO status at the UN and UNESCO levels.

To cite such examples at random is not to say that global civil society is describable as a para-governmental body. It is not a 'court society', of the kind that prevailed before the eighteenth-century emergence of civil societies, when concentric rings of social life were typically attached like barnacles to the hulls of monarchic states, which distributed favours and privileges to members of 'society' roughly in direct proportion to their proximity to the centres of administrative power.[5] The feisty institutions of global civil society are on the whole more dynamic and independent than the court societies of old. There is another key difference, which is that, unlike the early modern civil societies, which typically hatched within the well-established containers of empires and territorial states,

[3] Thomas Risse-Kappen, 'Transnational Actors and World Politics', in Walter Carlsnaes *et al.* (eds.), *Handbook of International Relations* (London, 2002).

[4] Lester Salamon, 'Government and Nonprofit Relations in Perspective', in the publication of the Urban Institute, *Nonprofits and Government: Collaboration and Conflict* (Washington, DC, 1999); the comparative findings cited in Peter Evans (ed.), *State–Society Synergy: Government and Social Capital in Development* (Berkeley, 1997); and on the funding of Japanese INGOs by the Ministry of Foreign Affairs and Ministry of Posts and Telecommunications, see Toshihiro Menju and Takako Aoki, 'The Evolution of Japanese NGOs in the Asia Pacific Context', in Tadashi Yamamoto (ed.), *Emerging Civil Society in the Asia Pacific Community* (Singapore, 1995). See Ken Conca, 'Greening the United Nations: Environmental Organisations and the UN System', *Third World Quarterly*, 16:3 (1995); and Margaret Clark, 'The Antarctica Environmental Protocol: NGOs in the Protection of Antarctica', in Thomas Princen and Matthias Finger (eds.), *Environmental NGOs in World Politics: Linking the Local and the Global* (London, 1994).

[5] The difference between civil society and a 'court society' (*sociedad de corte*) is noted in Victor Pérez-Diaz, 'La formación de Europa: nacionalismos civiles e inciviles', *Claves* (Madrid), 97 (November 1999), pp. 10–21.

global civil society has emerged and today operates in the absence of a global state, a world empire, or comprehensive regulatory structures that are describable in the state-centred terms of political 'realism'.

Some observers quickly conclude from this generalisation that the term 'global civil society' is meaningless; for them, the term is logically the Siamese twin of the term 'global state'. The point that they want to drive home is: no global state, no global civil society.[6] Such reasoning is unconvincing, if only because it overlooks the utter novelty of our situation. It is true that there is currently no global state. It is also most improbable that in future one could be developed, even on the doubtful assumption – made by groups that champion a World State with a World Police, like the *Weltbürgervereinigung*[7] – that it would be desirable to do so. Our situation is different, and without historical precedent. The current growth spurt of global civil society under 'anarchic' conditions certainly outpaces governments of all descriptions, but that is why it contains within it a pressing constitutional agenda which must be conceptualised in fresh ways: the need to go beyond the present clutter of global political institutions, in order to find new governing arrangements that enable something like effective and democratically accountable government, the rule of law and more equitable and freer social relations, to develop on a global scale.

The challenge is daunting, and it is not made easier by the fact that conventional political wisdom has little to say on the matter. If one looks at the literature in the fields of international relations and political theory, it is evident that a string of political questions has been left dangling, knotted and neglected: Who does the governing in today's world? Through which institutions do they govern, in the sense that their decisions structure and confine the fields of judgement and action of actors within global civil society, even forcing them – through law, diplomacy, sanctions, violence – to do things that otherwise they would not do? Can governing institutions in this sense be given a name? How do they compare to previous typologies of government? In whose interests do these institutions operate? What key decisions do they make, where are they made, and who makes them? In short, through which administrative, legal, military/police and other structures do some people determine how others get what, when and how at the global level? How much authority do these institutions enjoy within their respective domains? To what extent are they perceived as legitimate?

---

[6] Chris Brown, 'Cosmopolitanism, World Citizenship, and Global Civil Society', *Critical Review of International Social and Political Philosophy*, 3 (2000), pp. 7–26; and the remarks of Klaus von Beyme on the 'unthinkability' of a civil society without the concept of 'a state' in 'Die Liberale Konzeption von Gesellschaft und Politik', unpublished paper (Wien, 2001).

[7] See www.weltbuergervereinigung.de and Ernst Heinrichsohn, *World State, World Citizenship: How a New Consciousness Can Save the World from Self-Destruction* (New York, 2000).

Could they become (more) publicly accountable – even more democratic in the eyes of the constituents of a global civil society? If so, how?

Despite much recent talk of 'globalisation', plausible answers to such questions have not been forthcoming. Something like a numerical – rather than a visually imaginable – theory of global politics prevails. 'Hundreds of organizations now regulate the global dimensions of trade, telecommunications, civil aviation, health, the environment, meteorology, and many other issues', a prominent international relations analyst typically observes.[8] This quantitative model – counting up the numbers of political institutions with a global reach – usually leads to the conclusion that a term like 'global government' is inappropriate. This conclusion, in turn, has given a boost to two different, but related intellectual trends. One of them emphasises the need for more 'realism'. Despite all recent talk of 'globalisation', it is argued, our world in reality is still in the grip of territorial states, whose reliance upon the trimmings of flags and embassies are signs of substantive – not just nominal – independence. 'Globalization is a process that cannot easily be applied to politics', writes Eric Hobsbawm. 'We can have a globalised economy, we can aspire to a globalised culture, we certainly have a globalised technology and a single global science, but politically speaking, we have a world that remains in reality pluralist and divided into territorial states.' He concludes: 'The reality is that there are no global political institutions.'[9] Other 'realists' dig in their heels more deeply. They insist that at the heart of the international system is the institution that Thomas Hobbes famously called the 'mortall God', the armed lawmaking territorial state that is capable of unleashing violence upon both its own subjects and its neighbours. These states are functionally similar and interact in an anarchic environment. They are constrained only by their interaction with other states; otherwise, they act in their own self-interest, even if this entails the development of two-faced comity, transgovernmental co-operation and other forms of 'international society'.[10] At a minimum,

---

[8] See Joseph S. Nye, Jr., 'Globalization's Democratic Deficit', *Foreign Affairs*, 80:4 (July–August 2001), p. 3.

[9] Eric Hobsbawm, *On the Edge of the New Century* (New York, 2001), p. 43.

[10] Another species of *étatisme* relies upon the concept of a society of states to emphasise that so-called realism is in fact not realistic enough. The world is indeed clothed in a system of states, but these states together fashion rules and regulations – international laws, diplomatic conventions, customs and immigration procedures, even rules of war – that have the effect of protecting and nurturing the states system itself. This system is certainly prone to changes that stem from either persuasion, or threats, or the actual use of armed force; yet it is not a system of anarchy, in which the strong out-muscle the weak and each helps themselves for the sake of themselves. Even the weaker members of the system can bolster their security by taking advantage of international norms, rules

states 'seek their own preservation and, at a maximum, drive for universal domination'.[11]

In a strange and round-about way, the second intellectual trend – let us call it the global governance school – agrees with this conclusion. But rather than being preoccupied exclusively with the unit of analysis called territorial states, it favours efforts to conceptualise the hotch-potch of international institutions as examples of 'governance without government'.[12] This school issues a direct challenge to the whole theory of global civil society. It claims that political life in the world is much more complex and messier than state-centric 'realist' observers make out. Nothing like a global political system or a global civil society exists, it is observed. Instead there is 'a multiplicity of governance systems or in-stitutional arrangements aimed at solving collective-action problems'.[13] The choice of the loosely formulated, rather vague term 'governance' is deliberate. It refers to any collective process of making and enforc-ing rules among interdependent actors. 'Governance' does not utilise formal organisations that we normally associate with government. It is suggested that the so-called system of 'global governance' does not really deserve the name 'system'. Our 'disaggregated' world of governance is better described (and in future would best function) as 'networked minimalism',[14] non-hierarchical arrays of governmental units, private firms and NGOs focused upon specific policy problems. It comprises a clutter of overlapping, sometimes conflicting institutions, *ad hoc* agen-cies and programmes, like UNICEF (United Nations Children's Fund)

---

and institutions. The world is governed by territorial states, but these states 'conceive themselves to be bound by a common set of rules in their relations with one another, and share in the working of common institutions' (see Hedley Bull, *The Anarchical Society: A Study of Order in World Politics*, New York, 1977, p. 13). A version of the same argument is presented by Anne-Marie Slaughter, 'The Real New World Order', *Foreign Affairs*, 75:6 (September–October 1997), pp. 183–97.

[11] Kenneth Waltz, *Theory of International Relations* (Reading, MA, 1979), p. 118.

[12] James N. Rosenau and Ernst-Otto Czempiel (eds.), *Governance Without Government: Order and Change in World Politics* (Cambridge and New York, 1992); see also Joseph S. Nye and John D. Donahue (eds.), *Governance in a Globalizing World* (Washington, 2000) and Danilo Zolo, *Cosmopolis: Prospects for World Government* (Cambridge, 1997).

[13] Oran R. Young, *International Governance. Protecting the Environment in a Stateless Society* (Ithaca and London, 1994), p. 17. It is worth noting that Young's attachment to the theory of governance is underpinned by a not-so-secret normative bias against govern-ment. He writes: 'the maintenance and operation of any government or public agency is costly, both in purely material terms (for example, the revenues required to run gov-ernment agencies) and in terms of more intangible values (for example, the restrictions on individual liberties imposed by governments' (Young, 1994, p. 16).

[14] Nye and Donahue (eds.), *Governance in a Globalizing World*, p. 14. Note their deep-seated, residual 'realism': 'the political world is organized largely around a system of unequal states' (p. 33). They draw from this observation the normative conclusion that 'the state will remain the basic institution of governance well into the century' (p. 36).

as well as intergovernmental structures with sectoral responsibilities, like the World Trade Organisation and the OECD, and the International Court of Justice (ICJ) and other global institutions seeking to enforce the rule of law. The hotch-potch system of governance, it is said, also includes global accords, treaties and conventions, such as the Montreal Protocol covering ozone levels; policy summits and meetings like the Davos World Economic Forum; and new forms of public deliberation and conflict resolution, like truth commissions, that have a global impact.

Cosmocracy

Summarising the dynamics of these various interacting and overlapping structures is admittedly not easy, but for various strong reasons that will become clear it can and must be done. Its necessary precondition is a bold leap of political imagination. Some groups within global civil society have spotted this. Transparency International's image of good global government as like a Greek temple – with foundations built from publicly shared values, pillars comprising separate branches of government and a roof structure that supports the world-wide rule of law and a sustainable, high-quality way of life – points in this direction.[15] A new theory of the emerging world polity is indeed urgently needed. And so a principal thesis of this book: our world is today coming under the influence of a new form of governmental power that can be called a *cosmocracy*. The neologism (from *kosmos*, world, order, universal place or space; and *kratō*, to rule or to grasp) is used here as an *idealtyp*. It describes in simplified form a type of institutionalised power that defies all previous accounts of different governmental forms – beginning with Aristotle's attempt to develop a typology of states and continuing today in various efforts to distinguish among 'Westphalian', 'post-modern' and 'post-colonial' states (George Sørenson) or 'modern', 'post-modern' and 'pre-modern' states (Robert Cooper). Although cosmocracy was not conceived as part of a grand design – it is much more a combined product of will, luck, accident and unintended effects – and although it has old roots, over time it has come to display a certain coherence and distinctiveness. Understood as an emerging system of political power, cosmocracy is without precedent. It defies all previous typologies because it is a form of government *sui generis*, with the following features.

Cosmocracy is the first-ever world polity. Despite the fact that it does not appear as such on maps of the world, cosmocracy is a system of

---

[15] Interview with Miklos Marschall, Executive Director of the Hungarian chapter of Transparency International (Berlin, 3 June 2002); and www.transparency.org.

world-wide webs of interdependence – of actions and reactions at a distance, a complex mélange of networks of legal, governmental, police and military interdependence at world-wide distances. These chains of interdependence are oiled by high-speed, space-shrinking flows of communication that have a striking effect: they force those who wield power within the structures of cosmocracy to become more or less aware of its here–there dialectics. The power structures of cosmocracy are constantly shaped by so-called 'butterfly effects', whereby single events, transactions or decisions somewhere within the system can and do touch off a string of (perceived) consequences elsewhere in the system. Those who wield power know not only that 'joined-up government' is becoming commonplace – that governmental institutions of various function, size and geographic location, despite their many differences, are caught up in thickening, fast-evolving webs of bilateral, multilateral and supranational relations.[16] They also know that 'splendid isolation' (Adam Watson) is impossible, that their decisions are potentially or actually unrestricted in scope and effect – that what they say and do (or do not say or do) impinges upon the lives of others elsewhere on the face of the earth. Both wilful and unintended political intervention in the affairs of others is a chronic feature of cosmocracy, as is meddling's opposite: regrets of abstentions and missed opportunities, even expressions of shame and public apologies (like that of President Clinton's to the survivors of the 1994 Rwandan genocide) for not having intervened politically in others' affairs.

Cosmocracy stands on the spectrum between the so-called 'Westphalian' model of competing sovereign states and a single, unitary system of world government. It functions as something more and other than an international community of otherwise sovereign governments. It is not understandable in terms of the nineteenth-century idea of balance-of- power politics. It is also wrong to understand it as a two-tiered, proto-federal polity that has been formed by the gradual 'pooling' of the powers of territorial states under pressure from arbitrage pressures and cross-border spillovers.[17] Cosmocracy is much messier, a far more complex type of polity. It is better understood as a salmagundi of multiplying, highly mobile and intersecting lines of governmental powers. It is *a conglomeration of interlocking and overlapping sub-state, state and suprastate institutions and multi-dimensional processes that interact, and have political and social effects, on a global scale.*

[16] See Slaughter, 'The Real New World Order', pp. 184–6.
[17] Examples of this commonplace way of thinking include the introduction by Daniele Archibugi and David Held to *Cosmopolitan Democracy* (Oxford, 1994), and the preface by Henry J. Aaron *et al.*, 'The Management of International Convergence', in Miles Kahler, *International Institutions and the Political Economy of Integration* (Washington, DC, 1995), pp. xxi–ii.

Cosmocracy (1)

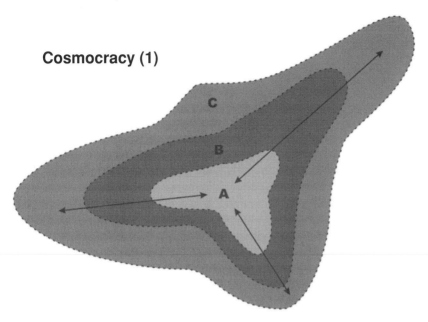

Figure 3.1

Viewed vertically, cosmocracy resembles a series of unevenly-shaped, tree trunk-like concentric circles (see figure 3.1). Its inner core (A) includes the political, legal and military structures governing the peoples of North America, Japan, South Korea, the Council of Europe countries, and Australasia. Here the webs of governmental interdependence are the longest and thickest and most dynamic; the density of efficient telecommunications is heaviest, and land and sea barriers to the movement of people, goods, decisions and information are consequently least meaningful. In the era of cosmocracy, the ability to move information, things and people at high speed – a specialty of the inner core – are decisive sources of power. That is a key reason why, within this inner core of cosmocracy, governmental structures are the most interdependent. Mutual recognition, in the form of exchanges of information and consultations designed to constrain the formation of separate regulations and policies, is most highly developed. So too are monitoring and surveillance mechanisms – of the kind found in the IMF's and the Group of Seven's surveillance of exchange rate and macroeconomic policies. Patterns of explicit harmonisation, joint decisionmaking and continuous bargaining are also commonplace.

This inner core of cosmocracy, out of which thick and long webs of interdependence radiate, is embedded within, and functionally related to, three outer zones of political power. The second of the four zones (B) is a zone of populous, large-scale, quasi-imperial territorial states like China, India, Indonesia and the Russian Federation; except for India, these are not power-sharing democracies (two of them are in fact post-totalitarian regimes), but their governing structures, although jealous guardians of their own territorial 'sovereignty', are in important ways interlinked, both with one another, and with other zones and structures of the cosmocracy, in the form of push-and-pull, pressure-reverse pressure, more or less conflictual relationships. Examples of this interdependence readily spring to mind: Russia, the world's second largest arms peddler and an observer-member of NATO, has its most developed supplier–buyer relationships with India, China and Iran; the Shanghai Co-Operation Organisation, a body that aims to monitor Islamic groups and movements, includes China, Russia, Kazakhstan, Tajikistan, Kyrgyzstan and Uzbekistan; the ongoing, behind-the-scenes consultations and bargaining among the 'big powers' at the UN Security Council; and the fact that the major global organ, the WTO, with the recent admission of China, now encompasses nearly all parts of the two inner zones of the cosmocracy.

Moving further away from its core, a third zone (C) within the cosmocracy is encountered: an agglomeration of interrelated, territorially bound units. Some of them (like Brazil) are potentially powerful actors on the global stage, but most of them – Nigeria, Bahrein, the Philippines, Thailand – are less powerful small states, or proto-states. Although some of these governments are beginning to cluster, in the form of regional bodies like ASEAN and CARICOM and within recent agreements like the Free Trade of the Americas, it is generally true that within this peripheral zone the webs of governmental interdependence are thinnest and most frayed. A few of them, like Zimbabwe and Pakistan, are failing states that totter on the extreme outer margins of the cosmocracy, where worldwide webs of governing institutions give way to no-go areas in which cosmocratic power is unwelcome. Feelings are often mutual. Voices from within the cosmocracy often denounce these no-go areas as a danger to world order, thereby confirming the old rule that successful regime-building requires identification and definition of a threat. These outer fringes of the cosmocracy tend to live up to the stereotype. They include regimes that actively refuse what they call 'Western imperialism' or 'neo-colonialism', and are hyper-jealous of their territorial integrity. Despite some important connections with the rest of the world – in matters of drugs and guns, for instance – their authorities avowedly turn their backs on the whole rotten process of globalisation. Sometimes they are openly hostile to cosmocracy, like the governments of Burma and North Korea.

Cosmocracy (2)

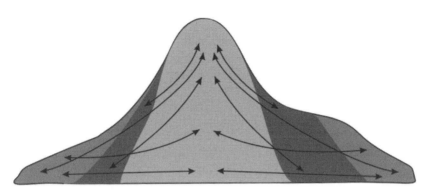

Figure 3.2

This outer zone, beyond the bounds of cosmocracy, also includes the landscapes of war (Juan Goytisolo): blood-soaked, scorched-earth, land-mined, ruined and rubbled territories, like Chechenya, Sierra Leone, southern Sudan and the ill-named Democratic Republic of Congo, where peaceful and effective structures of government hardly exist.

When viewed horizontally, the distinctiveness of the system of cosmocracy is not fully apparent. Its peculiar features become much clearer when viewed in profile, from a horizontal perspective (see figure 3.2). Cosmocracy becomes understandable as a modularised system of government in which decisionmaking power, especially in its core, is distributed among three different – but linked – forms of governmental spaces. For the sake of convenience, these can be described as *micro-government*, *meso-government* and *macro-government*.

The first-mentioned term, *micro-government*, refers to sub-territorial state institutions, like local and regional governing institutions, whose decisionmaking powers, either on an *ad hoc* or more permanent basis, have felt effects elsewhere in some or other corner of the globe. The strengthening tendency of local courts to examine and prosecute symbolically 'foreign' acts of wrongdoing is an example. Cosmocracy also comprises *meso-governments*, whose immediate constituents number anything from a few to many hundreds of millions. *Meso-governments* include territorially defined states and actual or proto-regional institutions, like the European Union, CARICOM and the ASEAN pact. These too are interlinked and have effects at a distance, an enduring symbol of which was the 1995 ruling of the South African Supreme Court – which cross-referred to court decisions in Hungary, Tanzania, Canada, India, Germany and the European Court of Human Rights – that the death penalty was unconstitutional. Then, finally, cosmocracy is structured by *macro-governments*, supranational institutions, whose power to make and enforce decisions is directed at all or many of the peoples of the world. While macro-governing bodies are often the product of bargaining and agreements among meso-governments, experience shows that their global reach derives from their strong tendency to develop their own 'autonomous' institutional logic. They are not merely passive agents and footservants of territorial states. They develop distinct organisational styles and ways of working; they develop self-interests; and they can be creative, energetic catalysts of change. More recent examples of macro-government include the 1999 OECD Convention on Combating Bribery of Foreign Public Officials in International Business Transactions – a convention that has been ratified by nearly thirty countries, including the world's major exporters, and that commits signatory countries to pass laws that criminalise the bribing of officials abroad[18] – and the International Criminal Tribunal for the Former Yugoslavia, established in 1993 after a unanimous vote of the UN Security Council.

Despite the geographic distance separating these differently sized and territorially located governments, their institutions are more or less tightly *linked*. The fashionable talk in international relations and elsewhere of security communities, global governance, 'spillover effects', 'arbitrage pressures', interdependence and the internationalisation of states is symptomatic of this trend towards linkage. It is evident not only in the growth of 'joined-up' local government under pressure from 'spillover' problems and 'arbitrage pressures'[19] and in the globalisation of military power, but also in matters as diverse as the harmonisation of immigration and extradition laws, environmental protection and economic policy. Naturally, as a new form of polity, cosmocracy is laced through with various modern communications technologies, which have the combined effect of nurturing its operations by greatly reducing, sometimes nearly to zero, time and space barriers.

Cosmocracy is a dynamic polity. It is a conglomeration of institutions shaped by several structuring principles, whose resultant reminds its subjects and observers alike, or at least gives them the impression, that

---

[18] See Arnold Heidenheimer and Holger Moroff, 'Controlling Business Payoffs to Foreign Officials: The 1998 OECD Anti-Bribery Convention', in Arnold Heidenheimer and Michael Johnston, *Political Corruption: Concepts and Contexts* (New Brunswick, NJ, 2001), pp. 945–61.

[19] See the various contributions to Robert J. Bennett (ed.), *Local Government in the New Europe* (London and New York, 1993).

these institutions have one thing in common: their particular power to shape and re-shape people's lives has *global* effects. Sometimes this sense is lost in immediacies, which is understandable considering that cosmocracy is a polity of many sides in motion. Among the principal problems confronting a theory of cosmocracy is to choose appropriate similes for picturing and interpreting its multi-structured dynamics. Consider several possibilities. Cosmocracy may for instance be described as a polymerous form of rule. Chemists are familiar with compounds whose molecular structure is formed out of a large number and variety of lower-order compounds. Analogously, cosmocracy has no single organising principle, and for that reason it defies comparison with the standard treatments of different regime types that have associated aristocracy with virtue, oligarchy with wealth, tyranny with lawlessness, despotism with fear. For that reason of hybridity – to switch to a simile from genetics – cosmocracy is a *dynamic* polity comprising 'recombinant' structures, which are themselves products of a constantly changing, permanently unfolding hybridisation of existing processes and decisions. The recombinant qualities of cosmocracy ensure that it is a polity on the move. It produces, among subjects and observers alike, a persistent sense of 'newness' – a sense that it is a moving target that produces unforeseen consequences. Finally – to switch to architectural analogies drawn from research on European integration processes – cosmocracy is sometimes seen as a polity shaped by 'multi-level governance'.[20] Within its structures, power is not concentrated in any simple hierarchical way; it is rather distributed and dispersed across the interlocking micro-, meso- and macro-structures, and among the actors who operate within these respective domains. These different 'levels' are not interrelated in a simple zero-sum fashion. Micro-structures, like local governments and courts, can and do thrive along with the flourishing of macro-level institutions; and within the system of cosmocracy, territorial states and other meso-level institutions, far from either withering away or stubbornly retaining their precious 'sovereign' powers, find themselves melded into a multi-level polity that is highly differentiated and

---

[20] Some of the best literature on this subject includes Edgar Grande, 'Multi-Level Governance: Institutionelle Besonderheiten und Funktionsbedingungen des europäischen Mehrebenensystem', in Edgar Grande and Markus Jachtenfuchs (eds.), *Wie problemlösungsfähig ist die EU? Regieren im europäischen Mehrebenensystem* (Baden-Baden, 2000), pp. 11–31; Beate Kohler-Koch and Rainer Eising (eds.), *The Evolution and Transformation of European Governance in the European Union* (London, 1999); Gary Marks, Liesbet Hooghe and Kermit Blank, 'European Integration from the 1980s: State-Centric v. Multi-Level Governance', *Journal of Common Market Studies*, 34:3 (1996), pp. 341–78; and Fritz Scharpf, 'Introduction: The Problem-Solving Capacity of Multi-Level Governance', *Journal of European Public Policy*, 4 (1997), pp. 520–38.

linked both horizontally and vertically, from the micro- to the macro-domains.

Legality

Cosmocracy is a conglomeration of political power cemented together with laws and legal procedures. Especially since 1950, there has been a definite trend towards not only the *legalisation of governmental structures*, but also the development of new forms of *multilateral legal networks* that highlight the passing away of the fiction of the legal sovereignty of territorial states.[21] Talk of sovereignty and claims that it remains at the core of the world's political system certainly survive in the era of cosmocracy. Its protagonists point out that since the founding of the United Nations in 1948, the number of officially recognised states has nearly quadrupled, a state-centric trend that is reinforced by international law.[22] Appearances are however deceptive, or at least paradoxical. For in policy areas like the management of the commons (outer space, Antarctica and the oceans, for instance), or global crime, weapons systems and environmental protection, three highly complex, often overlapping forms of multilateral legal regulation are now becoming standard.[23] Some multilateral agreements, such as the Antarctic Treaty and the Montreal Protocol on the protection of the earth's ozone layer,[24] contain provisions that are aimed not only at the contracting parties, but at third parties as well. Other arrangements, exemplified by the International Tribunal for the Former Yugoslavia, the judgement of the European Court of Human Rights in

---

[21] The literature is vast, but see especially Yves Dezalay *et al.*, 'Global Restructuring and the Law: Studies of the Internationalization of Legal Fields and the Creation of Transnational Arenas', *Case Western Law Review*, 9:44 (1994), pp. 407–98; and Wilhelm Grewe, *The Epochs of International Law* (Berlin, 2000).

[22] The famous ruling of the Permanent Court of International Justice in the case of the *SS Lotus* is often cited: 'International law governs relations between independent States. The rules of law binding upon States therefore emanate from their own free will as expressed in conventions or by usages generally accepted as expressing principles of law and established in order to regulate the relations between these coexisting independent communities or with a view to the achievement of common aims.' See *The Case of the SS Lotus*, in *Permanent Council of International Justice*, Series A, Number 10, at 18. More generally on the life and times of the idea(l) of sovereignty, see Hendrik Spruyt, *The Sovereign State and its Competitors* (Princeton, 1994); Jens Bartelson, *A Genealogy of Sovereignty* (Stockholm, 1995); and Stephen D. Krasner, *Sovereignty: Organised Hypocrisy* (Princeton, 1999).

[23] Dinah Shelton, 'The Nature and Role of International Law in a Globalised World', paper presented to the conference, *Globalisation and Its Possibilities* (University of Sydney, 12–14 December 2001).

[24] *Antarctic Treaty* (Washington), 402 *United Nations Treaty Series*, 71, 12 UST 794, TIAS 4780; *Montreal Protocol on Substances that Deplete the Ozone Layer*, 26 *International Legal Materials*, 1541 (1987).

Al-Adsani v. *the United Kingdom*, and the well-known Pinochet case, are guided by the doctrine of *jus cogens*, according to which there are definable global norms – a 'common interest of humanity' – from which no dissent or derogation by governmental or non-governmental parties is justified.[25] Still other agreements, such as the UN General Assembly resolutions to ban driftnet fishing and the 1979 Bonn Convention on the Conservation of Migratory Species of Wild Animals, take the form of agreed measures, declarations, programmes, final acts and other types of non-legally binding 'soft law', whose purpose is to induce others to change or reinforce their behaviour.[26]

These polycentric forms of legal regulation have sprung up in a higgledy-piggledy or sector-by-sector fashion, in consequence of which the legal norms and jurisdictional boundaries of the cosmocracy are in a constant state of definition and re-definition, conflict and compromise. Their principal trajectories are nevertheless clear. Most obvious is that the various units of cosmocracy, including territorial states, are caught up in thickening webs of sub-national and intergovernmental and global law. There is also growing world-wide awareness that the whole process of ordering, enabling, restraining and legitimating the cosmocracy by means of law is taking on a life of its own and, for that reason, that it stands in need of more flexible procedures and rules. Rigid, difficult-to-amend treaty law tends to fall into disfavour, or to be supplemented with new legal strategies, such as interim applications, flexible amendment procedures and the commitment of some courts to the principle that legal obligations can and should be revised when norms change. There are calls as well for tighter synchronisation of currently conflicting laws and jurisdictions, perhaps even their 'harmonisation' (through initiatives like the Organization of the Supreme Courts of the Americas, ratified in 1996) by applying the principle of a hierarchy of global norms. This dynamism in the field of law, and the first efforts to coordinate it, help to explain why the nets of legal regulation are now beginning to be cast over various parts of global civil society, so that matters once considered 'private' or subject to territorial state prerogatives – from the migration patterns of birds, genocidal crimes and violence against women to corporate mergers and acquisitions and corruption in the world's diamond industry – are now subject to legal regulation.

---

[25] See *Le ius cogens international: sa genèse, sa nature, ses functions*, in *Collected Courses of the Hague Academy of International Law*, 17, III (The Hague 1982).

[26] Christine Chinkin, 'Normative Development in the International Legal System', in Dinah Shelton (ed.), *Commitment and Compliance: The Role of Non-Binding Norms in the International Legal System* (Oxford, 2000); and Wolfgang H. Reinecke, *Global Public Policy: Governing Without Government* (Washington, DC, 1998).

A pertinent example of this trend towards the 'legalisation' of global civil society is the regulation of the Internet. The healthy mix of self-regulation and no regulation that once characterised the medium is now withering away. So too is the presumption that the Internet abolishes both geographical boundaries and territorially based laws. In fact, a regulatory net is being cast over the Internet by three intersecting types of political institutions. *Territorial states* like South Korea have outlawed gambling websites; in Britain, the Regulation of Investigatory Powers Act has granted the police broad powers of access to e-mail and other online communications; and a French court has banned the Internet portal firm Yahoo! from providing French users with images of Nazi memorabilia otherwise posted on its American sites. Meanwhile, *supranational institutions* are also experimenting with their regulatory powers. A new EU law drawn from the Brussels Convention entitles consumers to sue EU-based Internet sites in their own countries, so long as it can be proved that the site was targeted at their countries; the Hague Convention aims to enforce foreign judgements in matters such as contractual disputes, libel and intellectual property claims; and the Council of Europe has drafted the world's first global treaty on cybercrime, which aims to harmonise laws against hacking, child pornography and Internet fraud. Finally, the complex pattern of multiple jurisdictions is reinforced by moves by e-commerce firms to claw back regulatory powers through so-called mechanisms of *alternative dispute resolution*: in effect, they are pushing for a new market-based system of private laws, which would enable companies to operate outside of the courts, within a minimum framework of 'safe-harbour' rules guaranteeing privacy and consumer protection.[27]

This trend towards the 'legalisation' of global civil society is by no means a zero-sum relationship in favour of governmental power. More legal attention is certainly being paid to non-state actors, coupled with expectations that their behaviour will be subject to norms and procedures previously applied to governments and their agents. But developments like the World Court Project (a coalition effort to obtain an opinion from the ICJ on the legality of nuclear weapons) and the UN-sponsored Indigenous Forum (comprising representatives of member states and of indigenous groups) point to a different conclusion: by being drawn into governmental affairs, parts of global civil society are now regularly exercising influence on the institutions of cosmocracy itself. This rule of effect and counter-effect certainly applies to the slow erosion of both the immunity of sovereign states from suit and the presumption that statutes do not extend to the territory of other states. There are many tendencies

---

[27] 'The Internet and the Law', *The Economist* (13 January 2001), pp. 25–7.

in this direction. INGOs are licensed by bodies like the Council of Europe and the United Nations. Non-governmental groups participate in election monitoring and as *amici curiae* in the proceedings of such bodies as the European Court of Justice (ECJ) and the Inter-American Court of Human Rights. War crimes cases are given global publicity, thanks to new bodies like the Hague Tribunal; an international criminal court has been agreed, and awaits the breath of life; and local courts, under pressure from citizens' groups, show ever greater willingness to prosecute symbolically 'foreign' acts of wrongdoing.[28] The empowerment of global civil society is also evident in the fields of power of the turbocapitalist economy. While criticisms of the 'anarchy' of 'unregulated' global markets remain justified, the domination of turbocapitalist firms is now routinely subject to contestation and resistance. Not only are they subject to the 'top-down' rulings of governmental institutions like the WTO, a free-standing body with legal personality (the same politico-legal status as that, say, of the United Nations) and self-executing dispute mechanisms that are binding on all its members. The turbocapitalist economy is subject as well to various legal pressures initiated 'from below', including plaintiffs' efforts in the United States to use the Alien Tort Claims Act to hold turbocapitalist firms liable for environmental damage and human rights violations in far-away countries like Nigeria, India, Burma and South Africa.

Clumsy government

As a compound form of government wrapped in law, cosmocracy has a definite durability. Especially within its heartlands, there is a strong tendency towards a stable and non-violent, if dynamic equilibrium. This stability is paradoxical, especially because, throughout the system, from the macro- to the micro-domains, there is a heavy preponderance, and sometimes deliberate reliance upon, decisionmaking procedures that involve 'muddling through' and 'clumsiness'. Cosmocracy might be described as a dynamic system of *clumsy institutions*.[29] Indeed, from either a strategic or a normative standpoint – the *idealtyp* of cosmocracy is used in this context primarily for the purpose of descriptive interpretation – much can be said in its favour. Clumsy government has all sorts of desirable features – like

---

[28] From the *Los Angeles Times* (August 11, 2000, p. A11) comes a random example: the order, applied during early August 2000 by a US District Court in Manhattan, requiring Radovan Karadzić to pay $745 million to a group of 12 women who filed a civil suit, accusing him of responsibility for killings, rapes, kidnappings, torture and other atrocities.

[29] Among the first usages of this term is Michael Schapiro, 'Judicial Selection and the Design of Clumsy Institutions', *Southern California Law Review*, 61 (1988), pp. 1555–69.

the power-sharing that comes with a plurality of institutions marked by 'useful inefficiencies' – certainly when compared with the unworkable normative ideal of designing institutions that are rigidly geometric in style and strategy.[30] There are certainly many policy areas in which clumsy governing structures enable civil society organisations and actors to practise the arts of *divide et impera* from below, so ensuring positive-sum effects. Working in the interstices of government, non-governmental bodies take advantage of its resources by finding ways of bending and manipulating that system for the purposes of strengthening the hand of global civil society itself.[31]

The processes through which this happens are highly complex. Many different governmental forms function as catalysts of global civil society. This consequently results in a wide continuum of different relations enjoyed by non-governmental bodies with their governmental counterparts. Hence, an important rule: that global civil society should not be thought of as the natural enemy of political institutions. The vast mosaic of groups, organisations and initiatives that comprise global civil society are variously related to governmental structures at the local, national, regional and supranational levels. Some sectors of social activity, the so-called anti-government organisations (AGOs), are openly hostile to the funding and regulatory powers of state institutions. In certain contexts, this resistance or cantankerousness of social organisations is important in loosening up and humbling governmental structures. Charter 77 in Czechoslovakia and KOR in Poland and similar bodies certainly had this effect during the last years of the Soviet empire, especially on its western fringes. Elsewhere, the gradual strengthening of NGOs, some of them directly linked to global civil society, has had the effect of questioning arbitrary and/or pompous exercises of governmental power – as in Japan, a country in which the old word for public (*ōyake*, literally the house of the emperor) and terms like *okami* (the government or the authorities, literally 'those

---

[30] The advantages of clumsy government and the need for constant institutional re-jigging in efforts to cope with environmental damage and clean-up are helpfully discussed in M. Verweij, *Transboundary Environmental Problems and Cultural Theory: The Protection of the Rhine and the Great Lakes* (London, 2000); F. Hendriks, 'Cars and Culture in Munich and Berlin', in D. J. Coyle and R. J. Ellis (eds.), *Politics, Policy and Culture* (Boulder, 1994); and Michael Thompson, 'Style and Scale: Two Sources of Institutional Inappropriateness', in M. Goldman (ed.), *Privatizing Nature: Political Struggles for the Global Commons* (London, 1998), pp. 198–228. See also C. Engel and K. H. Keller (eds.), *Understanding the Impact of Global Networks on Local Social, Political and Cultural Values* (Baden-Baden, 2000), and Michael Thompson *et al.*, 'Risk and Governance Part 2: Policy in a Complex and Plurally Perceived World', *Government and Opposition*, 33:3 (1998), pp. 139–66.

[31] Robert Wapner, 'The Normative Promise of Nonstate Actors: A Theoretical Account of Global Civil Society', in Robert Wapner and Lester Edwin J. Ruiz (eds.), *Principled World Politics. The Challenge of Normative International Relations* (Lanham, MD), p. 271.

above') and familiar proverbs like 'the nail that sticks out gets hammered' (*Deru kugi wa utareru*) once sat comfortably alongside popular maxims such as 'respect for authorities, contempt for the people' (*kanson minpi*).[32]

In other sectors of global civil society, for instance those in which the acronym NGO means rather (according to the South African joke) 'next government official', relations between social organisations and political power are openly collaborative. Civil society organisations either serve as willing contractors for governments or bodies like the World Bank, or aim at dissolving themselves into governmental structures.[33] Still other NGOs (so-called GRINGOs or GONGOs, like the International Air Transport Association and the World Conservation Union) are the dependent creations of state authorities. In between these two extremes stand those social actors (e.g. Médecins Sans Frontières, Oxfam, Greenpeace) who slalom between self-reliance and legal and political dependency. They form *ad hoc* partnerships with governments; lobby donor intergovernmental bodies like the World Bank to change their policies; and work with other NGOs in rich and poor countries, zones of peace and war alike.

Public–private partnerships between sectors of global civil society and governing institutions are strongly evident in one of the major supranational political developments of the twentieth century: the formation of the United Nations. Its history is often told from above, from the standpoint of the behaviour of governments and their diplomats. This is unfortunate because, during its gestation period, civic organisations took advantage of its arrival by playing a small but vital role in shaping its future identity. In the spring of 1945, for instance, the Roosevelt administration included some forty NGOs as 'consultants' within the American delegation to the UN Conference on International Organisation. Although the aim was to use these civil society groups to win public support for the UN Charter to be agreed in San Francisco, they were joined by others – an estimated 1,200 of them, from all around the world – who together went on to contribute to the drafting process itself. Meanwhile, inside the newly established Human Rights Commission, a small group of legal experts and diplomats led by Eleanor Roosevelt hammered out the world's first international bill of rights. As the major powers squabbled and concentrated on political methods of war prevention through new territorial guarantees and collective security arrangements, the declaration – written in a language that could not be dismissed as simply

---

[32] Masayuki Deguchi, 'A Comparative View of Civil Society', *Washington–Japan Journal* (Spring 1999), pp. 11–20.
[33] Judith Tendler, *Turning Private Voluntary Organizations into Developmental Agencies: Questions for Evaluation*, USAID Program Evaluation Discussion Paper, 12 (Washington, DC, 1982).

'Western' – won the necessary backing of religious and peace groups, legal activists, and political figures from smaller countries, all of whom were convinced that the disregard of civil and political freedoms and social justice had produced the barbarities of the Second World War.[34]

Considering that key powers, including the United States, were opposed to UN entanglements in the domestic affairs of states implied by NGO activity, the power of the supposedly powerless civil society actors was considerable. They were not merely an inspiration for a generation to come. Their immediate influence was evident in the inclusion of human rights provisions in the Charter: article 55(c) confirms, for example, that the UN will promote 'universal respect for, and observance of, human rights and fundamental freedoms for all'. Article 71 of the Charter affirms that the UN Economic and Social Council (ECOSOC) 'may make suitable arrangements for consultation with non-governmental organizations which are concerned with matters within its competence'. While such arrangements were subject to the approval of the member states and intergovernmental organisations, the formal legitimation of civil society involvement – note the striking contrast with the League of Nations, which lacked such a provision – was to set the rules for the subsequent growth of governmentally framed, cross-border civil initiatives. So article 71 served as the parent of the formation of the World Health Organisation (WHO), whose constitution and conduct fostered the involvement of civic organisations, and of UNESCO, under whose activist Director-General Julian Huxley provision was made for the 'consultation and co-operation' of INGOs and, in cases where they did not exist, time and money were invested to nurture new NGOs. Soon after its formation, UNESCO also convened a path-breaking conference on the protection of nature, at which global NGOs like the International Committee for Bird Preservation recommended that the problem of pesticides be tackled by calling upon the United Nations to establish a joint commission of its relevant agencies.

The catalytic effects of the United Nations during its earliest years should not be exaggerated. It certainly recognised the existence and information and nuisance values of NGOs, but little positive recognition was initially given to their potential role in structuring the post-war global

---

[34] See Dorothy B. Robins, *Experiment in Democracy: The Story of US Citizen Organizations in Forging the Charter of the United Nations* (New York, 1971), pp. 88–9, 102–6; Ruth Russell, *A History of the United Nations Charter* (Washington, DC, 1958), pp. 594–5, 800–1; Peter Willetts, 'Pressure Groups as Transnational Actors', in Peter Willetts (ed.), *Pressure Groups in the Global System* (London, 1982), p. 11; Rainer Lagoni, 'Article 71', in Bruno Simma (ed.), *The Charter of the United Nations: A Commentary* (New York and London, 1994), p. 904; and Mary Ann Glendon, *A World Made New: Eleanor Roosevelt and the Universal Declaration of Human Rights* (New York, 2001).

environment along the lines of a global civil society. The birth of the United Nations was nevertheless a symbol of hope for a more civilised world – a world that lay beyond the textbook descriptions of territorial state politics. In its early years, the United Nations was also a vital training ground for civil society organisations, many of which came to learn that political/legal regulation is often a vital precondition of their survival and effectiveness. The latter-day complexity within the patterns of regulation is staggering. Many thousands of civil society organisations are now officially recognised by the United Nations, and by supranational governing bodies, like the Antarctica Treaty System.[35] Political institutions and agreements meanwhile play a vital role in fostering the growth of turbo-capitalism, for instance the 'Final Act' of the Uruguay Round of trade negotiations, a 1994 agreement that had the backing of 145 states and that led to the establishment of both the WTO and the extension of the principle of freer trade into such areas as copyrights, patents and services. Governmental institutions also sometimes operate as important catalysts of non-profit activity within global civil society. This logic of catalysis was famously evident in the proliferation of human rights groups like Charter 77 after the 1975 signing of the Helsinki Accords, one of whose 'baskets' required signatories to guarantee the civil and political rights of their citizens. Similar catalytic effects resulted from the much-publicised 1992 Global Forum and Earth Summit, held in Rio de Janeiro, and the follow-up women's and population conferences in Beijing and Cairo; and the 1993 Vienna Conference on Human Rights, where 171 states reaffirmed their commitment to the principle of the 'universal nature of the rights and freedoms' specified in the International Bill of Human Rights.

Instabilities

There are rare times, in response to major global crises, like that of 11 September 2001, when the whole system of cosmocracy – resembling what is called in physics the Bose–Einstein condensate – is so chilled down with concern that its different components momentarily sing together in unison.[36] Under more normal conditions, however, the complex, multi-layered, dynamic and open-ended totality called cosmocracy

[35] Anne-Marie Clark et al., 'The Sovereign Limits of Global Civil Society: A Comparison of NGO Participation in UN World Conferences on the Environment, Human Rights, and Women', World Politics, 51:1 (October 1998), pp. 1–35; Roger A. Coate et al., 'The United Nations and Civil Society: Creative Partnerships for Sustainable Development', Alternatives, 21 (1996), pp. 93–122; and John Boli and G. M. Thomas (eds.), Constructing World Culture: International Nongovernmental Organizations Since 1875 (Stanford, 1999).
[36] Bose–Einstein condensates, so named and predicted to exist by Satyendra Nath Bose and Albert Einstein some seventy years before their actual laboratory creation, are bundles

displays several fault-lines. These zones of tension and slippage periodically produce shock-effects on the whole system, especially when they are highlighted as such by collective actors and journalists operating through communications media. Such instabilities strongly suggest that cosmocracy's description as a multi-level governance system or system of 'transgovernmentalism' is inappropriate. Theorists of multi-level governance and transgovernmentalism concede that complexity – multiple actors, variable patterns, unpredictability – are among its leading qualities, yet they tend to downplay or neglect the idea that a system of multi-level governance or transgovernmentalism can suffer destabilising contradictions. This idea is profoundly relevant for any examination of cosmocracy, which is currently marked by patterns of danger and deep incoherence that highlight the ways in which it is an inadequate form of government. The governing institutions of cosmocracy (as we have seen in the case of the United Nations) certainly have positive enabling effects, upon global civil society. But cosmocracy also chronically lets global civil society down. It does not bring peace and harmony and good government to the world, let alone usher in calm order. Its hotch-potch of rules and institutions produce negative – disabling and destabilising – effects.

What are these contradictions or *structural problems* of cosmocracy? What are their symptoms? To what extent do they have paralysing effects on the whole system? To answer these questions, we need to look carefully at the principal overlapping, but identifiably different, structural problems lodged within the structures of cosmocracy. A sample of four – they are among the most pertinent – are outlined below.

Political entropy

In affairs of government, as in physics, confusion and ineffectiveness are the offspring of *entropy*, the condition of inertness and self-degradation that results from formlessness. Whatever advantages bless its clumsy structures, the system of cosmocracy displays definite signs of entropy. In this sense it poses challenges that are the *opposite* of those confronted during recent centuries by the influential separation of powers doctrine. That doctrine, famously associated with Bolingbroke and Montesquieu, proposed solutions to the overconcentration of power that typically plagued the absolutist states of early modern Europe. Bolingbroke remarked: 'The love of power is natural; it is insatiable; almost constantly whetted; and never cloyed by possession.'[37] Montesquieu, marked by his training as a

---

of atoms that sing in unison, in that they lose their individual identities and join together in a single energy state after being cooled down to just a few billionths of a degree above absolute zero.

[37] Henry St John Bolingbroke, in *Craftsman*, 13 June 1730.

magistrate of a provincial *parlement*, added the prescription that power should be used to tame power.[38]

This kind of language may in future come to be strikingly relevant for the system of cosmocracy, but for the moment, and for the foreseeable future, this system is hampered by the *underconcentration of powers*. The serious lack of driving seats and steering mechanisms, and the ineffectiveness of many that currently do exist – note that no unfavourable comparison with an imaginary perfect form of state is here being secretly made – is one of cosmocracy's striking weaknesses. Cosmocracy has no proper functioning parliament or network of parliaments or regular forum – like a Civil Society Forum – through which the various and conflicting demands from global civil society could be peacefully channelled. There exists no executive power, for instance an elected, fixed-term and impeachable president of the world. There are no governing agencies capable of effectively negotiating and enforcing controls on either the global laundering of dirty money, or corporate accounting fraud, or hot money flows. The United Nations Security Council, once the hope of the world, is comprised of five permanent members who are together responsible for nearly nine-tenths of the world's arms exports. There are no political parties that campaign globally, on a regular basis, trying to gather support for certain policies among business and non-business NGOs and receptive governments.[39] There are still no well-publicised, global opinion polls. There is no global army or police force that could act decisively to bring about just order and maintain peace within and across the territorial boundaries of states and regions. There is not yet a global criminal justice system – with sharp teeth.[40] And there are still no global governmental agencies with a bark loud enough to prevent the destruction by repressive governments of whole ways of life – as in the Tibetan capital Lhasa, which is slowly being destroyed by an iron ring of Chinese military compounds, the demolition of historic buildings, both secular and Buddhist, and Beijing-backed occupation by the kind of Han Chinese who disdainfully walk counter-clockwise along Lhasa's sacred ways.

---

[38] Montesquieu, *De l'esprit des lois* (1748), ed. Victor Goldschmidt (Paris, 1979), book XI, chapter 4 ['Pour qu'on ne puisse abuser du pouvoir, il faut que, par la disposition des choses, le pouvoir arrête le pouvoir'].

[39] W. Kreml and Charles W. Kegley, Jr., 'A Global Political Party: The Next Step', *Alternatives*, 21 (1996), pp. 123–34; Richard Falk and Andrew Strauss, 'Bridging the Globalization Gap: Toward Global Parliament', www.globalpolicy.org/ngos/role/globdem/globgov/2001/0418gap.htm.

[40] The flourishing of a global (war) crime industry highlights the paucity of institutions designed to monitor, police and convict its criminals. Here the work of the great (but mainly forgotten) Dutch jurist Cornelis van Vollenhoven is relevant. He showed how the historical development of modern forms of supranational law had deep roots in the medieval world; how, after about 1500, the break-up of the medieval Christian world and

Where global steering mechanisms do exist within the cosmocracy, they are often hampered by four related impediments – which highlight their serious need of overhaul. First, they are often marked by impotence caused by *funding shortages, understaffing, jurisdictional disputes, ineffective sanctions and consequent lack of reputation*. A case in point is the ILO, which sets important employment standards but often lacks the sharp teeth required to enforce them. Another example is the main global agency for monitoring and preventing world-wide money laundering, the Paris-based Financial Action Task Force (FATF).[41] Set up by the Group of Seven governments in 1989, mainly to counter money laundering by global drug cartels, it operated (in 2001) with a staff of only five and a budget of only FFr 5.8 million (US$810,000). FATF provides no well-publicised white lists or black lists that rank leading global bodies for the least or greatest dirty money laundering. It has no effective carrots or sticks, and in practice it defers to the weak and corrupting principle of 'consolidated supervision', according to which each home country regulator of a turbocapitalist financial institution is solely responsible for exercising oversight on its global operations, despite its obvious strategic importance for turbocapitalism and cosmocracy, and despite its formal backing by the European Commission, the Gulf Co-Operation Council, and twenty-nine states (but not including important countries like Russia, Indonesia and Egypt).

Political entropy also results from *bureaucratic sclerosis* caused by *demarcation disputes* and the *opacity* that results from the tangled, rhizomatous (or rootstalk-like) structures of decisionmaking. Parts of the administrative organisation of the United Nations have a wide reputation for well-intentioned self-paralysis and a seasoned culture of doing nothing; wags have understandably defined the United Nations as an organisation that makes mission possible impossible. The documented examples

the rise of territorial states with unrestricted sovereignty as their ideal gave prominence to talk of the *ius belli*; and how, after three centuries, the re-birth of what Jeremy Bentham first called 'international law' led first to talk of a *ius belli ac pacis*, then to talk of a *ius pacis ac belli*. Van Vollenhoven was adamant that a subsequent phase – an age of *ius pacis* – was thinkable, but he was equally clear that it would be possible only if a global police force could be invented and deployed. He favoured keeping separate the right of military intervention from legal judgements and punishments of the crimes of the violent. What are peoples of the world to do in the event of an eruption of fighting? No need for a long dispute to find out who is right, or who is ready to give due assistance to those who are in need of protection, he thought. That should come at a later stage, van Vollenhoven argued. The first priority is to issue the threatening warning of the police order: stop fighting. If this order is not obeyed, the police itself must intervene, to separate the opponents, to put an end to the fighting of its own accord. Then comes the trial and punishment of the guilty, the attempted righting of wrongs, the provision of compensation for suffered losses.

[41] *Financial Times* (London), 3 October 2001.

readily spring to mind, including the UN freeze while 800,000 Tutsis and Hutu moderates were hacked to death in Rwanda, and the transformation of the United Nations into the administrator of the Serbian siege of Sarajevo. The slow-witted and negligent UN reactions during and after the brave efforts of the East Timorese to shield themselves against the genocidal attacks of the Indonesian army following the 1999 independence referendum counts as another – sad and drawn-out – example: the absence of a military plan for protecting the Timorese, despite foreknowledge of Indonesian army intentions to rip the local social fabric to shreds; frequent and often bumbling disregard for the physical safety of the UN's own staff; the senior staff habit of rejecting or ignoring bad news; examples of staff arrogance at all levels, laced with symptoms of laziness and incompetence; departmental run-arounds and pass-the-buck bureaucracy; insensitivity to environmental hazards; contracts for supplies and materials (like unreliable TATA vehicles) arranged through nepotism, without regard for local needs or conditions; and, at one point, instructions to starving villagers that they would be denied emergency food unless they agreed to end a rat plague – presumably, either by purchasing poison with non-existent cash, or by using their bare hands in the dark.[42]

Other examples of UN entropy are downright farcical, as in the difficult business of setting up the International Criminal Tribunal for the former Yugoslavia (ICTY). The establishment of the world's first-ever global war crimes tribunal (in May 1993) was delayed for fifteen months because of wrangling within the UN Security Council. When the Chief Prosecutor was eventually appointed, he had to pay out of his own pocket his first airfare to New York and the Hague. He was also soon informed that there was no budget for the tribunal, and that it would have to be approved by the Advisory Committee on Administrative and Budgetary Questions (ACABQ), who insisted that at least one indictment would have to be issued before funding could be approved. That forced on the fledgling tribunal a safe, but symbolically low-level indictment, Dragan Nicolić. It also necessitated many irritating and time-consuming meetings about organisational – budgetary and evidential – matters with UN officials, and with Secretary-General Boutros-Ghali, who expressed deep suspicions of the original decision of the Security Council to establish the Office of the Chief Prosecutor as an independent unit. Mechanisms were not put in place to arrest Radovan Karadzić and General Ratko Mladić, and

---

[42] See Michael Barnett, *Eyewitness to a Genocide. The United Nations and Rwanda* (Ithaca, 2002); correspondence with an anonymous UNTAET officer formerly stationed in East Timor (Sydney, 10 and 25 February 2002); and Michael Ignatieff, *The Warrior's Honor. Ethnic War and the Modern Conscience* (London, 1998), pp. 102–8.

indeed Admiral Leighton Smith, then commander of the United Nations Implementing Force (IFOR), adamantly opposed despatching troops to catch indicted war criminals. Even in the nasty business of suspected or confirmed mass graves, UN forces refused to get involved in search or night-watch duties; at one point, the tribunal engaged the services of a willing Norwegian NGO and their sniffer dogs to do that necessary work.[43]

Unaccountability problems

Quite a few of the institutions that comprise the system of cosmocracy are *publicly unaccountable*. Cosmocracy is not quite a species of absolutism, since its core contains rich networks of democratic procedures designed to expose and oppose hubris. Yet when considered overall, as an integrated polity, cosmocracy definitely has an affinity with authoritarian, rather than representative-democratic procedures. It is full of what the English call 'rotten boroughs', whose political processes are invisible to many millions of eyes.

The ingredients of representative democracy are in short supply, and often entirely absent. Time-limited power granted on the basis of open and equal electoral competitions, effective complaints and evaluation procedures, the obligation of power-wielders to solicit different, openly expressed opinions and to explain and justify their actions publicly to stakeholders (wherever they are on the face of the earth), and to re-sign in cases of gross mismanagement or misconduct – these vital rules, well outlined in initiatives like the Global Accountability Project and the Campaign for a More Democratic United Nations (CAMDUN),[44] are often flouted by the structures of cosmocracy, many of which are ob-scure and secretive. Its organisations tend to be dominated by cliques and clubs and networks of professionals whose power to decide the shape of the world is often wholly unresponsive to outsiders' perceptions and demands. Whether in Beijing or Berlin, those who wield power within these structures – like all exercises of power – tend to feed upon the two standard justifications for concealing its motives and moves. They say that it is foolhardy to reveal one's hand to one's opponents and enemies (let us call this the Rumsfeld Rule: 'In difficult situations, governments do not discuss pressing matters'[45]). They repeat as well some version

---

[43] Richard Goldstone, 'Crimes Against Humanity: Forgetting the Victims', The Ernest Jones Lecture (London), 25 September 2001; and his *For Humanity: Reflections of a War Crimes Investigator* (New Haven and London, 2000), esp. chapters 4 and 5.

[44] www.charter 99. org/accountability; www.oneworld.org/camdun.

[45] From a press conference featuring Donald Rumsfeld, United States Defense Secretary, *CNN* (7 October 2001).

of Plato's Rule that efficacious government requires commoners to keep their snouts out of the troughs of politics. They say that affairs of government are too complex and difficult to explain to publics, who would not in any case understand what is at stake. Sometimes these two alibis converge, as when the institutions of cosmocracy deliberately shield themselves from public scrutiny because their aim is openly to favour a certain power group within the global civil society, using such techniques as secrecy, spin and legal coercion.

There are unfortunately plenty of examples where, for instance, cosmocratic institutions resemble management boards for turbocapitalism. The tribunals set up under NAFTA – sarcastically condemned by the Canadian trade lawyer Steven Shrybman as 'revolutionary development in international law' – enable corporations to veto governmental restrictions upon corporate power by bringing a case before a tribunal that operates *in camera*. If a company considers that its commercial rights have been violated, and if the tribunal finds in favour of the company and its complaint, then a government is legally obliged to make a pay-out to the corporation.[46] Such authoritarian arrangements give a bad name to global governance. They fuel the suspicion that turbocapitalist firms, and the global economy in general, have been unfairly granted unlimited grazing rights that threaten the authority of democratically elected governments. The power of property feels unchecked; it seems that the global economy has become master to none, that hard-won citizens' rights at home are being gobbled up by unchecked world-wide 'market forces'. This conclusion easily fuels fatalism: as John Ralston Saul has pointed out, the *ad hoc* alliance between turbocapitalism and the enabling and compliant power of cosmocratic institutions potentially destroys the one institution that citizens can identify with as their own: representative government.[47] A sense spreads that governments are powerless in the face of mysterious forces operating 'out there', in the buccaneering, nineteenth-century-style global economy.

Within the system of cosmocracy, these familiar alibis of unaccountable power are regularly supplemented by two less familiar dynamics. One of them is related to the issue of complexity: the fragmentation of political authority, combined with a technocratic mind-set among officials and

---

[46] The suit brought by the Canadian company Methanex before a NAFTA tribunal during 2001 is an example. Methanex produces a gasoline additive that accidentally leeched into the municipal water supply of the city of Santa Monica. Most of its wells had to be shut down. The state of California reacted by imposing a ban on the additive, which prompted Methanex in turn to take its case to NAFTA, claiming almost a billion dollars' compensation from the US government. The case is detailed in Linda McQuaig, *All You Can Eat: Greed, Lust and the Triumph of the New Capitalism* (Toronto, 2001).

[47] John Ralston Saul, *The Unconscious Civilization* (Concord, 1995).

a lack of public-friendly, well-trained administrative staff, ensures that many parts of the cosmocracy are closed off from either mutual or public scrutiny of any kind. They come to feel like an impenetrable jungle of acronyms. Matters are worsened by the tyranny of distance: despite the noblest of public-spirited motives, decisionmakers tend to lose track of their decisions, which are whizzed around in a cyclotron of global structures and events, with many different and unpredictable effects. Governing at a distance tends to 'disjoin remorse from power' (Shakespeare). Responsibility is overpowered. It becomes just a word.

A dominant power

The body politic of cosmocracy contains a destabilising anti-body: a dominant power, the United States. Like all previous modern dominant powers – from Habsburg Spain to the *Pax Britannica* of the nineteenth century – this one seeks mastery over the whole system. Yet the United States differs from these previous dominant powers in two fundamental ways. It is the first such power in human history that finds itself in a position, partly thanks to a measure of historical luck, of being in the position to lay claim to world hegemony. It is also unusual because it is a dominant power equipped with a revolutionary world-view: a vision of itself, and the whole world, as a unique constitutional order based upon the republican, federal, democratic principles first crafted in the 1776 revolution. In its embrace of the Philadelphia model, America differs, say, from the House of Habsburg, which was a dynastic confederation of states (stretching from Portugal and the Netherlands to Naples and Milan through to Bohemia and Hungary) that gathered at the altar of international Catholicism. The new dominant power also differs from nineteenth-century Britain, the driving force behind the previous phase of globalisation. Even at the height of its power, those who governed Britain sensed the folly of risking everything, including its fleet, to conquer the world. Where they perceived that they could not intervene successfully, in continental Europe or South America, they refrained from doing so.[48]

The United States shows few signs of acting in this way. Like revolutionary France and Soviet Russia before it, the United States is a territorial power dedicated to transforming the whole world in its favour. True, its political leaders and diplomats are often embarrassed by talk of 'empire'; they speak and act as if the United States were only one state among others. Such efforts of an empire to masquerade as a state are nevertheless wearing thin: the days when it could be said (by Gore Vidal and

---

[48] Hobsbawm, *On The Edge of the New Century*, pp. 46–57.

others) that the success of the American empire depends in part upon keeping it a secret are coming to an end. Its leaders now see themselves more and more as the world's first unchallenged global imperial power, as a sequel and effective replacement of the old system of nineteenth- and twentieth-century imperial powers that once ruled the world, and have now collapsed.

The United States tends to behave in this way, despite historical evidence that all previous dominant powers produce geopolitical instability, and despite growing evidence, reinforced by the theory of global civil society, that the world has become too large and complicated to be governed by a single power. The dominant power often operates bullishly,[49] and it does so because its governing class perceive strength as the principal way in which it can secure its flanks and protect its dominant power privileges, if need be by exercising the right of direct intervention into others' affairs.[50] This perception is not inaccurate. Considered as a political sub-system of cosmocracy, the dominant power is the engine and deficit-of-last-resort of the turbocapitalist economy (despite the fact that its share of world production has fallen from one-third to one-fifth since 1950); the driving force of the global telecommunications and entertainment industries; and the homeland of the mightiest army in the world. During the Clinton presidencies, it completed the transformation of its strategy of global containment into the capacity 'nearly simultaneously' to fight two major regional wars.[51] The Gulf War of 1991, the Bosnian pacification of 1995, and the overthrow and arrest of Milosević after the war in Kosovo all showed that decisive military action at the global level depended on the United States. So too did the 2001 war against the government of Afghanistan, which collapsed quickly under the impact of the most advanced military technology known to humanity: state-of-the art bombing, missiles fired through doorways by unmanned Predator aircraft, interception of the enemy's every telephone call and radio

---

[49] One example: during the first eight months of 2002, the Bush Administration publicly rejected the Anti-Ballistic Missile Treaty, the Kyoto Protocol, the Rome Statute of the International Criminal Court, a convention on the sale and transfer of small arms, and a protocol to the Biological Weapons Convention.

[50] In 1986, after a terrorist bombing of a Berlin discothèque frequented by American servicemen, Secretary of State George Schultz explained that it was 'absurd to argue that international law prohibits us from capturing terrorists in international waters or airspace; from attacking them on the soil of other nations, even for the purpose of rescuing hostages; or from using force against states that support, train and harbour terrorist or guerrillas'. See his 'Low-Intensity Warfare: The Challenge of Ambiguity', Address to the National Defense University (Washington, DC, 15 January 1986), reprinted in *International Legal Materials* 25 (1986), 204 at 206.

[51] Department of Defense, *Annual Report to the President and Congress, 1994* (Washington, DC, 1994), p. 16.

transmission, bombs that bust open the deepest bunkers. The dominant power's war-fighting budget for 1999 was only two-thirds of what it was in 1989, but still it accounts for 35 per cent of the world's total military spending (Russia's share was ten times less); expenditure on the armed forces is equal to the sum total of the next largest eight states in the world. The United States has meanwhile consolidated its role as the biggest arms dealer, with sales in the year 2000 worth US$18.6 billion, more than half the US$36.9 billion global arms trade figure.[52]

The dominant power can and does throw its weight around – most recently, in Serbia and Afghanistan. Its leaders know that money, information, kilobytes, blood and iron count in world affairs. Its politicians are tempted, like every previous dominant power of the modern era, to act as a vigilante power, to see their power as the ability, especially when push comes to shove, to measure their strength against all of their rivals combined.[53] They do so partly through arrogant presumptions – summarised in the closing words of presidential speeches, 'May God bless the United States of America' – and straightforward designs of aggrandisement and neglecting or cherrypicking international agencies and agreements at their own convenience; and partly through the quite different insistence that everybody has an 'urgent and binding obligation' to 'answer history's call', to gather beneath the stars and stripes, and to march forwards with America in its world-wide struggle for democratic freedoms.[54]

Cosmopolitan democracy?

When comparing monarchies and republics, the great Dutch political commentator, Jan de Witt, claimed that the former (in line with Machiavelli's *Il principe*) encouraged princes to act using the force of lions and the cunning of foxes. By contrast, de Witt said, those who are elected and in charge of republics are encouraged to act with stealth, like

---

[52] *New York Times*, August 21, 2001; *The Economist*, 20 June 1998; *Washington Post*, August 13, 1998.

[53] Martin Wight, *Power Politics*, eds. Hedley Bull and Carsten Holbraad (Leicester, 1978), pp. 30–40. A small example that summarises this attitude: On 11 October 2001, in a widely reported television interview, Richard Armitage, the deputy secretary of state in the Bush Administration, when asked about Osama bin Laden's repeated insistence that US troops should be nowhere near Muslim holy places, ignored the question. He went on to say that the troops were there to protect Persian Gulf oil sites, and that anyone who asked this kind of question was playing bin Laden's ballgame.

[54] From the speeches of President George Bush, Jr. at the United Nations, as reported in *Financial Times* (London), 23 November 2001, p. 13, and *Guardian* (London), 12 September 2002, p. 1.

cats, which are both 'agile and prudent'.[55] De Witt's rule-of-thumb today
retains its heuristic value. For whether the United States will succumb
to the temptation of lion-and-fox world aggrandisement, or whether, like
the British before them, it will instead take measures to behave carefully, like a cat, and to avoid hubris, for instance by playing the role
of catalyst of a more effective and democratic form of cosmocracy, is
among the great, if dangerous political issues of our time. Its resolution
will help to determine the life-span of global civil society. If the hege-
monic power turns out (unusually) to be a self-limiting global force for
'constitutional order' guided by principles like power-sharing, multilat-
eralism and the rule of law, then global civil society could well thrive
during the coming years.[56] If, on the other hand, the American empire
consistently behaves as if it is morally entitled to run the whole world,
and to act on its behalf, then almost certainly that roguery would have
the effect of stirring up geopolitical troubles. That roguery would in turn
work against global civil society, perhaps even wrecking the chances of its
survival.

The problem of whether (or how) the dominant power can be tamed
is compounded by the pressing need to develop a more effective and legitimate form of cosmocracy. What can be done to tame and control the
zones of unaccountable power within the actually existing cosmocracy?
Following the world's largest death squad atrocity directed at two key
symbols of the emerging global civil society and cosmocracy, it is to be
hoped – forlornly, in all probability – that the classical tactic of tyrant-
killing by monarchomachs, as the Scot Barclay famously called it, has lost
all legitimacy.[57] Whatever transpires, the search for solutions to the problem of unaccountable power on a global scale will continue; the members
of global civil society cannot expect the perpetrators of incompetence and
hubris to be destroyed automatically by the angry gods. Other, human,
all-too-human remedies will be needed.[58]

---

[55] Cited in Franco Venturi, *Utopia e riforma nell'illuminisimo* (Turin, 1970), pp. 35–6.

[56] This is the expectation of G. John Ikenberry, *After Victory* (Princeton, 2001), and his
'Getting Hegemony Right', *The National Interest*, 63 (Spring 2001), pp. 17–24. See also
Joseph S. Nye, *The Paradox of American Power: Why the World's Only Superpower Can't
Go It Alone* (Oxford and New York, 2002), and the thesis that governments that are in
highly interdependent relations with others are less likely to resort to violence, presented
in Bruce M. Russett and John R. Oneal, *Triangulating Peace: Democracy, Interdependence
and International Organizations* (New York, 2001).

[57] A rather pessimistic view of the rise and proliferation of death squads under modern
conditions is presented in Bruce B. Campbell and Arthur Brenner (eds.), *Death Squads
in Global Perspective. Murder with Deniability* (New York and Basingstoke, 2000).

[58] See Ernst-Otto Czempiel, 'Governance and Democratization', in James N. Rosenau and
Ernst-Otto Czempiel (eds.), *Governance Without Government: Order and Change in World
Politics* (Cambridge and New York, 1992), pp. 250–71.

It is obvious to many that a pressing constitutional agenda confronts both the actually existing cosmocracy and global civil society: the need to find the appropriate methods for enabling something like effective, publicly accountable government to develop on a global scale. Alas, there is currently no consensus about what form this agenda might take. This is partly because of the inordinate strength of the neo-liberal forces that champion free market turbocapitalism *über alles*. It is also partly because some of their opponents slam 'globalisation' in the name of stronger and more nationalist territorial states, or by means of vague notions of 'de-globalisation' and the 'deconcentration and decentralization of institutional power' through 'the re-empowerment of the local and the national'.[59] Matters are not helped by the far-fetched thinking that foolishly turns its back on the actually existing system of cosmocracy, in order to predict (and in the process recommend) the arrival of 'world government'.[60] Meanwhile, political thinkers are divided about what should or could be done. Some defend the principle of a transnational democratic legal order, a community of all democratic communities, something resembling a global *Rechtstaat*, of the kind implied in article 28 of the Universal Declaration of Human Rights: 'Everyone is entitled to a social and international order in which the rights and freedoms set forth in the Declaration can be fully realised.' Others anticipate a second-best scenario that owes everything to Emmerich de Vattel: a complex international system of nominally sovereign, democratic states that are the voting members in a variety of international fora. Still others foresee a new compromise between these two options: a cosmopolitan process of democratisation, through which citizens gain a voice within their own states and in sites of power among their states.

This latter approach – the neo-Kantian appeal to 'cosmopolitan democracy' – currently enjoys some popularity in academic circles.[61] Its early exponents (Archibugi, Held and others) imagined a 'system of geo-governance unlike any other proposed to date'. The approach (without considering the archaeology of its concepts) tried to bring a rather unconventional meaning to the word 'cosmopolitan', to indicate 'a model of political organization in which citizens, wherever they are located in the world, have a voice, input and political representation

---

[59] Walden Bello, 'The Struggle for a Deglobalized World', www.igc.org/trac/feature/wto/8-bello.html (September 2000).

[60] During the early 1970s, this prediction was at the centre of the World Order Models Project, as Saul Mendlovitz explains in the 'Introduction' to Johan Galtung, *The True Worlds* (New York, 1980), p. xxi.

[61] See especially the Introduction (from which all the following quotations are drawn) to Archibugi and Held (eds.), *Cosmopolitan Democracy*, pp. 1–16.

in international affairs, in parallel with and independently of their own governments'. This cosmopolitanism measured itself against historical examples. It aimed to steer a course between and beyond, on the one hand, NATO-style arrangements, whose trans-national power structures are a law unto themselves, and at odds with the mainly democratic structures of their member states; and, on the other hand, Congress of Vienna-style arrangements, which displayed the inverse mismatch: generous interstate consultative mechanisms among states that were mostly autocratic. Cosmopolitan democracy looked forward instead to 'the parallel development of democracy both within states and among states'. It noted that this double democratisation required the building of 'authoritative global institutions', like the reform of the Security Council, the creation of a second chamber in the United Nations, the strengthening of international law, even the creation of 'a small but effective, accountable, international military force'.

The early version of the theory of cosmopolitan democracy was stimulating, but unconvincing. Its definition of democracy was vague and tautologous ('the distinctive feature of democracy is . . . not only a particular set of procedures [important though this is], but also the pursuit of democratic values involving the extension of popular participation in the political process') and it rested ultimately on the questionable, arguably out-dated principle that democracy equals 'popular participation'.[62] And note, above all, its not-so-secret attachment to an originally Kantian, two-level or 'double democratisation' schema. 'What is necessary', it was argued, 'is to deprive states of some of their more coercive and restrictive powers: in the former case, those powers which are deployed against the welfare and safety of citizens; in the latter case, those powers which are deployed to forestall or inhibit collaborative relations among states on pressing transnational questions'. Then came a revealing conclusion: 'Cosmopolitan institutions must come to coexist with the established powers of states, overriding them only in certain, well-defined spheres of activity.'

The implied goal of peaceful co-existence between two levels of government is problematic, if only because, empirically speaking, the complex and contradictory structures of cosmocracy are against it. The early model of cosmopolitan democracy supposed that we are still living in the age of Kant – or the age that spawned Tennyson's vision of 'the Parliament of Man, the Federation of the World', a vision that has since resurfaced in John Rawls' image of 'representatives of liberal peoples'

---

[62] See my *Whatever Happened to Democracy?* (London, 2002) and *A History of Democracy*, forthcoming.

making 'an agreement with other liberal peoples'.[63] The early vision of cosmopolitan democracy rested, unfortunately, upon what can be called the Law of the Excluded Middle: an object of theoretical reflection, it is supposed, can or may be here or there, but not in both places in once. It can be A or not-A, but not both, or not somewhere in between. Things, events, people have their place: they belong to separate and pure realms. Such dualistic thinking is unhelpful in the task of theoretically understanding how substantially to increase the level of public accountability of governmental institutions on a global scale. Such a theory not only needs to be much clearer and more persuasive about the normative meanings of democracy and how strategically it can be built; on descriptive grounds, it also needs to be much more sensitive to the 'messy', self-contradictory, criss-crossing, dynamic networks of mediated power that are a basic feature of cosmocracy.

The failure of the early cosmopolitan approach to deal with such problems provides a clue for understanding its subsequent flights of ethical fancy.[64] Its more recent formulations rely upon arbitrarily chosen regulative principles that are claimed to be universal (or could become universal, through 'open-ended interaction, uncoerced agreement and impartial judgement' guided by the 'force of the better argument'): core principles that oblige the reciprocal recognition by free and equal individuals that each person 'should enjoy the impartial treatment of their claims'. The starting point of this revised cosmopolitanism, as it might be called, is to insist that ethical principles that cannot serve as guides for a plurality of different actors should be rejected; and, conversely, that ethical principles must be *universally* applicable. This categorical imperative or Cosmopolitan Moral Law runs something like: 'Act in all situations and at all times only in accordance with the maxim that all human beings enjoy the status of equal moral value, reciprocal recognition, and an equal chance to have their claims impartially considered.' Note the guileless thinking: the ethical worthiness that is supposed to be measured by a process of 'reasonable rejectability' and by acting 'out of duty' to universalisable principles in fact looks suspiciously like a species of liberal humanism born of the Atlantic region. Daoist celebrations of natural, virtually anarchistic spontaneity and Legalist defences of centralised political order through carefully controlled punishments and rewards – to mention two randomly chosen but important Chinese intellectual traditions – do not see eye to eye with such 'cosmopolitan' regulative principles. Why

---

[63] John Rawls, *The Law of Peoples* (Cambridge, MA and London, 1999), part 1.

[64] See, for example, David Held, 'Globalization, Corporate Practice and Cosmopolitan Social Standards', *Contemporary Political Theory*, 1 (2002), pp. 64, 65–6, 67, 74; and his *Cosmopolitanism* (Cambridge, 2002).

should they? Why should they or the rest of the world even engage in a reasoned public debate with cosmopolitans, whom they might (understandably) dismiss out of hand or instead suppose, wielding their own plausible reasons, to be wrong-headed, or utterly mistaken? Cosmopolitanism is ill-equipped to handle such retorts, which not only expose (as the final section of this book shows) the *historical particularity* of its norms. Revised cosmopolitanism's flight of fancy rests upon bad political sociology and poor history. Empirical applications of the concept of global civil society – a concept whose emphasis upon pluralism sticks a pin in the bottom of cosmopolitan universalism – are virtually absent. The whole approach presupposes that once upon a time there was a nation-state system but that 'national states and national governments are now embedded in complex networks of political power at regional and global levels'. It also ignores the structural problems that currently dog the system of cosmocracy. Revised cosmopolitanism supposes, secretly but implausibly, that the world is in the tightening grip of something like a teleology of normative progress. So it draws a happy conclusion: 'a cosmopolitan covenant is already in the making as political authority and new forms of governance are diffused "below", "above" and "alongside" the nation-state, and as new forms of international law, from the law of war to human rights law and environmental regimes, begin to set down universal standards.'

Fatalism

Cosmocracy is a much more complex and self-contradictory polity than revised cosmopolitanism supposes. Cosmocracy is an intricate system of power that cannot be understood by means of empty moralising or metaphors like 'levels' or emergent cosmopolitan covenants, or the like. Its multiple sites of decisionmaking, on the contrary, are better understood by the political interpreter as cross-roads, as 'quasi-objects' situated at the intersection of an ensemble of other 'quasi-objects'.[65] One could say, to put the point pithily, that for this reason a theory of global civil society needs less Kant and more Althusius. The work of Johannes Althusius (1557–1638), especially his *Politica* (1614), is today deserving of a revival. His writings belong to those of which Bacon once said: 'They are to be chewed and digested.' This is because, despite various weaknesses and anachronisms, Althusius has much to say to us about the need to think normatively and strategically, in more nuanced ways, about complex systems of power. Cosmocracy resembles a thoroughly modern

---

[65] See Bruno Latour, *We Have Never Been Modern* (Cambridge, MA, 1993).

version of the political world pondered by Althusius, a strangely 'neo-medieval' mélange of overlapping legal structures and political bodies that come in all shapes and sizes – a many-sided world of overlapping and potentially conflicting political structures, primordial groups, differently sized political associations, and federalist strivings for both particularism and universalism, ecumene and community.[66]

It may be that our latter-day Althusian world of cosmocratic structures will facilitate a Global New Deal: a multi-layered global political settlement defined by a core of governing institutions designed to rein in the most destructive behaviours, and a periphery of governing institutions based on more voluntary and non-coercive regulations.[67] This is the undecided future. Whatever comes to pass, it is safe to say that the global polity of the future will defy the simplifications and confusions of prevailing theories of globalisation that think in the old-fashioned terms of (potentially) 'sovereign' territorial states, or of 'multi-level governance' or 'cosmopolitan democracy'. Beyond that probability, nothing is certain, which is why it should not be supposed that long-lasting remedies for the weaknesses of cosmocracy can be found within the cupboards of contemporary political acceptability. Brand new democratic thinking – implicit in the theory of global civil society – is required, even if there are no guarantees of success. That lugubrious thought prompts a final few words about historical analogies and the pitfalls of fatalism in any theory of global civil society.

It is common in discussions of the system of global governance, or cosmocracy as I have called it here, that the word 'system' frequently comes in for a battering. It is often greeted with puzzlement, or outright derision, mainly because *prima facie* the tangled mess of governmental and para-governmental institutions that have global effects seem to defy both systematic description and normative judgement. This so-called global system of governance seems to be a global system of anarchy: it seems that no institution or body regularly occupies the seat of power. Its complex and contradictory logic seems to be: *sauve qui peut*. There seem to be no secure rules or regulations; nobody seems to be in charge. Little wonder, then, that most languish in its presence. It seems to defy description, and so to induce a faint feeling – even a feeling of fatalism before the powers that be.

---

[66] See Johannes Althusius, *Politica Methodicè digesta atque exemplis sacris & profanis illustrata* (Herborn, 1614), and the classic commentary of Otto von Gierke, *The Development of Political Theory* (New York, 1966 [1880]).

[67] Michael Edwards, *Future Positive. International Co-Operation in the 21st Century* (London, 2000), chapter 9.

This fatalism is an enemy of both global civil society and of the goal of injecting positive-sum powers and public accountability into the system of cosmocracy that frames it. The fatalist, who comes in two types, is generally someone who feels overwhelmed or overpowered by the world. One of them, the ignoramus, is simply ignorant, and confident in that ignorance, often supremely so in the straightforward conclusions that are drawn. They know who rules the world: it is the rich and powerful, or the big multinational corporations, or the United States of America, for instance. And that's that. Nothing more to be said – and nothing more can be done, at least for the time being. There is another species of fatalist: the more cautious type. They haven't a clue about who runs the world, and they aren't much troubled or intrigued by their ignorance. This blasé fatalist does not know who rules the world; when asked, they readily admit to their ignorance, and quickly add, with a sigh, that they don't much care. They divine from their ignorance the conclusion that the effort to define who holds the reins of power is a waste of time. For – here the two species of fatalists join forces – it is said that there's no point in wasting words on the subject, for no matter what is said and attempted the governing forces always get their way. Here the two types of fatalists spread their sails and drift together in the ancient waters of Greek mythology, where fatalism appears in the shape of old women who sit patiently spinning the threads and ropes of worldly events that are bound to happen. Fate was represented as both external and internal to the individual. One's fate was 'spun', and so given, from the outside; but fate was at the same time intensely personal, something experienced from the inside. It left the individual no other option but to yield to what was felt outside and inside. The Romans called this inner and outer experience of necessity *fatum*. It literally meant 'a thing said', something that is reported before it actually happened. Fate is a forewarning of an event or chain of events that cannot not happen. The *fatum* is irreversible. It cannot be changed by a millimetre or a gramme. Fatalists are those who believe or accept this. They embrace fate – their unfreedom – as theirs. Fate is *their* fate.

The contemporary sense that fate has power over our lives is under-standable. A moment's reflection reveals that human beings are never to-tally in control of everything that happens to their lives. They chronically feel forced to go along with things, to accept or to do things against their will. The compulsion, complexity and contradictoriness of the system of cosmocracy arguably reinforces this feeling. All this is understandable. But when the recognition and acceptance of fate hardens into dogma, fa-talism takes hold of the individual, or group, cruelly and without mercy. Fatalism distorts and paralyses visions and actions: it makes it seem that nothing can be done, that everything is foreordained. That is why fatalism is a principal curse of the twin projects of nurturing global civil society and democratising the system of cosmocracy. Fatalism produces inattention towards the framework of governance within which this society has sprung up, and today flourishes. Fatalism is the silent enemy of political thinking about global civil society. It conjures necessity from contingency. Fatalism feeds wistfulness. It turns its back on the job of naming and mapping these governing institutions, in order that they may better be judged, defended, reformed, or fundamentally transformed.

We know from historians that among the principal reasons why the last major growth spurt of 'globalisation' failed was because no effective or efficient or legitimate structures of global government were put in place.[68] By the 1930s, people and political institutions like the League of Nations, its Economic and Financial Organisation, the ILO, and the Bank for International Settlements were overwhelmed by the intense contradictory pressures of a globalised world. Governing institutions were overburdened by economic crises and long-standing political resentments, including the bitter politics of reparations and war debts. Luckily, the essential ingredients of a 1920s-style endogenous revolt against democratic forms of globalisation are today missing. There are today no Soviet Unions or Third Reichs on the horizon. The thought that defenders of *souverainisme* (the term used by French protesters in Seattle for the defence of the territorial state), or the Taliban or the Burmese junta or Chinese-style capitalism in post-totalitarian form serve as universal counter-models to cosmocracy in more democratic form is laughable. Fatalism, however, is no laughing matter. It is the favourite liquor of idiots, and kicking its habits is for that reason – as de Gaulle reportedly commented after spotting a Free French tank daubed with the words 'Death to Idiots!' – a vast task. Fatalism is our principal threat. That is why its refusal initially requires a strong dose of clear thinking about the web of governing institutions that presently cover the earth. This is what the theory of cosmocracy seeks to do. Whether and to what extent it can or does succeed is for others to decide.

---

[68] Harold James, *The End of Globalization: Lessons from the Great Depression* (Cambridge, MA, 2001); see also Andrew Gamble, *Politics and Fate* (Oxford, 2000).

Paradise on earth?

Higher education

Exactly because global civil society consists of a vast mosaic of socio-economic groups, organisations and initiatives that are variously related to governmental structures at the local, national, regional and supranational levels, its organisations and actors are pushed and pulled in various and often contradictory directions: not only towards and away from businesses and non-profit civic organisations, but also towards and away from governmental institutions. Government-funded systems of mass higher education – now linked together across borders by shared languages, common teaching and research methods, staff and student exchanges, and compatible hardware – illustrate well these messy, sometimes productive tensions built into government-enabled civil organisations.

During the past half-century, the role of governing institutions in fostering higher education has had spectacular effects. Driven by a variety of policy objectives and hunches – military capability, national pride, liberal beliefs in the importance of education, but above all by expectations that during coming decades perhaps half of all jobs in the post-industrial turbocapitalist economies will require a minimum of sixteen years' schooling and training – governments of all kinds in all continents have invested heavily in the business of higher education. The huge increase in the numbers of state-funded students on various patches of the earth has definitely helped to create an impression that higher education is a world-wide development. It is easy to see why. The total numbers of higher education students world-wide have grown exponentially in recent decades – from 51 million in 1980 to 82 million in 1995, an increase of 61 per cent. The numbers now top 90 million. A majority of these students is concentrated in the richer OECD countries, where around half of the 18–23 age group is now enrolled in some form of higher education. In some OECD countries, change has been especially rapid. German student numbers have increased by 80 per cent since 1977; a similar pattern of expansion has been evident in France, where the number of higher education students jumped from less than 150,000 in 1955 to a record 2.2 million in 2002. Outside the bloc of wealthy OECD states, similar trends, although patchy and in a state of flux, are evident. During the past twenty-five years, the number of higher education students in Saudi Arabia increased more than twenty times; there has been a tripling of the number of university students in Iran since the overthrow of the Shah; many states in the South East Asia region have embarked on vigorous programmes of expansion; while some twenty states, half of them in so-called developing countries, now boast at least a million higher education students.[1]

The image of higher education as an important 'global' phenomenon is reinforced by another, more striking and consequential development: the qualitative growth of cross-border chains and loops in the field of higher education, whose institutions arguably are now far more 'worldly' than any other institution, including turbocapitalist firms themselves.[2] The outward-looking university is of course not new. Thomas Jefferson's decision in 1824 to recruit faculty members from Germany to teach at the University of Virginia serves as a reminder that the trend has a long and respected history. Yet we are living in a time of the unprecedented globalisation of higher education. Everywhere there are signs that teaching and administrative staff and students themselves accept that in the field of higher education inward-looking strategies are unproductive, that they may even lead to organisational stagnation, or decline. What are the main indicators of this trend? Cheer-leading for the cause of higher education, for learning that is more universally accessible on a global scale, is championed by bodies like UNESCO.[3] The higher education industry plays the role of host at thousands of annual conferences, research institutes and teaching and publishing programmes – to the point where it should not be surprising that the institutions of higher education are the epicentre of a vigorous global debate about 'globalisation' itself. Then there are various policies and strategies designed for winning contracts, students and prestige within global civil society. There are schemes that aim to nurture scientific knowledge, languages, technologies, business methods, teaching skills and personal and professional contacts across borders. A prominent example is Universitas 21: it has announced plans to set up a global online university in partnership with Thomson, the

---

[1] Jan Sadlak, 'Globalization and Concurrent Challenges for Higher Education', in Peter Scott (ed.), *The Globalization of Higher Education* (Buckingham and Philadelphia, 1998), p. 101.

[2] See J. Currie and J. Newson (eds.), *Universities and Globalization: Critical Perspectives* (London, 1998).

[3] UNESCO, *Policy Paper for Change and Development in Higher Education* (Paris, 1995).

Canadian electronic publishing group, to be run by the University of Melbourne, to operate accreditation schemes and to share external examiners among a network of large, similar-profile public universities elsewhere in Australia, New Zealand, Canada, the United States, Singapore and the United Kingdom.[4] Other notable examples include the student mobility schemes ERASMUS and SOCRATES, which have so far assisted more than half a million European Union students to spend a meaningful period of their studies in another member state. Meanwhile, franchising deals *à la McDonald's* flourish.[5] Efforts are made to internationalise qualifications. Joint courses are pioneered. Course credits are accumulated and transferred across borders.

Needless to say, these and other schemes have been enabled by revolutionary developments in communications, most notably the Internet, which is the propolis of higher education. High-tech reality has descended on higher education, and the virtual university is its interim masterpiece. There is a steady increase in the number of institutions offering virtual degrees: in the United States, in 1998, more than 300 colleges and universities offered online courses to over 700,000 cyberstudents. Three years later, fuelled by companies like Blackboard.com, Campuspipeline.com and the Global Knowledge Network, the numbers of tertiary students enrolled in e-Ed courses was 2.3 million. Future growth seems probable, especially because the professoriate can benefit – companies like UNext, Harcourt-Brace and Thinkwell offer academic staff attractive financial deals – and because distance learning is an effective – and potentially profitable – means of providing retraining and upgrading courses that do not involve time-consuming travel and severe disruption of professional employment.

Finally – this is perhaps the most eye-catching and consequential development – there is a vast increase in the numbers of students who now pack their bags in search of improved qualifications in foreign lands. By the mid-1990s, more than 1.5 million foreign students, half of them from less developed regions, were enrolled in higher education in some fifty host states. During the past twenty-five years, student mobility across borders has grown by over 300 per cent, and some observers predict a continuing

---

[4] 'A World Wide Web of Elite Universities', *Times Higher Education Supplement*, 13 March 1998.
[5] 'It's a big world. Somebody has to run it', says the advertisement for TRIUM, the 'only truly integrated, truly global' executive MBA offered by New York University's Stern School of Business, the London School of Economics and Political Science and the Parisian HEC School of Management. Participants earn a joint degree in sixteen months by attending concentrated two-week study modules at the flagship schools, plus one week each in São Paulo and Hong Kong. Distance learning and team projects continue between class sessions.

massive increase during the next twenty-five years.[6] The patterns are of course distributionally skewed, so that more than three-quarters of study abroad takes place within ten host states, led by the United States (more than 30 per cent of all foreign students), France (more than 11 per cent) and Germany (about 10 per cent) and including Canada and Belgium (less than 2.5 per cent each), and Switzerland (about 2 per cent). Yet the aggregate trends are impressive, as are new initiatives, like those of the People's Republic of China, where in recent years the number of foreign students has grown most dramatically.

The ivory tower?

For some observers, all these trends, especially the globalisation of student mobility, represents an important renewal and universalisation of the original mission of the *universitas*. This founding mission of higher education, they point out, was expressed in the medieval European practice of the *studia generalia* – students wandering from Bologna to Paris to Salerno (perhaps the first European university, founded in the ninth century AD) to Edinburgh and to Oxford, in search of knowledge – and in the much earlier Islamic *madrasah* colleges – like those in Bukhârâ, Cairo, Damascus, Hillah and Timbuktu – that attracted students from far and wide.[7] In Europe, in its earliest stage of development, the university was a scholastic guild, formed on the analogy of the trades guilds and the guilds of aliens in foreign cities.[8] Composed to a great extent of students from foreign countries, the *universitas* was a combination formed for the protection of its members from civil and papal authority, from the extortion of townsmen and from other annoyances linked to being resident in a foreign country and studying subjects beyond those offered by the monastic and cathedral schools. Seeing the hand of the past in the present, these same observers praise the growth of student mobility for offering large numbers of young students a taste of what in former times only a privileged elite handful tasted: the experience of higher education as an 'ivory tower', a modern-day equivalent of the Roman *eboreum*, an exotic place of temporary seclusion, or withdrawal from the harsh realities of the world.

---

[6] See the figures and predictions cited in D. Blight, *International Education: Australia's Potential Demand and Supply* (Canberra, 1995) and UNESCO, *Policy Paper for Change and Development in Higher Education*. The latest tables on higher education foreign student numbers are available at http://unescostat.unesco.org/yearbook/ybframe.htm.

[7] J. M. Cameron, *On the Idea of a University* (London, 1978); Marshall G. S. Hodgson, *The Venture of Islam*, vol. 2 (Chicago and London, 1977), pp. 438–45, 555.

[8] H. S. Denifle, *Die Universitäten des Mittelalters bis 1400* (Berlin, 1885), i, pp. 1–29.

There is admittedly much seductive charm left in the image of the cosmopolitan ivory tower. Observe a moment's silence for the Kaiser Friedrich Wilhelm Universität, founded in Berlin in 1809 under the rectorship of Johann Gottlieb Fichte, a seat of learning that helped regenerate German cultural life during the nineteenth century. Admire the boldness of Kant's *Der Streit der Fakultäten* (1798), with its plea for a philosophy faculty 'that is independent of the government's command with regard to its teachings; one that, having no commands to give, is free to evaluate everything, and concerns itself with the interests of the sciences, that is, with truth: one in which reason is authorised to speak out publicly'.[9] Stroll through the quadrangle and across the Backs of King's College, Cambridge. Enter the mirror-lined, space-age library of the beautiful ocean-side, eucalyptus-dotted campus of the University of California at San Diego. Sit peacefully in the frescoed library of Bologna's oldest university. Surely these are places of Universal Knowledge? Spaces of personal self-discovery emancipated from the burdens of *Brotstudium* – studying for the sake of a career – and thus open to the disinterested pursuit of truth? Settings in which (as Karl Jaspers said) people 'do not have to bear responsibility for current politics, precisely because they alone bear unlimited responsibility for the development of truth'?[10] They are not. The classical ideal of the *universitas* – an ideal of a disinterested body of scholars devoted to learning and teaching defended a generation ago by such prominent scholars as Ortega Y Gasset, Karl Jaspers and Sir Walter Moberly[11] – is obsolete because its natural habitat – a setting freed from the pressures of the market and the state – has been destroyed.

Pressured by various domestic and globalising forces, described above, colleges and universities everywhere suffer metamorphosis through fragmentation. The boundaries of the late medieval university were clearly demarcated; its walls and quadrangles looked inwards, as if to encourage students and teachers to turn their backs on the world. By contrast, institutions of higher education today are outward-looking, ultimately 'global'. Little wonder, for they are pushed and pulled in many

---

[9] Immanuel Kant, *Der Sreit der Fakultäten* (Berlin, 1798), pp. 26–8. Kant here distinguished between the university's 'lower' faculties, areas of scholarship unencumbered by state censorship, such as 'historical knowledge' and 'pure rational knowledge' (history, geography, philology, the empirical knowledge of the natural sciences, the humanities, pure mathematics and pure philosophy), and the 'higher' faculties, such as theology, law and medicine, in which scholars are instruments of government policy and therefore 'not free to make public use of their learning as they see fit'.

[10] Karl Jaspers, *The Idea of the University* (London, 1960), p. 132.

[11] José Ortega Y Gasset, *Mission of the University* (Princeton, 1944); Jaspers, *The Idea of the University*; and Walter Hamilton Moberly, *The Crisis in the University* (London, 1949).

contradictory directions, to the point where talk of 'the university' or 'the college' is both inappropriate, even obfuscatory. This development is not at all describable as the growth of either an 'attenuated university' or a multi-purpose 'multiversity'.[12] It is far more complicated, and destructive than that. Thanks to domestic and global pressures, and in no small measure because of its contributions to the globalisation of civil society, higher education is torn apart. Its ideals and institutions suffer dispersal. It becomes, at one and the same time, an apparatus of nation-state, regional and transnational power; a profit-seeking market corporation; a self-monitoring, self-administering body; a public space of open debate and independent enquiry; and a force for cosmopolitan institutions and values.

So, for example, territorial states now vie with local and regional governments for greater policy and managerial control over the internal workings of institutions of higher education; boxed in by quality assessment exercises, monitoring, and financial inspections, one could be forgiven for thinking of universities and colleges as integral components of government apparatuses. They are no longer places where only scholars pass judgement on scholars (Kant). An audit culture spreads: in the name of quality, everything seems subject to external political scrutiny and evaluation. In practice, the audit culture is fed not only by fiscal constraints, but also by competitive market pressures. The truth is that higher education is pushed one way by governmental power, and pulled in the opposite direction, towards civil society, by the market-driven forces of turbocapitalism. Gone forever are the days when (as the old joke had it) academics were voted into chairs only at the age at which they had forgotten the meaning of the word 'irrelevant'. Gone too is the once-common feeling among academic staff that they could have done better outside education, in the real world of 'business'. Higher education becomes big business, or the tool of business. Institutions are expected to become 24/7 enterprises that pay their way: they must balance their books, or even make a surplus. Press officers work overtime to market their 'brand' of higher education on the global market. Students find that they have to pay (more) for their degrees. Research designed to yield technology transfers and patents ('patents, not papers') is privileged. Encouragement from the top is given to start up enterprises that are capable of commercially exploiting the institution's stocks of knowledge in, say, informatics

---

[12] The notion of an 'attenuated' university is developed in R. Cowen, 'Performativity, Post-Modernity and the University', *Comparative Education*, 32:2 (1996), pp. 245–58. The once-popular idea of the 'multiversity' is traceable to the Godkin lectures delivered at Harvard University in 1963 by Clark Kerr, and later published as Clark Kerr, *The Uses of the University* (Cambridge, MA, 1972).

and biotechnology. Academics market themselves as consultants. Teaching becomes a saleable commodity, packaged for students in bite-sized learning packs and easy-to-open handouts.

Many higher education institutions try to stake out still different options. Some try to protect themselves against the contradictory forces of government and the market by reacting strategically, or defensively; they tighten their internal controls, pinch and squeeze themselves from within through successive rounds of re-organisation, hoping that experiments in self-regulation and the adaptation of the latest techniques of the 'new public management' will improve their administrative efficiency and fiscal position. Such moves towards self-regulation often produces internal misery – endless meetings, hundreds of emails, peer group assessments, and in general the loss of professional freedoms of academics.[13] Then there are those areas of higher education which commit themselves to neither governments, nor markets, but to the principle of civic engagement with the less powerful groups and communities of civil society. In the United States, there is a long and rich tradition of these institutions with their sleeves rolled up (as they are called), dating from the 1862 Morrill Act, which ushered in land grant colleges, and including more recent initiatives like agricultural extension services, the GI Bill, the Campus Compact (endorsed by more than 600 university and college presidents), and schemes, such as the Democracy Collaborative at the University of Maryland at College Park, that are publicly committed to 'building democracy and strengthening community'.[14]

These cross-cutting trends within higher education naturally diversify, in some cases to the point of incoherence, the roles of students and staff alike. Four decades ago, being a university student meant sex, drugs, rock 'n'roll, rioting, a bit of reading if time permitted: we called it learning. In the Atlantic region, today's students are more socially diverse and they do many and more varied things: they still like to consume pills and spend their time between sheets, or at their favourite clubs, but most feel cut off from governments and party politics and consequently worry more about the meaning of life, or about doing something socially useful in an NGO, or finding a part-time or full-time job that pays enough for them to survive, or in future thrive. As for managerial staff, a similar diversification of roles is obvious. 'The university has become the multiversity and

---

[13] M. Bottery, 'The Challenge to Professionals from the New Public Management: Implications for the Teaching Profession', *Oxford Review of Education*, 22:2, 1996, pp. 179–97.

[14] See *The Democracy Collaborative: Engaged Scholarship and Informed Practice for a Democratic World. Progress Report* (The University of Maryland, College Park, 2001); and Diane Ravitch and Joseph P. Viteritti (eds.), *Making Good Citizens. Education and Civil Society* (New Haven, 2002).

the nature of the presidency has followed this change', commented Clark Kerr. 'The president of the multiversity is leader, educator, wielder of power, pump; he is also officeholder, caretaker, inheritor, consensus seeker, persuader, bottleneck. But he is mostly a mediator.' In the new era of higher education, the president of the institution is all these, and more: s/he is as well government agent, corporate executive, salesman, politician, citizen, media star, spin doctor, humanist, realist, labour relations expert, psychologist, lawyer, local patriot, travelling cosmopolitan, ironist.

All these trends are difficult to summarise, so puzzlingly difficult in fact that they prompt some observers to conclude that higher education is now a 'ruined institution'.[15] Like Edward Gibbon, sitting amidst the crumbling stone columns of the once-great Roman Empire, some even ask whether it is possible to dwell in the ruins without lapsing into romantic nostalgia. There is a growing consensus that the possibility is slim. Many feel that paradise has been lost, that higher education, despite its unprecedented resources and growth, is directionless, and certainly that it is incapable of inspiring itself and others with clearly enunciated goals, like those of 'reason', 'knowledge' and 'universalism'. There are definite signs of listlessness and melancholia, even flights of fancy, evident for instance in the self-reassuringly long acknowledgements sections of many scholarly works. Then there are those who dig in their heels, turn away from the world, almost as if they treat worldly failure as the mark of success and worldly success the sign of failure. They deny tenure to those who concentrate upon teaching or write textbooks; spread whispers about academic authors of commercially successful 'pop-books'; and rail against 'distance learning' in defence of 'real learning' based on proximity and presence. All these reactions are questionable. They ignore the *positive* implications of the fragmentation of higher education: that it cannot any longer pretend to speak through the grand narratives of Truth and Knowledge, but is instead confronted with the fact that it is a divided community that both contains rival conceptions of what constitutes success and competitor institutions – think tanks, research laboratories, educational TV channels, corporate campuses, e-learning or webucation providers[16] and other 'knowledge societies'[17] – that challenge its intellectual authority from outside. (So too do government initiatives, like

---

[15] B. Readings, *The University in Ruins* (Cambridge, MA, 1996), p. 169.

[16] The global e-learning market is expected to exceed $23 billion by 2004, up from $1.7 billion in 1999. There are an estimated 2,000 corporate universities – most are American suppliers with names like SmartForce, Click2Learn, DigitalThink, Global Knowledge Network, NETg, and Saba – and the numbers are expected to grow to some 3,700 by the end of the decade; see 'E-learning On Course for Strong Growth', *Financial Times* (London), 6 June 2001.

[17] Nico Stehr, *Knowledge Societies* (London, 1994).

the UK government's University for Industry, which has signed contracts
with BT, The Royal Air Force, Sainsbury, the TUC, and its recently
announced University for the National Health Service.) The field of
higher education is flung into a cyclotron of conflicting aspirations and
meanings and achievements – and even forced to come to terms with
the political problem of how to handle multiplying and often conflicting
perceptions of 'reality'.

Jean-François Lyotard, when invited by the Conseil des Universités of
the province of Québec to report on the state of knowledge in the Western
world, drew similar conclusions in his *La condition postmoderne: rapport sur
le savoir* (1979). Yet Lyotard, suffering from political wistfulness, could
draw only obscure conclusions. 'Let us wage a war on totality', he wrote,
'let us be witnesses to the unpresentable; let us activate the differences
and save the honour of the name'. He did not see just how helpful
and necessary the perspective of global civil society is in rescuing higher
education from its own ruination. Higher education is no longer exclusively a place for the formation of the self-conscious middle classes,
symbolised by the independent teacher/scholar/intellectual motivated by
an inner calling to query everything related to commonplace worldliness and (Hegel's early critique of the unreason of *bürgerliche Gesellschaft*
is an example[18]) the vulgarities and confusions of civil society. Higher
education instead becomes potentially a friend and supporter of global
civil society, principally because both have an intrinsic interest in the
nurturing and extension of the structures and ideals of non-violent pluralism. The point could be sharpened, to say that higher education is
potentially a principal catalyst and defender of global civil society and its
ethos. As we shall see in the concluding section of this book, among the
appropriate norms of global civil society are flexibility and openness, the
willingness to be humble and to respect others, self-organisation, curiosity
and experimentation, non-violence, peaceful networking across borders,
a strong sense of responsibility for the fate of others, even long-distance
responsibility for the fragile biosphere in which we and our offspring are
condemned to dwell.

Research and teaching in most institutions of higher education currently do not measure up to these norms of self-scrutiny and scrutiny of
the wider world, of course. There is cynicism and demoralisation. And,
alas, there is still plenty of old university arrogance, of the kind revealed
in the well-known story about the group of Englishwomen going about
the countryside recruiting soldiers at the outbreak of the First World

---

[18] G. W. F. Hegel, *Grundlinien der Philosophie des Rechts* (Berlin, 1821). Compare the different understanding of universities within civil society settings in Emil Brix and Jürgen
Nautz (eds.), *Universitäten in der Zivilgesellschaft* (Wien, 2002).

War. Sweeping into Oxford, they confronted a don in his Oxonian master's gown, reading Thucydides in the original Greek. 'And what are *you* doing to save Western civilisation, young man?', one of the women demanded. Drawing himself up to his full height, the don looked down his nose, and replied: 'Madam, I *am* Western civilisation!' Graduates are today living between arrogance and humility. They are inadequately taught the arts of dealing with diversity and coping with conflict, handling adversaries, nurturing skills of self-reliance and courage, in the face of the unexpected, the unfamiliar, or the unknown. Almost everybody is just getting by, bobbing up and down on the surface, pulled hither and thither by a flood of meetings, memoranda, travel schedules, league tables, business plans, research applications, publishing commitments, long teaching weeks, mountainous piles of assignments, due tomorrow, and for marking the following day. Yet thanks to its 'ruination', higher education can (and is already beginning to) resonate to the theme of self-scrutiny and scrutiny of the world. Pushed and pulled hither and thither, faced with a surfeit of data, and conflicting frameworks of interpretation, higher education is becoming a field in which 'supercomplexity' is recognised.[19] It is called on by the world to ditch its metaphysical past, even to abandon talk of the republic of science (or dreams of public collusion of science-minded industrialists and financiers to establish a world republic, as outlined in H. G. Wells' classic tract, *The Open Conspiracy*, 1928). The field of higher education is forced to become more humble, to be the responsible bearer of bundles of norms that have a strikingly similar, if contradictory ring: the organised suspicion of Truth; the realisation instead that our lives and the world itself can be interpreted in multiple and different ways; the search for commercially viable knowledge; the resistance to commercialism; suspicion of ideologies and speaking out independently against prejudice; criticising the powerful; supporting the weak; emphasising the ironies of the human condition... and taking seriously the ethos of pluralism, even giving it institutional force, so placing higher education and its graduates on a collision course with the principal threats to global civil society.

Ideologies

Although it does not turn it into paradise on earth, the spread of higher education arguably helps to stabilise and strengthen global civil society. It adds to some of its best qualities, and highlights the need for clear-headed strategic thinking about how best to strengthen them further.

[19] Ronald Barnett, *Realizing the University in an Age of Supercomplexity* (Buckingham and Philadelphia, 2000).

The outlines of these actually existing qualities have gradually surfaced in this book, and can be summarised in a few propositions. Global civil society enables individuals, groups and organisations to organise and to deploy their powers across borders, despite remaining barriers of time and distance. This society provides non-governmental structures and rules which enable individuals and groups to move and to decide things, to follow their inclinations, to bring governmental powerholders to heel, to engage in many kinds of mutually beneficial exchanges, even to work for the socialisation of market economies so that production for social need, rather than for profit, prevails. This society makes it easier and cheaper for trades unions and campaigners against hunger to coordinate their actions, for companies in Seoul to ship goods to Italy, for the aboriginal peoples of northern Canada to keep in touch with their brothers and sisters in southern Africa; it enables the residents of Melbourne to visit relatives in Athens, for activists in Vancouver to challenge the timber-cutting policies of Indonesians and Brazilians, and for large banks in Frankfurt and Tokyo to manage their world-wide foreign-exchange positions around the globe, from one branch to another, always staying ahead of the setting sun. Global civil society (as Michael Walzer has said so aptly[20]) resembles a project of projects. It resounds of liberty, with all its multifariousness, awkwardness, challenge and hope. Its civilities tend to be independent-minded and active, rather than deferential. It is rich in freedoms within and beyond borders: for example, to keep in touch with others who are loved and valued; to accumulate money and wealth; to consume products that were once considered exotic, in any season; to travel, to make friends across borders, and to reunite with others, virtually or actually; and to re-build damaged infrastructures by recovering memories, protecting the vulnerable, raising hopes and generating new wealth and income. Global civil society offers other possibilities: 'spaces of hope'[21] in which to warn the world of threats to its security and to denounce and to reduce violence and uncivil war; the freedom to press the principle that social and political power beyond borders should be subject to greater public accountability; and, generally, the opportunity to rescue the culture of 'cosmopolitanism' from its negative connotations of jet-setting, leisured individuals loyal to no one and bent on selfishly sampling all cultures at will – replacing such connotations through the defence of a *worldly* politics that cultivates the need for transnational mobility of viewpoint and action in support of justice and freedom for all of the earth's inhabitants. In this way, the three little words 'global civil society' potentially enable millions of people

---

[20] Michael Walzer, 'The Concept of Civil Society', in *Toward a Global Civil Society* (Providence and Oxford, 1995), p. 27.
[21] David Harvey, *Spaces of Hope* (Edinburgh, 2000).

to *socialise* definitions of our global order – even to *imagine* its positive reconstruction.

Unfortunately, such freedoms or 'spatial opportunities' (Micheline Ishay) are currently unfolding in a hell-for-leather, Wild West fashion, and are also very unevenly distributed. The freedoms of global civil society are exclusionary and fail to produce equalities; in other words, global civil society is not genuinely global. It is not a *universal* society. Vast areas of the world, and certainly the large majority of the world's population, are excluded from active involvement. True, they 'participate' within this society in the minimal sense that they are sometimes seen fleetingly, by the privileged, mostly as anonymous television or newspaper images and broken voices and reported tales of woe. In an era of rapid communications, the marginalised know that the world is a ladder on which some go up and most go nowhere, or down. They see and feel their abjectness refracted through their encounters with the guardians of power and prosperity. The wretched of the earth come to develop a world-wide reputation for malnutrition, disease, homelessness and death.

They are seen as well as victims robbed of a voice by the cruel facts of communication poverty. It is common knowledge that three-quarters of the world's population (now totalling 6 billion) are too poor to buy a book; that a majority have never made a phone call in their lives; and that only 5 per cent currently have access to the Internet.[22] It is less common knowledge (according to US State Department figures) that as many as 4 million men, women and children annually are being bought, sold, transported and held against their will in slave-like conditions. For its victims, global civil society means the freedom of others to exploit them – in quick time, at great distances. It means as well rising vulnerability to the destructive or infectious powers of others: whereas smallpox, first discovered in the Nile Valley 1,300 years ago, reached the continent of Australia only during the nineteenth century, the AIDS virus took merely three decades to penetrate to all four corners of the earth. The global epidemic has so far left 50 million people infected, of whom 16 million have died. Around 14 million children have consequently been orphaned; and in countries like Lesotho and Zimbabwe, where one-fifth of all children have lost their parents, whole social fabrics are torn by crumbling household structures.

From their side, the excluded and victimised 'participate' within global civil society in a second minimal sense: thanks to aid programmes, television and Hollywood films, they know something about the lives of the rich and powerful of the world. Struggling to make ends meet, they are

---

[22] John Keane, *On Communicative Abundance* (London, 1999).

aware of how insubstantial is their share of the world's wealth and power and style. They sense that their lives are permanently under the shadow of 'Westerners' and things 'Western': They are subjected to crude and aggressive prejudices of those who shadow them. They feel scorned, like a 'wrongful' majority. They know that being marginal means being condemned to a much shorter life. They are made to feel like victims of a predatory mode of foreign intervention: they feel shut out from global civil society, or uprooted by its dynamism, or imprisoned within its discriminatory structures and policies, like unpayable debt-service payments, or victimised by hunger or scores of uncivil wars.[23]

Others – many Muslims say – feel profound disappointment, tinged with anger and righteous indignation. They reason that the enormous potential of global civil society to expand dialogue among civilisations, to 'affirm differences through communication', is being choked to death by the combined forces of global markets and military might, manifested for instance in the long-standing and dangerously self-destructive alliance between the United States and Israel[24]; some deeply religious Muslims influenced by 'salafi' ideology blast that alliance as world-threatening. They reject foreign ideals such as democracy and urge violent action leading to the establishment of an Islamic order based upon the 'sovereignty of shari'a' (Taqiuddin An-Nabhani). Still others are gripped by feelings of humiliation: of being crushed into impotence that derives from the failure to be understood, the simple inability to make their voices heard, to be recognised as the potential makers of their own histories. Then, finally, there are the damned who curse quietly or express open hatred for this civil society – or who join Dostoevsky's underground man by drawing the defiant conclusion, against all things 'reasonable' and 'Western', that two plus two indeed equals five. From there, it may be only a step or two to picking up a gun – to fight for the cause of ridding the world of the hypocrisy and decadence of an immediate aggressor, or a pseudo-universal way of life.

All these reactions serve to fuel the conclusion that global civil society today resembles a string of oases of freedom in a vast desert of localised injustice and resistance. The metaphor – familiar in the Arabic contrast between *al-mujtama' al-madani* (civil society) and *al sahara*, the desert, with its connotations of savagery, the unpolished and unrefined – can be prolonged for a moment, in order to draw another necessary conclusion:

---

[23] Fred R. Dallmayr, 'Globalization from Below', *International Politics*, 36 (September 1999), pp. 321–34, Richard Falk, *Predatory Globalisation. A Critique* (Oxford, 1999), chapter 8; and Orhan Pamuk, 'The Anger of the Damned', *The New York Review of Books*, November 15, 2001, p. 12.

[24] Interview with Professor Abou Yaareb al-Marzouki, Hammamet, Tunisia, 18 April 2001.

that it is important as well to see that the privileges within this oasis cannot be taken for granted. Global civil society currently suffers a serious deficit of legitimacy: not only does it generate enemies who make a fist in their pockets, but it is also marked by the absence of widely held 'common values'. There is certainly plenty of moral 'spirit' within this society: movements, organisations, groups and individuals project and defend ideas and values that bear crucially upon the ways the world should be organised. Yet the old rule that a common sense of belonging is necessary for a community to survive and thrive does not apply – or so far does not hold – for global civil society. It contains no 'self-evident truths' (in the sense of the American revolutionaries) and indeed any attempt to project a particular bundle of norms as candidates for 'Common World Values' – to do with such familiar modern versions of principles as Race, Religion, History, Nation – appears both reactionary and divisive. Global civil society is at best bonded together by norms that are strongly procedural – commitments to due process of law, political democracy, social pluralism – and also by norms – like civility and the commitment to non-violence – that have a highly variable content or are revocable under certain conditions. The upshot is that this society is highly vulnerable to the charge that it contains no binding moral Esperanto or 'world values', and that consequently 'many people feel as though they have lost control of their lives'.[25] And so, unsurprisingly, the plural freedoms of global civil society are threatened constantly by the fact that it is a breeding ground for manipulators who take advantage of its available resentments and freedoms by waving the sword of ideologies above the heads of others.

The growth of borderless economic exchanges encourages certain winners, some global corporations for instance, to cultivate talk that slakes their thirst for power over others. Free market ideology linked with turbocapitalism – talk of deregulation, capital account liberalisation, stable money, budgetary restraint, structural adjustment, the privatisation of the public sector, opportunity, risktaking, performance, consumer choice – has a strong affinity with these corporate winners. This ideology, sometimes called the 'Washington consensus' (a term first used by the economist John Williamson), encourages those who believe in it to turn a blind eye to the contradictions of turbocapitalism. It puts business on a tall pedestal. 'The problem for capitalism', writes one of its ideologists, 'is that many people – including many capitalists – seem to have forgotten that it's the most powerful force for good the world has seen'. Global business reduces poverty, raises employment standards, and

---

[25] From the speech by Amitai Etzioni to the colloquium, 'Diversity Within Unity' (Centre for the Study of Democracy, London, 25 April 2002).

promotes human rights and democracy. 'So it's time for the capitalists and anti-capitalists to make common cause', concludes the ideologist. 'It's time that campaigners for social justice and environmental protection saw business as their ally, not their enemy.'[26] Such talk massages the conscience of the rich, if they have one. It encourages them to feel invincible. They are charmed into believing that they are clear winners, that they no longer have to sit at the same table with their trade union or consumer critics. Clustered around turbocapitalist firms and their servicing professions, the new rich even come to feel that they have no 'need' of the new poor – even that the freedoms of civil society themselves are a tradeable commodity.

Borderless exchanges also produce strong political reactions in favour of the local and national. Sometimes these localist reactions are dogmatic. They are often led by public figures – Patrick Buchanan, Pim Fortuyn, Pauline Hanson, Vladimir Zhirinovsky – who behave like the albatrosses of globalisation. Harbingers of political storms, they rail against the whole dirty business of 'Euro-globalisation' (Jean-Marie Le Pen). It stands accused of robbing 'us' of 'our' jobs because of competition from low-paid 'foreign' labour and cheap 'foreign' imports. The dogmatists play on the fact that in various parts of global civil society, except Japan, the number of foreign-born workers has been rising in recent decades. More than 7 million Mexican-born people are now living in the United States; and in the European Union, there are an estimated 20 million legal (and 3 million illegal) immigrants. The 'anti-globalisation' dogmatists bowdlerise the point: they ignore the fact that most trade is between the richest countries, and that (for example) unskilled and low-paid jobs in these countries are typically in the service sector, which for obvious reasons is comparatively insulated from global competition and often suffers labour shortages. The dogmatists play on protectionist impulses. They warn citizens that 'their' own country is already 'full', and that (as Pim Fortuyn said repeatedly before his assassination in 2002) 'foreigners', with their peculiar, bigoted beliefs, are diluting the precious culture of tolerance for which civil societies are renowned.[27] Sometimes the dogmatists preach revenge. 'Why should we create suffering for ourselves?', Vladimir Zhirinovsky once asked. The answer was quick: 'We should create suffering for others.'[28]

---

[26] Steve Hilton 'The Corporatist Manifesto' *Financial Times Weekend* (London), 20–21 April 2002.

[27] Correspondence with Percy Lehning (Amsterdam), June 2002. On the general problem of nationalism, see my *Civil Society: Old Images, New Visions* (Oxford and Stanford, 1998), pp. 79–113.

[28] *Financial Times* (London), 9 December 1993.

Such unpleasant proto-nationalist talk reminds us that global civil society (as Ulrich Beck has observed[29]) is not some new kind of meganational society that contains and dissolves all national identities into itself. It is rather a vast landscape of multiple and non-integrated identities, including national identities that are produced and preserved in and through the communications systems of the society itself. No necessary harmonising effects are produced from within this landscape. Its losers sometimes react to their disempowerment resentfully, by taking revenge upon others, sometimes cruelly, guided by thoroughly modern ideological presumptions, like xenophobic nationalism or dogmatic religiosity. Racist ideology functions in a similar way. Although its roots are traceable to late medieval Europe, racism too began to flourish only from the time of the nineteenth century, mainly in the Western hemisphere, where the rejection of hierarchy as the governing principle of social and political life nurtured both the quest for meaning and a sense of self-worth and political aspirations for equality *in this world*. The term 'racism' began to be used only during the 1920s, when it signified, as it still does today, a rejection of the ideal of a civil society. Racists are those who react suspiciously against others in social spaces by concentrating on the different physical markings of their bodies and then wrapping them in fearful and arrogant, if inchoate presumptions of emotional and intellectual inferiority. Its arbitrary stereotypes are often self-confirming, but in every case they serve (as Loury puts it[30]) to 'spoil' the collective identities of civil society by treating others as dangerously different.

These grim incivilities reveal that the plural social spaces of global civil society, some of which are tissue-thin, are constantly threatened with ransacking or takeovers in the name of some or other organised ideology. Ideologies are upwardly mobile, power-hungry and potentially dominating language games. They make falsely universal claims. In so doing, they mask their own particular conditions of production, and attempt to snuff out the plurality of language games within the actually existing global civil society or surrounding state structures in which they were born.[31] The proponents of ideologies like free market competition, nationalism and racism take advantage of the growth of global civil society by roaming hungrily through its free social spaces; they try to convince the unconverted that 'it is often safer to be in chains than to be free' (Franz Kafka);

---

[29] Ulrich Beck, *What is Globalization?* (Cambridge, 1999), Introduction.
[30] Glenn C. Loury, *The Anatomy of Racial Inequality* (Cambridge, MA and London, 2002); see also George M. Frederickson, *Racism: A Short History* (Princeton, 2002).
[31] This revised understanding of ideology is developed in my 'The Modern Democratic Revolution: Reflections on Lyotard's *The Postmodern Condition*', in Andrew Benjamin (ed.), *Judging Lyotard* (London and New York, 1992), pp. 81–98.

they treat others as competitors, or as enemies to be defeated, or injured, or left to starve to death. In consequence, inequalities of power, bullying and fanatical, violent attempts to de-globalise are chronic features of global civil society. Understood normatively as a trans-national system of social networks of non-violent polyarchy, global civil society is a wish that has not yet been granted to the world.

The triangle of violence

The legitimation problems of global civil society should remind its friends of the need to examine carefully, as well as strategically confront, the principal threats to its survival and future growth. Violence against civilians – the unwanted physical interference with their bodies that typically causes them pain and mental anguish and, in the extreme case, death – is undoubtedly one of the greatest enemies of this society. Violence is anathema to its spirit and substance. This follows, by definition, because global civil society is marked by a tendency to non-violence. This stems from the fact that many of its participants – not all of them, it should be emphasised – share a peacefully cosmopolitan outlook on the world, for instance by displaying a strong distaste for war, a genuine interest in others' ways of life, a facility or respect for different languages, or a simple commitment to ordinary courtesy and respect for others, whatever their skin colour, gender or geographic background. This learned quality of non-violent openness is paradoxically reinforced by the fact that the daily lives of its participants are normally cloth-bound in inherited habits and structured routines that might seem banal in their repetitiousness, but are in fact highly intricate and complex in the way they work.[32] The existential foundations of daily life are the 'raw material' of civility. The members of global civil society are animals of erect stature. They find it painful to remain upside down for long and therefore not only have a common understanding of up and down, but prefer uprightness. They likewise have shared notions of left and right, of immobility or motion, and because they have bodies, arms and legs they comprehend what it means to move, to squash, to kick, to be hit by something hard. Conceptions of constraint come easily to these beings: they dislike it when others prevent them from talking, or swallowing, or obstruct their motion, or strike or physically hurt them. These dispositions are enmeshed in non-violent webs of more or less taken-for-granted commitments: conversations, gestures, washing their bodies, patience, laughter, sexual play, housecleaning, shopping for items produced in more than one country, planning journeys, tending crops and

---

[32] Thomas L. Dumm, *A Politics of the Ordinary* (New York and London, 1999), chapter 4.

plants, worrying about income, filling out forms, paying bills, preparing food, looking after others, watching television, reading newspapers, telling children about the world and putting them to bed.

We have seen that the contemporary revival of interest in civil society, and the corresponding invention of the new term global civil society, had much to do with such experiences of the past century as total war, aerial bombardment, concentration camps, and the threat of nuclear annihilation. Violence is a great catalyst – and vicious enemy – of civil society. And so it is necessary, if disconcerting and painful, to reflect for a moment on the problematic forms of violence which today surround and threaten global civil society. Quite aside from the ongoing tendency of local civil societies to produce troubling amounts of violence – rapes, muggings, gang-land crimes, murders[33] – linked to humiliation, poverty, frustration, physical and mental exhaustion, emotional abandonment and the loss of intimacy, there is also mounting evidence that global civil society, despite the end of the Cold War, is today falling under the shadow of an unstable *triangle of violence.*

One side of the triangle is the instability caused by nuclear-tipped states in the post-Cold War world system of cosmocracy. This system (as we have seen) is dominated by the United States, which can and does act as a vigilante military power backed by nuclear force. As a vigilante power, it is engaged in several regions without being tied permanently to any of them, but its manoeuvres are complicated by the fact that it is presently forced to co-exist and interact peacefully with four powerful states within the system of cosmocracy, three of whom are nuclear powers: Europe and Japan (zone A), and China and Russia (zone B) (see figure 3.1).[34] The geometry of this arrangement clearly differs from the extended freeze imposed by the Cold War, when (according to Raymond Aron's famous formula) most parts of the world lived in accordance with the rule, 'peace impossible, war unlikely'. With the collapse of bipolar confrontation, this rule has changed. There is no evidence of the dawn of a post-nuclear age, and the freedom from the fear of nuclear accident or attack that that would bring. Nowadays, as Hassner has explained, peace has become a bit less impossible and war a bit more likely, principally because a form of unpredictable anarchy has settled on the whole world.[35]

---

[33] See my *Reflections on Violence* (London and New York, 1996), esp. pp. 107ff.

[34] Barry Buzan, 'Rethinking Polarity Theory: Reflections on the Meaning of "Great Power"', unpublished paper (Centre for the Study of Democracy, London, March 2000).

[35] See the concluding interview in Pierre Hassner, *La violence et la paix: de la bombe atomique au nettoyage ethnique* (Paris, 1995), esp. pp. 23–61: 'In the past, the doctrine of deterrence matched the civil character of our societies: an invisible hand, or abstract mechanism,

It may be that nuclear weapons have so reduced the need for mass mobilisation of troops that they have enabled a permanent 'civilianisation' of daily life in some Western states.[36] Insofar as these weapons have also tended to make unlikely war between the dominant powers, it may be true as well that the probability of a nuclear apocalypse, in which the earth and its peoples are blown sky-high, has been permanently reduced.[37] Perhaps. Yet the actors and institutions of global civil society need to be on guard: perpetual peace is a very long way off in the future. There are various reasons for this. The key political powers are currently preoccupied with seeing through a possible 'revolution in military affairs',[38] in which military forces will be geared increasingly to electronic intelligence gathering, computerised communications networks, protective screens and highly destructive, precision-guided or 'smart' weapons capable of use anywhere on the globe. It is highly doubtful whether such weapons can eliminate 'frictions' (von Clausewitz) from battles. There are doubts too about whether the claimed level of precision can be affordably and reliably achieved, or about whether civilians uninterested in military heroism will be prepared to witness, in silent gratitude, the violent elimination of others by remotely piloted vehicles, nano-weapons and sophisticated information systems. Major wars using these and more old-fashioned weapons remain a long-term possibility, including even the use of nuclear-tipped weapons in conflicts that originate in local wars and conflicts.

took charge of our security, and we did not have to bother our heads with it. But today the nuclear issue can no longer be considered in isolation, it is inextricably mixed up with everything else.' A more activist perspective is provided by Helen Caldicott, *The New Nuclear Danger* (New York, 2002).

[36] Paul Hirst, *War and Power in the 21st Century. The State, Military Conflict and the International System* (Oxford, 2001), p. 39.

[37] A classic reflection on the problem is Hans Morgenthau's *Politics Among Nations: The Struggle for Power and Peace* (New York, 1954). Following the nuclear attack on Japan, he claimed that the avoidance of a nuclear Third World War required the structural transformation of the anarchic territorial state system into a world state. He saw that requirement as necessary, but as impossible to satisfy. No world state – except one that was imposed in the aftermath of a Third World War – could be built unless it was built upon a sense of world community nurtured by shared moral and political values. Morgenthau concluded that such a world polity was unlikely, since no such community of values was available, either in the present or in the foreseeable future. Some observers, including the American 'realist' scholar Kenneth Waltz, have turned Hans Morgenthau's conclusions upside down, to argue that the gradual spread of nuclear weaponry is more to be welcomed than feared, principally because the rising dangers of accident or attack will spawn the growth of global self-restraint in all matters nuclear. See Jonathan Schell, 'The Folly of Arms Control', *Foreign Affairs* 79:5 (September–October 2000), pp. 29–30.

[38] The policy trends are analysed in M. O'Hanlon, *Technological Change and the Future of Warfare* (Washington, DC, 2000); E. A. Cohen, 'A revolution in warfare', *Foreign Affairs* 75:2 (March–April 1996), pp. 37–54; and in the contributions to J. Arquilla and D. Ronfeldt (eds.), *In Athena's Camp: Preparing for Conflict in the Information Age* (Santa Monica, 1997).

Surgeons speak of enucleation to describe the process of removing tumours from shells. The same term could be used to describe a basic political priority of the friends of global civil society: the systematic removal of nuclear weapons and weapons-making systems and materials from its structures of government. The priority will be hard to realise; alternative scenarios are equally likely. Global civil society is embedded within a risk-producing system in which the possibility of a damaging theft or spillage of nuclear materials, or nuclear reactor meltdown or the open use of nuclear weapons is chronic. A taste of things to come is perhaps the routine dropping of depleted uranium shells on the victims of war. Meanwhile, nuclear weapons abound – the arsenals of the United States and the Russian Federation each contain somewhere around 7,000 nuclear warheads.[39] And despite the 1972 Anti-Ballistic Missile Treaty, nuclear capacity, as can be seen in the nuclear arms races between Pakistan and India, and between Israel and the Arab states, is spreading, despite any prior agreements about the rules of nuclear confrontation and despite the fact (revealed in the so-called National Missile Defense system planned by the Bush administration) that the issue of nuclear weapons is now deeply implicated in the so-called 'modernisation' of weapons systems. American officials, aware that their old Cold War rival is no longer so, now like to speak of a 'generic' threat, a bundle of potential dangers that might well arise at any moment, somewhere else in the world. Hence the investment, since the early 1980s, of some $60 billion in the project of developing a National Missile Defense programme that takes aim at 'rogue' powers equipped with nuclear weapons. One trouble with this project is that there are potentially large numbers of rogues – the US State Department currently lists forty-four governments endowed with nuclear weapons' capacity – and that the world of cosmocracy is already confronted by rivalries between newcomer nuclear governments. The world's first nuclear confrontation unrelated to the Cold War – five tests conducted by India in May 1998, followed by seven tests by Pakistan – has been reinforced by a long sequence of new and equally threatening developments: the Iraqi government's expulsion of UN weapons inspectors; North Korea's ongoing efforts to build weapons; continuing doubts about Russia's ability to keep safe its nuclear weapons and materials (despite American contributions of $2.3 billion per annum under the Nunn–Lugar legislation); and American assurances that it will not object to China's plans to expand its nuclear arsenals – which would lead to the end of the current world-wide moratorium on nuclear testing, as codified in the Comprehensive Test Ban Treaty. Like the seeds planted by Cadmus,

[39] *The Times* (London), 10 February 2001, p. 16.

nuclear armaments appear to be breeding nuclear armaments. Talk of 'throw-weight gaps', 'windows of vulnerability' and 'missile gaps' admittedly no longer echoes through the corridors of cosmocracy. Yet ominous signs are everywhere. New revelations of past and present administrative carelessness and 'normal' nuclear accidents are streaming into public circulation. Disturbing compensation claims against the malfeasance of nuclear-tipped governments are finding their way into the cosmocracy's courts. Plans are afoot to develop 'mini-nukes', precision-guided, low-yield nuclear weapons that suppose that the principle of casualty-free battle can be extended to nuclear war. The sequence of developments actually runs longer and deeper than this, and is by definition (like the future) uncertain. But the conclusion is unavoidable: global civil society is framed by a cosmocracy that produces a risk-producing rabble of self-interested nuclear powers sharply opposed to the aim of either reducing or abolishing outright nuclear weapons systems.

Uncivil war

Global civil society is threatened as well by the violence unleashed in uncivil wars: armed conflicts that rip apart political institutions, poison the institutions of civil society, and fling their combatants into self-preoccupation with survival.[40] Examples of this second side of the triangle of violence are to be found in abundance, and include two decades of fighting in the Sudan, fuelled by constant imports of arms that reach the hands of state and non-state actors, who struggle to use these arms in highly complex ways to preserve or acquire land, cattle, wealth and power. The conflict has resulted in the death of at least 2 million people and another 4 million are refugees in their own country – internally displaced people, in the jargon of the INGO world.[41]

Despite many differences, uncivil war zones of the Sudanese kind are marked by similarities. Those who are caught up in their maelstroms of violence suffer a shrinking of existential horizons caused by unimaginable cruelties: armies, militias and rag-tag criminal gangs rape, pillage and murder to the point where all remaining islands of civility are wrecked, beyond repair. The violence is typically fuelled by global flows of arms, money and men, who take advantage of the fact that local political institutions are crumbling and competitor power groups are jostling for territory

[40] Uncivil wars are analysed in my *Reflections on Violence*, pp. 131ff.
[41] See Francis Deng, *War of Visions* (Washington, DC, 1995); Abdelwahab El-Affendi, *For a State of Peace. Conflict and the Future of Democracy in Sudan* (London, 2002); and the report by the International Crisis Group, *God, Oil and Country. Changing the Logic of War in Sudan* (Brussels, 2002).

and resources. Whole populations are consequently dragged down into dark holes of violence. The results can hardly be described or analysed as 'civil war', a term that supposed that the combatants were locked into a violent but disciplined struggle for control over the key resources of territorial state power. Civil wars are carefully planned and executed struggles to seize or to preserve the means of state power by using rational-calculating violent methods. They are considered civil because civilians participate in the struggles for state power; and they are considered to be wars because violence is used as a tactical means by all parties.

The problem here with the concept of civil war is its inability to grasp the ways in which struggles for political power can and do easily become a euphemism for the most terrible experience of criminal anarchy, destruction and death. The Sudan, Sierra Leone, Kashmir, the ill-named Democratic Republic of the Congo are just a few of the many conflicts just beyond the boundaries of global civil society in which combatants' violent struggle makes a terrible descent into hell – towards a place where the means and acts of violence seem to take on a life of their own, so that violence becomes a grisly end in itself. It is as if the violent can affirm their identity only through violence projected onto others. The violent need enemies who appear to threaten them with extinction, and who therefore must be persecuted, tortured, mutilated and annihilated. In uncivil war zones, violence has a profound functional advantage. Rivalries, jealousies, quarrels within the community of the violent are projected outwards, onto others, in life-affirming acts of desperate cruelty against 'surrogate victims'.[42] All sober restrictions governing the ground rules of war are swept aside. The enemy is demonised as all-powerful, as all-threatening, as all-violent. Hence, the rituals of violence against them are repeated endlessly, shamelessly. Acts of violence become gratuitous. The killers' faces look blank. Sometimes they smile. Their words are cynical, or clichéd accounts of their private or group fantasies. There are plenty of alibis, certainly, but the laws of engagement are unnervingly transparent: murder and counter-murder innocents, sever the hands and genitals of the enemy, cut out their tongues or stuff their mouths with stones, destroy graveyards, rape women, poison or torch food, make sure their blood flows like water. Guarantee that there are no innocent bystanders. Punish waverers – like the moderate Hutu leader, Agathe Uwilingiyimana, who was murdered by her fellow Hutus for her moderation, her half-naked body left dumped on a terrace, a beer bottle shoved up her vagina.

---

[42] René Girard, *La violence et le sacré* (Paris, 1972); cf. the fine study of the uncivil war in the Lebanon by Samir Khalaf, 'The Scares and Scars of War', in *Cultural Resistance. Global and Local Encounters in the Middle East* (London, 2001), esp. pp. 201–33.

Everybody on the side of the violent must be baptised in blood, made into an accomplice of the crimes. Ensure that they witness rape, torture and murder. Make sure that they do not forget what they have done. Trouble global civil society with painful questions: what class of unreason prompts a Rwandan priest to set fire to his own church where terrified citizens have sought sanctuary, or Serbian bulldozer drivers to dig mass graves *before* murders begin? What instincts drive Bosnian Serb torturers to amuse themselves by forcing their Muslim victims to bite off the testicles of other Muslims? What manner of people are we who accept such degradation in our midst? Finally, when all is said and done: be prepared to boast to journalists or courts of law that the butchers are heroes, that the victims are fictions or that they deserved what they got – that this was no crime against humanity.

Terrorism

Every nook and cranny of global civil society, including its more local networked components, is threatened by another, relatively more recent form of violence: apocalyptic global terrorism. Terroristic violence of this kind arguably dates from the early 1980s. Of course, the phenomenon of terrorism – the word itself dates from the revolutionary *terrorisme* of the period from March 1793 to July 1794 in France – is not new. Its so-called 'classical' forms include operations that use (or threaten to use) violence to instil fear into others for the purpose of achieving defined political goals. While states can certainly be terrorist, in the sense that they can use assassins and other violent under-cover agents to govern through their subjects' fear of violent death, terrorism of the non-state variety is typically the work of fighters who are neither uniformed soldiers nor organised in elaborate hierarchical command structures. They are trained in the arts of handling explosives and light weaponry, usually within urban areas. Unlike guerrillas, such as the Revolutionary Armed Forces of Colombia (FARC), terrorists do not seek to occupy their enemy's territory; even though they too use lightning attacks and swift retreats, terrorists have neither the numerical strength nor military capacity nor the will to physically defeat their opponents. Like rats in a sewer, they operate in small and practically autonomous units within the more or less invisible channels of the local civil society, in order to wear down and demoralise their governmental enemy, whom they suppose – ultimately, despite everything – to be capable of negotiation, concession and retreat. New means of communication, such as mobile phones and the Internet, definitely enable terrorists to widen and multiply their contacts into all-channel networks, all the while keeping their activities invisible or 'private' in order – paradoxically – to win over public support for their case. Propaganda of the violent deed is among their specialties. So too is the struggle for victory by means of fear induced by measured acts of violence that have socially and politically disruptive effects.

The cruel but *measured* deployment of violence – not indiscriminate killing on a large-scale – was always and still remains a critical feature of classical terrorism. Basque, Irish and Colombian gunmen, hijackers and bombers mean business and want publicity, but the cruelty and panic they inflict is restrained. They do not wish to kill lots of people, which is why terrorism of the apocalyptic kind is a new departure. It is true that strongly 'classical' elements of terrorism are evident in the suicide attacks on American and French military facilities in Beirut in the early 1980s, the sarin attack on the Tokyo Metro, the bombing in early 1995 of the Federal Building in Oklahoma City, the simultaneous attacks on the American embassies in Dar es Salaam and Nairobi in August 1998, and the assaults on the Pentagon and the World Trade Center in September 2001. Each one of these attacks aimed at a fundamental change of the political order; and each unleashed violence in urban settings without however attempting to occupy its territory. Yet each one of these attacks also represented a rupture with past tactics. Their protagonists supposed that they were engaged in total war against an enemy unworthy of negotiation and incapable of compromise. The enemy was seen as both morally null and void and worthy of annihilation. Hence unlimited violence, bloodcurdling in its technical simplicity and witnessed by millions, is justified. The aim is to choose targets – key symbols of American power, for instance – and then to kill indiscriminately on a massive scale. The point is neither to win over public support nor to negotiate political deals. A deathly zero-sum game has to be played. Responsibility need not be claimed. The rottenness of the present-day world should be exposed. Nothing but catastrophe should result.

The politics of civility

Future historians may well look back on the past half-century and see in each of these depressingly violent trends not only the end of the distinction between war and peace. They may also record that we lived in times when the three sides of the triangle became so tightly linked that (as two Chinese military scholars, Liang and Xiangsui, have argued[43]) a new form of 'unrestricted warfare' swallowed up the whole world. Is the triangle of violence that now surrounds global civil society a prelude to

---

[43] Qiao Liang and Wang Xiangsui, *Unrestricted Warfare* (Beijing, 1999).

a more quarrelsome and barbarous Hobbesian world – perhaps even (as Guglielmo Ferrero first envisaged[44]) a regression into 'medievalism'? Are we fated to live in a global order riddled with violence, suspicion of enemies and restless struggles that produce universal fear – an order in which civil society institutions and customs have little or no place? Nobody of course knows. Perhaps indeed our fate has been so decided. Perhaps the capacity of the late modern world to draw a triangle around itself – a triangle bounded by apocalyptic terrorism, uncivil war and nuclear annihilation – and, within its bounds, to imagine and then to execute the end of its own existence, will prove to be self-confirming.

The challenge for the defenders of global civil society is to find fresh beginnings, to invent long-term remedies against violence, in order to prove that our fate has not yet been decided, and that this special form of society after all still has a future. A positive counter-trend in all this rather depressing reality should certainly not be overlooked. For among the most promising features of global civil society is its self-spun traditions of civilising politics – its actors' capacity to nurture networks of publicly organised campaigns against the archipelagos of incivility existing within and beyond its frontiers. These campaigns have a long history.[45] They extend well back in time, for instance to include the first transnational social movement in modern times: the campaign to abolish the slave trade, which had the backing of groups like the Pennsylvania Society for Promoting the Abolition of Slavery (formed in 1775), the Société des Amis des Noirs (formed in France in 1788) and the British and Foreign Anti-Slavery Society. This cross-border campaign – explicitly religious movements aside – was arguably the first moral entrepreneur to emerge out of the structures of civil society, to play a prominent role in world politics by pressing for new prohibition laws that would apply globally.[46] During the nineteenth century, networks of activists also sprang up to publicise the need to halt the trafficking in women and children within and across borders; in the same period, civil initiatives pressing for

---

[44] Guglielmo Ferrero, *Peace and War* (London, 1933), p. 96.
[45] See L. C. White, *International Non-Governmental Organisations* (New Brunswick, 1951); Chiang Pei-heng, *Non-Governmental Organizations at the United Nations. Identity, Role, and Functions* (New York, 1981), chapter 2; and Bill Seary, 'The Early History: From the Congress of Vienna to the San Francisco Conference', in Peter Willetts (ed.), *'The Conscience of the World': The Influence of Non-Governmental Organisations in the UN System* (Washington, DC, 1996), pp. 15–30.
[46] See Mary Stoughton Locke, *Anti-Slavery in America* (Cambridge, MA, 1901), pp. 87–98; Betty Fladeland, *Men and Brothers: Anglo-American Antislavery Cooperation* (Urbana, 1972), p. 258; David Brion Davis, *The Problem of Slavery in the Age of Revolution, 1770–1823* (New York, 1999); and Ethan A. Nadelmann, 'Global Prohibition Regimes: The Evolution of Norms in International Society', *International Organization*, 44 (1990), pp. 479, 495.

relief from the violence of war also became prominent. Prototypical was the International Committee of the Red Cross (first named the International Committee for the Relief of Wounded Soldiers). Born after the 1859 Battle of Solferino, its first outlines appeared after the Geneva Public Welfare Society voted to set up a committee in support of wounded soldiers. That committee called for the establishment of voluntary societies in every country of the world, and for an international conference of state and non-state delegates, subsequently held in 1864, at which approval was given to both the first-ever Geneva Convention and the committee that became the International Committee for the Relief of Wounded Soldiers.[47] The founding of The Save the Children Fund after the First World War is part of the same longer story of civil society initiatives against wanton violence. Médecins Sans Frontières, formed after the Biafran War, and Oxfam – established to provide civilian relief to Greece, when it was still under Nazi occupation, against the wishes of the British government – count as other examples.

Such civil initiatives against incivility, the attempts to nurture civility within global civil society and in turn to build 'bridgeheads' that expand the geographic reach of global civil society, are today a feature of all zones of violence. Some efforts, like protests against nuclear weapons and installations, engage in direct action, for the purpose of publicising to the world the grave risks linked to the global spread of nuclear technologies. A similar global focus is evident in the activities of organisations like Saferworld – a London-based research and lobby group that specialises in efforts to publicise the potentially deadly effects of global arms flows and to pressure bodies like the European Union into restricting arms sales to dictatorial states and armies that abuse human rights in uncivil war zones. Other organisations, like Human Rights Watch, actively 'witness' others' suffering in violent areas like Burma, Sierra Leone, Rwanda and southern Sudan. Or they push for the elimination of landmines, or biological weapons, or (like Amnesty International, which has more than 1 million members in 162 countries) campaign against political repression, especially maltreatment of the body and unfair imprisonment. Still others attempt to act as human shields against aggressors (in defence of the Palestinians against Israeli troops in the West Bank, for instance); or they negotiate ceasefires, or provide comfort for lives ruined when civilians are turned into refugees. And some groups – for their pains – find themselves targets of global criticism for prolonging or complicating

---

[47] James Avery Joyce, *Red Cross International and the Strategy of Peace* (London, 1959); and Martha Finnemore, 'Rules of War and Wars of Rules: The International Red Cross and the Restraint of State Violence', in John Boli and George M. Thomas (eds.), *Constructing World Culture* (Stanford, 1999), pp. 149–65.

uncivil wars, for instance by sheltering hostages, feeding aggressors, or serving as cover for warring armies.

A dilemma – and a strategy

Social campaigns to civilise global civil society – to democratise or publicly control the use of violent means[48] – are among the vital preconditions of its survival and growth. These campaigns throw into question the triangle of violence by robbing it of its supposed 'naturalness' or inevitability. Violence is seen to be a temporal, all too temporal affair. And the implication is clear: with will and effort, these means of violence could be eradicated from the world. This much is clear. Yet social campaigns to democratise the means of violence are presently hampered by complexities and countervailing trends, which are perhaps better described as a single dilemma that the defenders of global civil society need to recognise, to worry about, and practically to address.

Put simply, the dilemma that confronts global civil society is that it is incapable of bringing peace to the world through its own efforts. Global civil society thrives upon non-violence – yet it arguably requires violence to preserve and nurture its non-violence. Since it is vulnerable to various forms of violence, that stem either from within or without its boundaries, global civil society needs political/constitutional protection backed up by armed force. Quite aside from the deep uncertainty about whether adequate governing institutions can be developed at the global level to do this (see the earlier discussion of cosmocracy), its civilian members by definition do not have the available means of violence (police and standing armies) to eradicate that violence. Of course – as happens always at the point at which a civil society degenerates into an uncivil society – civilians can themselves resort to picking up guns, to point them at their violent opponents who lurk within or on the fringes of the global civil society. But that would undermine the shared culture of civility on which global civil society rests.

This institutional weakness of global civil society is compounded by its own plural freedoms: to the extent that global civil society enjoys such civil freedoms it can easily be taken for a ride by mercenaries, gangs, wired-up hooligans, mafia, arms traffickers, terrorists, private security agents and psycho-killers, all of whom cavort with the devil of violence by using, misusing and abusing the peaceful freedoms of that society.[49]

---

[48] The idea of democratising violence is explained in my *Reflections on Violence*.

[49] See Mark Findlay, *The Globalisation of Crime. Understanding Transitional Relationships in Context* (Cambridge and New York, 1999).

Global civil society is further threatened by the fact that the organised violence (potentially) needed to protect its citizens has a nasty habit of getting out of hand – arms breed hubris – thereby threatening everything that global civil society stands for. As the merchants of the early civil societies of the Italian city-states first recognised,[50] standing armies, with their sanguinary arrogance, are as dangerous as they are necessary. The citizens of global civil society thus require *limited* armed protection by authorities who can themselves turn against (or turn their backs on) those citizens, or act recklessly or foolishly, or contrary to their own and others' best interests.

Exactly what all this means in practice is context-dependent and cannot therefore be decided in advance, in accordance with some or other set of universal rules.[51] Every effort to reduce or to rid global civil society of violence must: pay attention to the degree of compatibility between the chosen means and the defined end; consider the possible or probable unintended consequences of a chosen course of action; be on the lookout for hubris in all its forms – and, as well, be alert constantly to the overriding need to preserve and nurture the non-violent plural freedoms of the global civil society itself. For this reason, despite contrary claims about imperatives of secrecy, the use of armed force, which always involves two-edged swords that easily slash fingers, is best guided by publicly scrutinised judgements, especially when it is used in the name of fostering civility. Gung-ho militarism and blind or one-eyed pacifism are enemies of global civil society. The awareness of complexity and dangerous unintended consequences is its friend.

Examples of this mode of political reasoning about violence easily spring to mind. Given that the act of ridding the world of nuclear weapons is desirable, how is this best achieved? What weapons systems would replace the bomb? How will nuclear plants and weapons be decommissioned, and can legal compensation and something like 'truth and reconciliation' processes help the world come to terms with the long history of suffering and long-term damage caused by the invention of the bomb? Given that the new form of apocalyptic terrorism operates like a deadly enemy from within the entrails of global civil society, what activist forms of surveillance, policing and military action are required to reduce the civil fear that it induces and to defeat it militarily? Are these means at all compatible with the preservation of the institutions and 'spirit' of civil society, which can suffer implosion and – under extreme

---

[50] See the remarks on the relationship between markets and organised violence by Harold D. Lasswell, *World Politics and Personal Insecurity* (Chicago, 1935), p. 23.

[51] See my *Reflections on Violence*, pp. 61–104.

conditions – suffer sociocide when threatened by fear and violence?[52] Are there other limits upon what can be achieved through the counter-violence of police and the armed forces?

These questions are challenging, and they suggest – in the case of uncivil wars – the need for bold and imaginative practical answers that must bite the bullet, quite literally. For among the most difficult political problems yet to be solved is if, how and when armed intervention can legitimately be used to put an end to uncivil war and so to keep alive, even to extend, the project of global civil society. Reactions to this 'Guernica paradox'[53] – the need to use violence to stop violence – range from suspicion to resistance. Activist supporters of global civil society understandably worry about the general erosion of civil freedoms that normally accompanies military and police action. Civilian life does not take kindly to the loss of sleep and frayed nerves induced by orders to strip and be searched, or by helicopter gunships hovering over the heads of urban residents, or by flag-waving and talk of the need for permanent war against evil. Political power may well grow out of the barrel of guns, but the velvet power of civil institutions thrives on permanent de-commissioning of weapons and strategies of social pacification. That is why many friends of global civil society understandably shy away from talk of violence: like the International Network of Engaged Buddhists, they have a principled commitment to active non-violence, or they have simply seen enough of violence, and therefore pragmatically prefer pacific means of protecting and nurturing the lives of defenceless citizens. Conventional 'realists', by contrast, doubt that civil society can become the good-natured cavalry of peace and freedom. They point out that might often triumphs over right. They defend the formula that sovereign are those who actually decide to use force to protect citizens, which begs hard normative questions about who *can* and who *should* shield our emerging global civil society from violence, and under what circumstances. The answer provided by the post-Shoah advocates of 'just' or humanitarian war – that the violent enemies of global civil society should be fought wherever they make a move – arguably legitimates eternal war, particularly in a world bristling with incivility. 'If wars should be waged everywhere that human rights are derided', comments one observer sarcastically, 'then they would embrace the whole of the planet, from Korea to Turkey, from Africa to China'.[54]

---

[52] See my 'Fear and Democracy', in Kenton Worcester *et al.* (eds.), *Violence and Politics. Globalization's Paradox*, pp. 226–43.

[53] Geoffrey Robertson, *Crimes Against Humanity. The Struggle for Justice* (London, 2000), chapter 11.

[54] Jean Clair, 'De Guernica à Belgrade', *Le Monde*, 21 May 1999, p. 16.

Does that necessarily follow? Arguably not, if only because the geo-military scope of non-nuclear humanitarian intervention is constrained by the fact that the United States, the world's dominant-power – despite its ability to act as a rogue power that can act with impunity – is presently forced, within the structures of cosmocracy, to co-exist and interact peacefully with the four great powers of Europe, Japan, China and Russia. Not only that, but especially under 'post-Vietnam', conditions, when log-rolling politicians' fear of casualties leads them to rely on the use of computerised, 'low-risk', aerial bombardment as their preferred means of 'humanitarian intervention', war can be waged only by the dominant power and its allies, in a very limited number of uncivil contexts: like those of Kosovo and Afghanistan, where the marauding forces to be bombed are geographically strategic but without powerful friends, and weak enough to be defeated easily but sufficiently strong to make the sensible calcula-tion to lay down their arms and refrain from using further violence.[55]

These preconditions of successful military intervention are exact-ing, to say the least. They imply that talk of the 'end of geography' (Paul Virilio) is premature; and that exaggerated contrasts between the nineteenth-century struggle for mastery over territory and the 'post-modern' weaponry of 'speed and facility of movement' (Bauman) must be doubted. The bitter fact is that there are presently *territorial* limits upon global civil society. That is not to say that the whole idea and nor-mative ideal of a global civil society is mere bunk – or that it has 'hardly started anywhere except in philosophers' study rooms'.[56] Global civil so-ciety has an *unfinished* quality about it. There are whole patches of the earth where its institutions and ethos have made little or no headway – Russia, China, Pakistan, North Korea, Algeria, Saudi Arabia – and where zones of uncivil war – Chechenya, Kashmir, the Democratic Republic of Congo – are effectively 'no-go' areas for military intervention. For the moment, in other words, all these geographic areas are safe in their out-right opposition to, or violation of, the principles and practice of global civil society.

Social pacification

There are perverse ironies in all this, above all that most uncivil wars are fuelled by armaments that are disproportionately produced and supplied

---

[55] See Edward Luttwak, 'No-Score War', *Times Literary Supplement*, 14 July 2000, p. 11. Other limitations of 'post-heroic' aerial bombardment are examined in Michael Ignatieff, *Virtual War* (London 2000), and in 'The New American Way of War', *The New York Review of Books* (20 July 2000), pp. 42–6.

[56] Zygmunt Bauman, 'Wars of the Globalization Era', *European Journal of Social Theory*, 4:1 (2001), p. 14.

globally by turbocapitalist firms based in the old civil societies of countries like the United States, France and Britain (which in 1998 alone sold weapons worth £9 billion). There are as well profound difficulties generated by efforts to stop uncivil war. In the limited number of cases where military ('humanitarian') intervention has put an end to those conflicts by force of arms, the political project of extending the reach of global civil society has had to learn the difficult art of social pacification. Military interventions, for instance those in Afghanistan and Kosovo, resemble hit-and-run affairs. Like a metal hammer that pounds a wooden stake into the earth, their aim is to beat the enemy into submission, in the expectation that the earthly elements of time will dissolve the sentiments that once nurtured the foe. The military action is reminiscent of nomads' strikes against their adversaries. Armed to the teeth, the attackers travel light; they rely on their ability to swoop down on their victims, to inflict the maximum harm, then to retreat, all the while knowing that there will be no retaliation by those who have been violated. One trouble with the strategy is obvious: the power to force others into submission does not translate spontaneously into the power of the survivors to form themselves into stable government and a law-enforced civil society. The psychic traumas, damaged tissues of sociability and ecological and infrastructural damage inflicted by the war of intervention are left untreated.

In some quarters of the victors' camp, nobody cares: when the job is done, the vanquished are tacitly written off (as Kipling once put it) as 'lesser breeds without the Law'. From the point of view of the survivors on the ground, things look rather different. It is as if the power to act in the world has stopped flowing through people's veins. Their trust in themselves and others, their ability to make long-term plans through households, partnerships, neighbourhoods and other associations, has been badly damaged. Efforts to build or re-build civil society out of the ruins of war start from this point.[57] So do the difficulties. Although the crafting of peaceful social relations is an essential antidote to the ruins left behind by uncivil war, talk of the need for a civil society is no all-purpose magic wand. Dahrendorf's sober warning is well-taken: 'It takes six months to create new political institutions, to write a constitution and electoral laws. It may take six years to create a half-way viable economy. It will probably take sixty years to create a civil society. Autonomous institutions are the hardest things to bring about.'[58]

---

[57] Compare the Commission of the European Communities document, *Linking Relief, Rehabilitation and Development* (Brussels, 1996), p. 6: 'Rehabilitation must be conceived and implemented as a strategy encompassing institutional reform and strengthening . . . People – both victims and participants – must be reintegrated into civil society.'

[58] Ralf Dahrendorf, 'Has the East Joined the West?', *New Perspective Quarterly*, 7:2 (Spring 1990), p. 42.

Why should civil society institutions – more broadly defined here than in Dahrendorf's use – be so difficult to reconstruct? There are several reasons. Turbocapitalist firms are often reluctant to play the role of economic wizards by taking risks and investing in the social and economic infrastructure wrecked by uncivil war. Meanwhile, in matters of relief and rehabilitation, compared with governments, NGOs are often comparatively flexible and innovative, low cost, and responsive to grass-roots pressures. But their qualities do not arise *spontaneously* or *automatically*. They are often constrained by counter-trends and unintended consequences. For instance, the task of rebuilding a civil society from the ground upwards is not a substitute for the essential task of building effective and legitimate governmental structures, which is why relief and development work is frequently scuppered by local warlords and armed gangs and private armies.[59] To the extent that civil society-building relies upon NGOs as conduits for aid money, in the expectation that this maximises sustainable development, it often turns them into hostages of fortune, with mixed dividends. Donor funding can and does overwhelm or distort the goal of creating a civil society. It tends to create local organisations that are excessively self-centred and blessed with power that is publicly unaccountable, partly because they are so heavily dependent on their donors; and partly because the staff of these NGOs (as the South African joke has it) En-J-Oy all sorts of privileges otherwise denied those living in misery around them. Finally, the institutional rules and organisations of civil society presuppose the emotional willingness of actors to get involved with others, to talk with them, to form groups, to change loyalties. In a civil society, this propensity of women and men to associate freely and to interact with others is not linked to any one particular identity or group, whether based on blood, geography, tradition or religion. The capacity for free association also requires women and men to renounce ideological groups,

---

[59] See I. William Zartman (ed.), *Collapsed States. The Disintegration and Restoration of Legitimate Authority* (Boulder and London, 1995) and D. Porter and P. Kilby, 'Strengthening the Role of Civil Society in Development? A Precariously Balanced Answer', *International Affairs*, 50:1 (1996), p. 32: 'civil society is not likely to thrive, unless there is an effective, strong state which can establish the rules of the game and provide some discriminatory framework for civil society activities.' Rather than speaking in the idealised Woodrow Wilsonian language of an 'effective, strong state' that is territorially sovereign, it would be much better to speak about the imperative of instituting 'governmental structures' that can tame lawlessness and bring violence to an end. In reality – the Lebanon is a case in point – so-called sovereign states can very often not be built at all; where they can, they are certainly not constructed overnight. The theory of cosmocracy anyway implies that our world is not principally composed of sovereign states; that the peaceful integration of political structures into governmental hybrid forms is a precondition of a global civil society; and that political order therefore can be restored in a variety of ways, not simply by chasing after the will-o'-the-wisp ideal of state integrity.

movements and parties driven by nationalism or xenophobic racism. A civil society supposes that women and men can live with a variety of others in complex ways, that they can control their vengeful impulses, that they are capable of *sociability* and therefore have in their hearts the ability to trust and be loyal to others – so loyal, in fact, that they feel strong enough to stand up to others and to organise against them. The trouble is that these dispositions can neither be agreed and written in round-table meetings or conventions, like constitutions, nor manufactured on assembly lines, like automobiles. These delicate 'civil' qualities take time to grow. They cannot be planned or legislated from above. They best hatch and grow in milieux like urban areas, where 'the transformation of the geography of fear into a culture of tolerance'[60] can take place through architectural design, the regeneration of small and large businesses, the staging of popular culture and the performing arts, and the promotion of curricular reform at schools and a wide variety of clubs and competitive sports.

Hubris

It is a well-known rule that the ambitious desire to have more than one's share of power is a chronic feature of social and political life, and one that inevitably produces disastrous effects.[61] The tendency towards hubris certainly applies to global civil society and its dynamics. The critics of global civil society, including those who question the very concept because there is 'no common global pool of memories; no common global way of thinking; and no "universal history", in and through which people can unite',[62] overlook or understate the advantages of its heterogeneity in warding off hubris. Global civil society resembles a bazaar, a covered kaleidoscope of differently sized rooms, twisting alleys, steps leading to obscure places, people and goods in motion. It is marked by increasing differentiation, thickening networks of structures and organisations with different but interdependent *modi operandi*, multiplying encounters among languages and cultures, expanding mobility,

---

[60] See Célestin Monga, *The Anthropology of Anger. Civil Society and Democracy in Africa* (Boulder and London, 1996); and the important reflections on efforts in urban settings to 'pacify the pathos' left behind by uncivil wars in Samir Khalaf, *Cultural Resistance. Global and Local Encounters in the Middle East* (London, 2001), esp. chapters 10 and 11.

[61] See the account of hubris in my *Václav Havel: A Political Tragedy in Six Acts* (London and New York, 2000), pp. 278–86.

[62] David Held, *Democracy and the Global Order. From the Modern State to Cosmopolitan Governance* (Stanford, 1995), p. 125. The same point is made in A. B. Bozeman, 'The International Order in a Multicultural World', in Hedley Bull and Adam Watson (eds.), *The Expansion of International Society* (Oxford, 1984).

growing unpredictability, even (despite growing numbers of full-time moderators and mediators) a certain depersonalisation and abstractness of its social relations. Such complexity is sometimes said to be a threat to democracy.[63] That is false, as John Dewey long ago emphasised, for the struggle against simplified definitions of social life and 'the social good' is a hallmark of a mature civil society.[64]

It is nevertheless true that complexity alone does not release global civil society from the laws of hubris. It is not only that the plural freedoms of global civil society are potentially disabled by the political framework of cosmocracy within which it operates. The problem of hubris is *internal* to global civil society as well: just like the domestic civil societies that form its habitats, global civil society also produces concentrations of arrogant power that threaten its own openness and pluralism. Stronger legal sanctions, governmental regulation and armed protection can ameliorate these inequalities, but are there additional ways of ensuring that its social freedoms can be nurtured and redistributed more equally at the world level?

The growth, since the mid-nineteenth century, of a globe-girdling, time–space conquering system of communications is arguably of basic importance in this respect.[65] Communications media like the wheel and the press had distance-shrinking effects, but genuinely globalised communications began only with inventions like overland and underwater telegraphy and the early development of Reuters and other international news agencies. The process has culminated in the more recent development of geo-stationary satellites, computer-networked media and the expanding and merging flows of international news, electronic data exchange and entertainment and education materials, thanks to giant firms like Thorn–EMI, Time–Warner, News Corporation International, Disney, Bertelsmann, Microsoft, Sony and CNN.

The globalisation of communications media has had several long-term effects upon global civil society. Most obviously, global media linkages have helped to do something much more persuasively than the maps of Gerardus Mercator ever did: to deepen the visceral feelings among millions of people that our world is 'one world', and that humans share some responsibility for its fate.

---

[63] Jessica Matthews, 'Power Shift', *Foreign Affairs*, 76:1 (January–February 1997), p. 64.
[64] The point is made in a little-known essay entitled 'Civil Society and the Political State', in Jo Ann Boydston (ed.), *John Dewey. The Middle Works, 1899–1924* (Carbondale and Edwardsville, 1978), pp. 404–33.
[65] Peter J. Hugill, *Global Communications Since 1844. Geopolitics and Technology* (Baltimore and London, 1999).

Eagle on the Moon

Consider just one watershed media event: the coverage of the day – Monday 20 July 1969 – two men openly defied the laws of gravity to set foot on the Moon's crinkled surface. 'Forty feet, down two and a half. Picking up some dust', crackled Buzz Aldrin's voice from the landing craft *Eagle* towards the Earth's radios and television sets. A few more minutes, a few more fuzzy words. 'Contact light. Okay. Engines stop.' After a string of procedures designed to 'safe' the vehicle, Neil Armstrong spoke: 'Houston, Tranquillity base here. The Eagle has landed.' An estimated world-wide audience of 600 million people, one-fifth of the world's population, watched the events of the rest of that day on television. The two-man crew of the Eagle told their navigators back on Earth that they weren't sleepy. So Aldrin and Armstrong were given permission to prepare for a two-hour expedition. They would collect rock samples, plant the Stars and Stripes, perform simple experiments, take more photographs, set up a television camera and solar-powered instruments to send information a quarter-of-a-million miles back to Earth. Just before ten o'clock that evening, American Central Daylight Time, Armstrong eased his white-suited bulk down a ladder. He paused, squinting through a gold-plated visor designed to reflect the sun's unfiltered glare. 'The surface appears to be very, very fine-grained as you get close to it', he said. 'It's almost like a powder.' He again paused, then carefully lowered his left boot onto the grimy black surface of the Moon. 'That's one small step for [a] man', he said excitedly, the first human ever to peer back towards Earth from the surface of the Moon, 'one giant leap for mankind'.[66]

Around the world, public reactions to these words varied. Confident euphoria predominated. Most commentators – echoing the words of John F. Kennedy when announcing, some years earlier, that an attempt would be made to get hold of the Moon and put it in our pockets – said that a page of human history had been turned. They spoke of the landing as a human triumph over nature, a challenge to go forward, a call to apply human know-how to the task of improving the human condition. Some saw it as a target of colonisation, a new holiday destination, a place where food could be grown in glasshouses, or some part of the

---

[66] Either because of a communications glitch, or because he forgot the article 'a', Armstrong's words were received on Earth as 'That's one small step for man, one giant leap for mankind'. He was later nonplussed and emphasised that the sentence was ungrammatical. That was so, but everyone understood its intended meaning. See Andrew Chaikin, *A Man on the Moon. The Voyage of the Apollo Astronauts* (London and New York, 1994), esp. pp. 206–19, and Charles Murray and Catherine Bly Cox, *Apollo. The Race to the Moon* (London, 1989), pp. 354–6.

world's population housed. Not everybody agreed. Some reacted flip-
pantly, or sarcastically. The words of Armstrong prompted women in a
north London neighbourhood to paint a large sign on a long brick wall,
proposing that since a man had now landed on the Moon, all men should
now be rocketed there. Others, bearing the weight of the world on their
shoulders, grew convinced that God no longer was prepared to keep
wolves and the Moon apart; amid the raw display of technological power,
they smelled hubris. 'I don't know whether you're frightened' remarked
Europe's most prominent philosopher. 'I am when I see TV transmissions of the earth from the Moon. We don't need an atom bomb. Man
has already been uprooted from the earth. What's left are purely technical
relations. Where man lives today is no longer an earth.'[67]

Arguably that view – that the Western project of human lordship over
nature had taken an arrogant, twenty thousand-league stride forwards and
upwards into the air – proved incorrect. The 'step forward for mankind'
served to bolster public perceptions, however vague, about the breathtak-
ing scale and complexity of the universe in which planet Earth is embedded. Such perceptions are different, say, than those commonly expressed
at the end of the nineteenth century, when human beings unimpressed
by religion did not know where they had come from, where they were,
indeed did not even realise that they did not know any of this. Matters of
that kind were seen to be the subject of metaphysics, or of meditations,
like those found in Blaise Pascal's *Pensées* (1670), on the 'disproportion-
ality' of humankind in comparison with the infinity of the solar system.
By contrast, the expedition to the Moon bolstered many people's feeling of smallness and insignificance. They sensed not only that Earth is a
modestly sized planet, but also that our galaxy, the milky ribbon that is
barely visible to the naked eye on moonless nights, is itself part of a group
of around thirty galaxies, the so-called Local Group, that measures some
4–5 million light years in diameter and is separated from other galaxies
by huge distances of black space.

So, although this was not intended, the expedition to the Moon fed
feelings about how, from simple beginnings, the universe has spawned
ever more intricate structures, of which human life on Earth is one result.
Astronomers have supported these feelings by pointing out that we have
reached something like a natural limit in our ability to see beyond our
horizons within the universe as we know it. This is not for lack of more
powerful instruments, but because far-distant objects – and the light trails
they leave – are moving away from our Earth and its Moon faster and

---

[67] From a posthumously published interview with Martin Heidegger in *Der Spiegel*, 23
(31 May 1976), pp. 193ff.

faster, some of them at or beyond the speed of light.[68] The 'event horizon', they say, is proving to be a natural limit upon what we can know of our environment. We know only that our universe has boundaries of which we are condemned to know little or nothing. That ignorance contradicts the unduly pessimistic, strangely homocentric conclusion that the Moon landing endangered humanity by tempting it to play dice with God – today the Moon, tomorrow the universe.

That conclusion proved to be wrong on another front, for the most astute witnesses of the Moon landing foresaw that it would have the un-intended effect of breathing new life into the old principle – vital for global civil society – of human responsibility for the Earth. Buzz Aldrin himself later captured something of this implication by pointing to a paradox: while standing on the Moon, he and Armstrong were farther from the Earth than anybody had been, he said, and yet both of them at the time had felt an almost mystical sense of closeness and unity with the rest of humankind.[69] Why was this so? The Moon landing arguably had the effect of making life on Earth seem more fragile. Not only did it serve as yet another reminder that only in the last tick of geological time did humans appear on Earth – that our world is but a parenthesis in eter-nity. The landing also served as a humbling reminder that human life rests precariously on an unknowable foundation of deep time – perhaps 4.5 billion years – within a vast universe of unknowable extent. Conse-quently, human life seemed more closely bound up with the fate of the world as we experience it: the world of rocks and rivers, birds and flowers, winds and clouds. The Gaia hypothesis developed by James Lovelock – Gaia was the Greek goddess of the Earth – is one version of this sense that humans and nature are in it together.[70] The hypothesis underscores the tightly coupled quality of Earth's physical and biological systems. The living organisms that comprise its biota of living plants, birds and ani-mals do not simply adapt passively to the material environment, which comprises the atmosphere, the oceans and surface rocks; these organ-isms change it constantly by selectively taking advantage of it. The Gaia hypothesis sees humanity as merely one element within this constantly changing process of cycling and recycling. It thereby warns against the simple-minded presumption that Earth is the slave of humanity. Although humans are latecomers to the world scene, it implies, we are currently doing things that may well have incalculably large effects on the biota, the physical environment, and upon ourselves as well. Earth could well take

[68] Armand Delsemme, *Our Cosmic Origins. From the Big Bang to the Emergence of Life and Intelligence* (Cambridge and New York, 1998).

[69] Chaikin, *A Man on the Moon*, p. 213.

[70] James Lovelock, *The Ages of Gaia. A Biography of our Living Earth* (Oxford, 1995).

its revenge on humanity. Indeed, the tight coupling of the environment of the Earth makes it impossible to predict the effects of such developments as the quickening depletion of natural resources, the extinction of other organisms at about a thousand times the natural rate, or the rising carbon levels in the atmosphere. That same tight coupling rules out simple solutions, like proposals that humans be stewards of the Earth. Given their history of heavy-handedness towards Earth, the hypothesis suggests, humans are as qualified to be its stewards as goats are to be gardeners. This leaves but one thing certain: that nothing is certain except that humanity must stand more humbly in the presence of Gaia.

Global publics

Granted that media coverage of the Moon expedition helped nurture our sense of worldly interdependence, what else can be said about the relationship between communications media and global civil society? It goes without saying that today's global communications system is an integral – aggressive and oligopolistic – sector of the turbocapitalist system. Ten or so vertically integrated media conglomerates, most of them based in the United States, dominate the world market.[71] They prioritise advertising-driven commercial ventures: music, videos, sports, news, shopping, children's and adults' filmed entertainment. Programme-making codes, in the field of satellite television news for instance, are consequently biased along turbocapitalist lines. They are subject to specific rules of market *mise-en-scène*. For instance, special emphasis is given to 'news-breaking' and 'block-busting' stories that concentrate upon accidents, disasters, political crises and war. And the material fed to editors by journalists reporting from or around trouble spots (called 'clusterfucks' in the vernacular) is selected – many stories are judged a non-story – shortened, simplified, repackaged and transmitted in commercial form. Staged sound-bites and 'live' or lightly edited material are editors' favourites; so, too, are 'flashy' presentational technologies, including the use of logos, rapid visual cuts, and 'stars' who are placed centre-stage. News exchange arrangements – whereby subscribing news organisations exchange visual footage and other material – then take care of the rest, ensuring a substantial homogenisation of news stories in many parts of the globe, circulated at the speed of light.

---

[71] R. Burnett, *The Global Jukebox* (London, 1996); A Mohammadie (ed.), *International Communication and Globalization* (London, 1997); and Edward S. Herman and Robert W. McChesney, *The Global Media: The New Missionaries of Corporate Capitalism* (London and Washington, DC, 1997).

These trends lead some observers to conclude that global communications media produce turboprogrammes for turbocapitalist audiences who are politically inactionary. They warn of the *embourgeoisement* of the skull. They insist that American-style, turbocapitalist culture is becoming universal because it is universally present. Algerian-desert dwellers smoke Marlboro. Nigerian tribespeople huddle around their televisions watching hand-me-down *Dallas*. Chinese peasant workers dream of driving a Chrysler. So global civil society is under great pressure to adopt more or less unaffordable turbocapitalist living standards adjusted to local conditions, many of them originally American, like automobility, Windows xP, Nike trainers, skateboards, Mastercards, shopping malls and endless chatter about 'choice'. If during the eighteenth century a cosmopolitan was typically someone who thought *à la française*, who in other words identified Paris with cosmopolis, then three centuries later, thanks to turbocapitalism, a cosmopolitan might turn out to be someone whose tastes are fixated on New York and Washington, Los Angeles and Seattle. Turbocapitalism produces 'McWorld': a universal tribe of consumers who dance to the music of logos, advertising slogans, sponsorship, brand names, trademarks and jingles.[72] 'The dictatorship of the single word and the single image, much more devastating than that of the single party', laments Eduardo Galeano, 'imposes a life whose exemplary citizen is a docile consumer and passive spectator built on the assembly line following the North American model of commercial television'.[73] Using ugly words, others express similar concerns about 'monoculture of the mind' (Vandana Shiva) or 'global cultural homogenization' in the form of 'transnational corporate cultural domination': a world in which 'private giant economic enterprises pursue – sometimes competitively, sometimes co-operatively – historical capitalist objectives of profit making and capital accumulation, in continuously changing market and geopolitical conditions'.[74]

Such laments correctly warn of the dangers of cultural monopolies, but they are overdrawn, partly for reasons to do with the marketing

---

[72] Benjamin Barber, *Jihad vs. McWorld: How Globalism and Tribalism are Reshaping the World* (New York, 1995).

[73] Eduardo Galeano, cited as the epigram in Herman and McCheshey, *The Global Media*, p. vi. More prudent assessments are presented in Aihwa Ong, *Flexible Citizenship: The Cultural Logics of Transnationality* (Durham, 1999); Richard Packer, *Mixed Signals: The Prospects for Global Television News* (New York, 1995); Michael Schudson, 'Is There a Global Cultural Memory?', unpublished paper (University of California at San Diego, 1997); and Mike Featherstone, 'Localism, Globalism and Cultural Identity', in R. Wilson and W. Dissanayake (eds.), *Global–Local: Cultural Production and the Transnational Imaginary* (New York, 1996), pp. 46–77.

[74] Herbert Schiller, 'Not Yet the Post-Industrial Era', *Critical Studies in Mass Communication*, 8 (1991), pp. 20–1.

process itself: as we have seen already, the retailing of consumer products like McDonald's, Dominos and Pepsi, if anything, has had the effect of *accentuating* cultural diversity within global civil society. Partly this is because profit-seeking, turbocapitalist retailers themselves see the need to tailor their products to local conditions and tastes (hence the statements by Coca-Cola: 'We are not a multinational, we are a multi-local'). It is also partly because local consumers of commercial media reciprocate: they display vigorous powers of reinterpreting these commodities, of giving them new and different meanings. True, globally marketed culture is not the product of an equal contribution of all who are party to it, or exposed to it. Few are consulted in its manufacture – and yet, despite everything, that culture, disproportionately Atlantic in style and content, remains permanently vulnerable to the *universal* power to make and take meanings from it. The American golf star Tiger Woods, who once described himself as 'Cablinasian' (a blend of Caucasian, black, Indian and Asian), is one symbol of this power.[75] Boundary-crossing cultural mixtures – 'creolisation' in the form of chop suey, Irish bagels, Hindi Rap, Sri Lankan cricket, 'queer *jihad*', veiled Muslim women logging on to the Internet, the fusion of classical European, aboriginal and Japanese themes in the scores of Peter Sculthorpe – are consequently widespread. Examples of the survival and flourishing of diasporic culture are also commonplace, as are the commercial global successes of cultural products from peripheral contexts – like Iranian and Chinese films, Brazilian telenovelas (exported to more than eighty countries) and the Mexican soap opera 'Los Ricos Tambien Lloran' ('The Rich also Cry'), which was among the biggest television hit in early post-communist Russia. The consequence: culturally speaking, global civil society is a hotch-potch space of various blends and combinations, fusions and disjunctions.

The globalisation of media constantly produces social hybridities. But especially from the time of the world-wide protest of youth against the Vietnam War, the globalisation of media has also had unanticipated *political* effects: it has contributed to the growth of a plurality of differently sized public spheres, some of them global, in which many millions of people witness mediated controversies about who gets what, when, and how.[76] Global media conglomerates create global products for imaginary global audiences: simultaneously, they suppose and nurture a *theatrum*

---

[75] *International Herald Tribune* (Paris), 24 April 1997, p. 3.

[76] See John Keane, 'Structural Transformations of the Public Sphere', *The Communication Review*, 1:1 (1995), pp. 1–22. Adam Michnik has suggested that the recent growth of global public opinion can be seen as the rebirth in different form of an earlier parallel trend, evident within nineteenth-century socialist internationalism, that came to an end with the First World War (interview, Washington, DC, 21 April 2001).

mundi. There is something necessary about this development, in that journalists and broadcasters must presuppose the existence of 'a public' that is listening, reading, watching, chatting, on- or off-line. They know that witnesses of media programmes and outputs are required – that these outputs cannot play for long to an empty house. Of course, not all global media events – sporting fixtures, blockbuster movies, media awards, for instance – sustain global public spheres, which is to say that public spheres are not domains of entertainment or play. They are scenes of the political: within their imagined bounds, power conflicts and controversies erupt and unfold before millions of eyes and ears. They are made possible by wide-bodied jet aircraft, computerised communications and satellite broadcasting with large footprints, thanks to which the public practice of non-violently monitoring the exercise of power across borders has taken root. These global public spheres – the term is used here as an *idealtyp* – are sites within global civil society where power struggles are visibly waged and witnessed by means other than violence and war: they are the narrated, imagined, non-violent spaces within global civil society in which millions of people at various points on the earth witness the powers of governmental and non-governmental organisations being publicly named, monitored, praised and condemned, in defiance of the old tyrannies of time and space.

Global public spheres are still rather issue-driven and more effective at presenting effects than probing the intentions of actors and the structural causes of events. Global public life is also highly vulnerable to implosion: it is neither strongly institutionalised nor effectively linked to mechanisms of representative government. It is a voice without a body politic. Yet in spite of everything, global public spheres have begun to affect the suit-and-tie worlds of diplomacy, global business, intergovernmental meetings and INGOs. Helped along by initiatives like the People's Communication Charter and Transparency International, and nurtured by around-the-clock broadcasting organisations like CNN (available in over 800 million households and many thousands of hotels) and the BBC World Service (which attracts 150 million viewers and listeners each week), global publics have several interesting effects. Few of these are reducible to the dynamics of rational–critical argumentation about matters of sober truth and calm agreement, although this sometimes happens.[77] Some

---

[77] Some limits of the rational communication model of the public sphere, originally outlined in the important work of Jürgen Habermas, *Strukturwandel der Öffentlichkeit: Untersuchungen einer Kategorie der bürgerlichen Gesellschaft* (Neuwied, 1962), are sketched in John Durham Peters, 'Distrust of Representation: Habermas on the Public Sphere', *Media, Culture and Society*, 15 (1993), pp. 541–71, and my 'Structural Transformations of the Public Sphere'.

of their effects are 'meta-political'. Global public spheres, for instance, interpolate citizens of the new global order, in effect telling them that unless they find some means of showing that global civil society is not theirs, then it is. In this way, global public spheres function as temporary resting places beyond familiar horizons; they give an entirely new meaning to the old watchword of Greek colonisation, 'Wherever you go, you will be a *polis*.' 'Dwelling is the manner in which mortals are on the earth', wrote Heidegger,[78] but the implication in that passage that mortals are bound to geographic place misses the new spatial polygamy that global publics make possible. Within global public spheres, people rooted in local physical settings increasingly travel to distant places, without ever leaving home, to 'second homes' within which their senses are stretched. They live locally, and think globally.

Thanks to media narratives that address audiences and probe the wider world in intimate (if ironic) tones, the members of global civil society become a bit less parochial, a bit more cosmopolitan. This is no small achievement, especially considering that people do not 'naturally' feel a sense of responsibility for faraway events. Ethical responsibility often stretches no farther than their noses. Yet when they are engaged by media stories that originate in other contexts – when they are drawn into the dynamic of a global public sphere – their interest is not based simply on prurience, or idle curiosity, or *Schadenfreude*. They rather align and assimilate these stories in terms of their own existential concerns, which are thereby altered. The world 'out there' becomes 'their' world. Global publics are taught lessons in the art of what can be called flexible citizenship: they learn that the boundaries between native and foreigner are blurred, that their commitments have become a touch more multiversal. They become footloose. They are here and there; they learn to distance themselves from themselves; they discover that there are different temporal rhythms, other places, other problems, other ways to live. They are invited to question their own dogmas, even to extend ordinary standards of civility – courtesy, politeness, respect – to others whom they will never meet.[79] Global public spheres centred on ground-breaking media events like Live-Aid (in 1985 it attracted an estimated 1 billion viewers) can even be spaces of fun, in which millions taste something of the joy of acting publicly with and against others for some defined common

[78] Martin Heidegger, 'Building Dwelling Thinking', in *The Question Concerning Technology and Other Essays* (New York, 1982), p. 146.

[79] See Stephen Toulmin's useful reflections on civility as the antidote to dogma in 'The Belligerence of Dogma', in Leroy S. Rounder (ed.), *Civility* (Notre Dame, 2000), pp. 94–100.

purpose. Global publics, staged for instance in the form of televised world news of the suffering of distant strangers, or of multimedia initiatives in campaigns of the kind that led to the UN Declaration for the Elimination of Violence Against Women,[80] can also highlight cruelty; and global publics can also be sites of disaster, spaces in which millions taste unjust outcomes, bitter defeat and the tragedy of ruined lives. The old motto that half the world does not know how the other half lives is no longer true. Media representation spreads awareness of others' damned fates. Its portrayal of disasters does not (automatically, or on a large scale) produce ethically cleansed cynics, lovers of entertainment sitting on sofas, enjoying every second of the blood and tears. The publics that gather around the stages of cruelty and humiliation make possible what Hannah Arendt called the 'politics of pity'[81]: by witnessing others' terrible suffering, at a distance, millions are sometimes shaken and disturbed, sometimes to the point where they are prepared to speak to others, to donate money or time, or to support the general principle that the right of humanitarian intervention – the obligation to assist someone in danger, as contemporary French law puts it – can and should override the old crocodilian formula that might equals right.

The public spheres housed within global civil society have other political effects. Especially during dramatic media events – like the nuclear meltdown at Chernobyl, the Tiananmen massacre, the 1989 revolutions in central-eastern Europe, the overthrow and arrest of Slobodan Milosević, the terrorist attacks on New York and Washington – public spheres intensify audiences' shared sense of living their lives contingently, on a knife edge, in the subjunctive tense. The witnesses of such events (contrary to McLuhan and others) do not enter a 'global village' dressed in the skins of humankind and thinking in the terms of a primordial 'village or tribal outlook'.[82] As members of a public sphere, audiences do not experience uninterrupted togetherness. They instead come to feel that the power relations of global civil society, far from being given, are better understood as 'an arena of struggle, a fragmented and contested

---

[80] Charlotte Bunch *et al.*, 'International Networking for Women's Human Rights', in Michael Edwards and John Gaventa (eds.), *Global Citizen Action* (Boulder, 2001), pp. 217–29.

[81] Hannah Arendt, *On Revolution* (Harmondsworth, 1990), pp. 59–114; and the development of Arendt's idea by Luc Boltanski, *La Souffrance à Distance* (Paris, 1993).

[82] See the introduction to Edmund Carpenter and Marshall McLuhan (eds.), *Explorations in Communication* (Boston, 1966), p. xi: 'Postliterate man's [*sic*] electronic media contract the world to a village or tribe where everything happens to everyone at the same time: everyone knows about, and therefore participates in, everything that is happening the minute it happens . . . This simultaneous sharing of experiences as in a village or tribe creates a village or tribal outlook, and puts a premium on togetherness.'

area',[83] the resultant of moves and counter-moves, controversy and consent, compromise and resistance, peace and war. Public spheres not only tend to denaturalise the power relations of global civil society. They most definitely increase its self-reflexivity, for instance by publicising conflicting images of civility, civilisation and civil society. Publicity is given as well to the biased codes of global media coverage, and to hostile coverage of global civil society itself, for instance by airing claims that it is a soft term without specific gravity, a Western dogma, a mere smokescreen for turbocapitalism, that is, a mere vehicle for 'the useful idiots of globalisation'.[84]

In these various ways, global public spheres heighten the topsy-turvy feel of global civil society. Doubt is heaped upon loose talk that anthropomorphises global civil society, as if it were a universal object/subject, the latest and most promising substitute for the proletariat, or for the wretched of the earth. Global public spheres make it clearer that 'global civil society', like its more local counterparts, has no 'collective voice', that it is full of networks, flows, disjunctions, frictions, that it alone does nothing, that only its constituent individuals, group initiatives, organisations and networks act and interact. Global publics consequently heighten the sense that global civil society is an unfinished – permanently threatened project. They shake up its dogmas and inject it with energy. They enable citizens of the world to shrug off bad habits of parochialism, to see that talk of global civil society is not simply Western bourgeois ideology – even to appreciate that the task of painting a much clearer picture of the rules of conduct and dowries of global civil society, a picture that is absent from most of the current literature on globalisation, is today an urgent ethical imperative.

The contemporary growth of global publics certainly points to the need to bring greater democracy to global civil society.[85] By throwing light on power exercised by moonlight, or in the dark of night, global publics keep alive words like freedom and justice by publicising manipulation, skulduggery and brutality on or beyond the margins of global civil society. Global publics, of the kind that in recent years have monitored the fate of Aung San Suu Kyi or Yasser Arafat, muck with the messy business of

[83] Margaret E. Keck and Kathryn Sikkink, *Activists Beyond Borders. Advocacy Networks in International Politics* (Ithaca and London, 1998), p. 33.

[84] David Rieff, 'The False Dawn of Civil Society', *The Nation*, February 22, 1999.

[85] The exclusion of the theme of public spheres from virtually all of the current literature on globalisation is criticised by Tore Slaatta, 'Media and Democracy in the Global Order', *Media, Culture and Society*, 20 (1998), pp. 335–44. A similar point is made implicitly by Arjun Appadurai, 'Grassroots Globalization and the Research Imagination', *Public Culture*, 12:1 (2000), pp. 1–19.

exclusion, racketeering, ostentation, cruelty and war. They chart cases of intrigue and double-crossing. They help audiences to spot the various figures of top-down power on the world scene: slick and suave managers and professionals who are well practised at the art of deceiving others through images; kingfishers who first dazzle others then stumble when more is required of them; quislings who willingly change sides under pressure; thugs who love violence; and vulgar rulers, with their taste for usurping crowns, assembling and flattering crowds, or beating and teargassing them into submission.

Global public spheres can also probe the powers of key organisations of global civil society itself. While the multiple voices of this society function as vital checks and balances in the overall process of globalisation and cosmocratic government, very few of the social organisations from which these voices emanate are democratic.[86] Publicity can serve as a reminder to the world that these organisations often violate the principle of public accountability. Reminders are served to those who read, listen and watch that its empty spaces have been filled by powerful but unaccountable organisations (such as FIFA and the International Olympic Committee, IOC) or by profit-seeking corporate bodies (like Monsanto) that permanently aggravate global civil society by causing environmental damage, or swallowing up others by producing just for profit, rather than for sustainable social use. Global public spheres can help to expose malfeasance – accounting and stock market frauds of the kind (in the United States, during 2002) that rocked the industrial conglomerate Tyco International, the energy trader Enron, the cable company Adelphia, and the telecommunications giant WorldCom. Global publics can as well help question some of the more dubious practices of some non-profit INGOs: for instance, their bureaucratic inflexibility and context-blindness, their spreading attachment to market values or to clichés of project-speak, or their mistaken belief in the supply-side, trickle-down model of social development. Public spheres can point to the post-colonial presumptuousness of some INGOs, their bad habit of acting as their brothers' keepers, like missionaries, in so-called 'partnerships' that are publicly unaccountable. And public spheres can criticise their smartly-dressed, self-circulating, middle-class elites, sometimes dubbed the 'Five Star Brigade', whose privileges and privileged behaviour contradicts the principles for which global civil society should otherwise be rightly cherished: its diversity of equal organisations, its open toleration of differences,

---

[86] See the important introductory remarks by Michael Edwards in Michael Edwards and John Gaventa (eds.), *Global Citizen Action* (Boulder, 2001), esp. pp. 6–8.

the speed and flexibility with which it forms complex, shifting alliances around a plurality of shared values and interests.[87]

Exactly because of their propensity to monitor the exercise of power from a variety of sites within and outside civil society, global public spheres – when they function properly – put matters like representation, accountability and legitimacy on the political agenda. They pose questions like: Who benefits and who loses from global civil society? Who currently speaks for whom in the multiple and overlapping power structures of global civil society? Whose voices are heard, or half-heard, and whose interests and concerns are ignominiously shoved aside? How could there be greater equality among the voices that emerge from the nooks and crannies of this society? And through which institutional procedures could these voices be represented? By formulating such questions, sometimes succinctly, global publics can help to ensure that nobody monopolises power at the local and world levels. By exposing corrupt or risky dealings and naming them as such; by wrong-footing decisionmakers and forcing their hands; by requiring them to rethink or reverse their decisions, global public spheres help remedy the problem – strongly evident in the volatile field of global financial markets, which turn over US$1.3 trillion a day, 100 times the volume of world trade – that nobody seems to be in charge. And in uneven contests between decisionmakers and decisiontakers – as the developing controversies within bodies like the IOC show – global public spheres can help to prevent the powerful from 'owning' power privately. Global publics imply greater parity. They suggest that there are alternatives. They inch our little blue and white planet towards greater openness and humility, potentially to the point where power, whenever and wherever it is exercised across borders, is made to feel more 'biodegradable', a bit more responsive to those whose lives it shapes and reshapes, secures or wrecks.

---

[87] Some of these undemocratic tendencies within NGOs – satirised in the South African joke that those lucky to have an NGO job can 'En-J-Oy' life – are discussed in Stephen N. Ndegwa, *The Two Faces of Civil Society. NGOs and Politics in Africa* (West Hartford, CT, 1996), esp. chapter 6; Brian H. Smith, *More than Altruism: The Politics of Private Foreign Aid* (Princeton, 1990); and Steven Sampson, 'The Social Life of Projects', in Chris Han and Elizabeth Dunn (eds.), *Civil Society: Challenging Western Models* (London, 1996).

Ethics beyond borders

A travelling ideal

In recent decades, the growth of cross-border publics has led to a rising awareness of the factual growth of global civil society.[1] This awareness, like a shell covering a kernel, contains another insight: that the emerging civil society on a world scale is breathtakingly complex. That is perhaps an understatement, because in reality global civil society is so complex that it appears to our senses as an open-ended totality whose horizons are not fully knowable. Those who try to survey and summarise its contours have the feeling that they are blind geographers. The global circulation of books and magazines, Internet messages, and radio and television programmes combine to spread the sense that this civil society resembles a kaleidoscope of sometimes overlapping or harmonious, sometimes conflicting and colliding groups, movements and non-governmental institutions of many different, often changing colours. Perhaps it is better to speak of global civil society as a dynamic space of multiple differences, some of which are tensely related or even in open conflict. It resembles the inner structures and dynamics of global cities like New York, London, Berlin, Paris or Sydney: a complex and dynamic three-dimensional landscape of buildings of all shapes and sizes, sought-after and down-market areas, organisations of all descriptions, cheerfulness and cursing, public generosity and private thuggery, millions of people on the move, using many forms of transport, in many directions.

This being so, a vital philosophical question with practical implications arises. It is this: given that global civil society has its enemies, and that in any case it contains a plurality of actors living by different norms, is there an ethical language that is politically capable of normatively justifying this civil society? Can a straight answer with a straight face be given to the question, often asked by critics, 'What's so good about global civil society, anyway?' In short, is there an ethic that can do two things: reply

---

[1] See my 'Global Civil Society?', in Helmut Anheier *et al.* (eds.), *Global Civil Society 2001* (Oxford and New York, 2001), pp. 23–47.

forcefully and unambiguously to the doubters and critics of global civil society; and speak to the civil society itself, with the aim of strengthening its reputation, showing its constituents why they should non-violently stand up for their freedoms, work together to observe their duties, strive for mutual recognition and reconciliation, thereby helping to add calm and rigour to the confused or 'battlefield' atmosphere within global civil society – in short, to make it a more liveable space of many kinds of different civil organisations and ways of life?

The search for a new ethic of global civil society is difficult, for several reasons. To begin with, there are few theoretical precedents to fall back on. Research on global civil society is generally undeveloped and nowhere is this more so than within the subject of ethics. When the subject arises, the most common reaction – among the friends of global civil society, at least – is to provide a list of its supposed good qualities, in no special order, often in quite general formulations that sometimes trail off into vagueness. Global civil society is said to be a value-laden term – a 'progressive anticipatory concept'[2] – that is guided by 'normative expectations of a more humane and inclusive world'. There is talk of 'the possibility of an ethical consensus' about the need to support 'global level aspirations for human rights and the rule of law, peace, sustainability, and social justice'. It is also observed that global civil society is a safe haven for values 'like non-violence, tolerance, solidarity, compassion, and stewardship of the environment and cultural heritage'. What these values might mean, whether they are mutually compatible, why they might be desirable, and what practical implications they might have in the hands of a diverse audience of researchers, activists and policymakers – none of this is normally made clear in discussions of the ethical dimensions of global civil society.[3] There is instead quiet agreement that a global civil society is a good ideal. Why it should be so regarded, and how and why its citizens should behave well, and in what sense, are matters left for the birds of this world.

The consequence is that global civil society becomes a heavily contested term, normatively speaking. The contestation is partly due to its strange elusiveness. Exactly because it implies, minimally, greater dignity and freedom among equals on a global scale – their freedom from bossing, violence, and injustice – the ideal of a global civil society demands more than humans seem willing or are capable of giving. What we call global

---

[2] Klaus von Beyme on the 'unthinkability' of a civil society without the concept of 'a state' in 'Die Liberale Konzeption von Gesellschaft und Politik', unpublished paper (Wien, 2001).
[3] See the remarks of Helmut Anheier, 'Measuring Global Civil Society', in Helmut Anheier *et al.* (eds.), *Global Civil Society 2001* (Oxford, 2001), p. 224.

civil society is never 'pure' or 'authentic'. There is never enough of it. It often seems too weak, or absent. We are always chasing it around corners, through halls of mirrors, across uncharted landscapes, up into blue skies. Improvement, perfectibility – and failure – is inscribed within the very ideal of a global civil society.

The job of answering questions about why global civil society is to be preferred is also hampered by the confused and confusing range of divergent claims that are usually marshalled in its favour. That confusion is a definite hurdle in the search for an ethic of global civil society. The confusion may be said to be the end game, or the end result, of a long historical process, dating from the end of the nineteenth century, when the ideal of a civil society was strongly linked with the bourgeoisie, a group that comprised only about one-eighth of the Western population. Its critics had a field day in pointing out that bourgeois values, especially their appeal to 'conscience' and 'charity' and 'self-government', were often a veil thrown over the lust for money and control of others. That was true, but equally undeniable was the wide social impact of its values. The bourgeoisie got involved in public affairs – at the level of local government, for instance – and its arrogance was often tempered with self-doubt about ideals it considered universal. It disliked action based on aggressive impulses. Considered as a whole, it was troubled by the beating of children, the maltreatment of servants, the exploitation of workers and the execution of criminals. So it strongly disliked the passions of the poor and the aristocratic fetish of organised murder that they called war...

In retrospect, we can see that the ethic of a civil society gradually lost its direct link with urban 'bourgeois' social groups and instead became 'scattered' across an ever-widening variety of social and political supporters, who are now located geographically in all four corners of the earth. This scattering of civil society values may be interpreted as the social basis of 'the continuing stability and attractiveness of civil society as a societal model'.[4] It certainly puts paid to the reductionist view that civil society is a merely 'bourgeois' or 'liberal' phenomenon. The standard version of this view goes something like this: the ideal of a civil society evolved within the Western tradition of political thought. It found its empirical moorings in the emerging liberal, bourgeois societies of the eighteenth and nineteenth centuries, especially in the liberal wing of the property-owning classes. Talk of civil society especially flourished in countries distinguished by a stable conjunction of limited constitutional government and private economic enterprise. That continues to be the case, which shows – so

---

[4] Guido Hausmann and Manfred Hettling, 'Civil Society', in Peter Stearns (ed.), *Encyclopedia of European Social History From 1350 to 2000* (New York, 2001), p. 495.

the argument runs – that both the idea and the ideal of civil society is historically specific, a contextually specific good that can be transported to other contexts only at the price of exposing its 'liberal' or 'bourgeois' biases. It thus makes no sense to speak of an ethic of civil society in India[5]; or in China[6]; or in Africa[7]; or even in Poland.[8] It is even less sensible to imagine an ethic of *global* civil society.

In contrast to these reductionist views of global civil society as a 'liberal' or 'bourgeois' ideal, the following reflection on the subject of ethics and civil society takes a more nuanced – and positive – view. It rejects the backward-looking essentialism of those approaches and instead explores the possibility of understanding civil society as a socially mobile ideal with a good deal of travelling potential – with perhaps even a propensity to become a *global* ideal. Once upon a time, talk of civil society was certainly associated with 'the better sort', good decent men, many of them propertied, some of them willing to support revolutionary acts, or instead to crush revolutionaries in the name of a property-owning civil society. Two hundred years later, things are different. The language of civil society has become 'unhinged' from its middle-class and professional and aristocratic origins; like the veritable genie that escaped its bottle, it has wandered off, in several directions. At the risk of sounding old-fashioned, the change that has come over the language of civil society can be put in the terms of the railway simile popularised by Max Weber: given that socio-economic and political groups are self-interested, the norms associated with civil society are the switchmen (*die Weichensteller*) that determine the rails on which their self-interested group action moves. The fact that these railway routes now fan outwards in the shape of global networks means not only that the normative 'reach' of the language of civil society has been greatly extended, certainly when compared with the one-hundred

---

[5] David L. Blaney and Mustapha Kamal Pasha, 'Civil Society and Democracy in the Third World: Ambiguities and Historical Possibilities', *Studies in Comparative International Development*, 28:1 (Spring 1993). A non-standard view – which still shares the reductionist view of civil society as a 'liberal' phenomenon – asserts that civil society, considered as 'a historical phenomenon as well as a theoretical concept', was 'tied to the rise of liberalism', but that today it is important to ask 'the intriguing question of whether it makes sense to think about nonliberal or even nonpluralist civil society' (see the editorial introduction by Simone Chambers and Will Kymlicka to *Alternative Conceptions of Civil Society*, Princeton, 2002, p. 5).

[6] David L. Wank, 'Civil Society in Communist China? Private Business and Political Alliance, 1989', in John A. Hall (ed.), *Civil Society: Theory, History, Comparison* (Cambridge, 1995), pp. 55–79.

[7] Peter Lewis, 'Political Transition and the Dilemma of Civil Society in Africa', *Journal of International Affairs*, 46:1 (Summer 1992), pp. 31–54.

[8] Adam B. Seligman, *The Idea of a Civil Society* (Princeton, 1995); and his 'Civil Society as Idea and Ideal', in Chambers and Kymlicka (eds.), *Alternative Conceptions of Civil Society*, pp. 13–33.

year period 1750–1850, the century of its birth and popularisation.[9] It implies as well that the meanings of this ethical language perforce multiply, essentially because the numbers of locomotives that are steered by this language have greatly expanded, as have the goods and passenger carriages in their tow to all four corners of the earth.

From an ethical standpoint, this globalisation of the language of civil society is a mixed blessing.[10] While it brings hope to millions whose lives are otherwise smothered in violence, poverty and bigotry, it also potentially multiplies the ethical meanings of civil society to the point where the ideal becomes self-contradictory and publicly unconvincing – and publicly attacked as a universally modish weasel word.[11] It is true that there are some signs that this pluralisation of meanings across the globe functions as the condition of a fruitful cross-interrogation of these conflicting meanings and, hence, serves as the prelude to a more cosmopolitan understanding of the ethics of civil society. Certainly, a more cosmopolitan understanding of civil society – of the kind that this theorisation of global civil society is attempting – is much needed. But in the interim, prudence counsels that the recent globalisation of the language of civil society renders it highly vulnerable to the more or less pessimistic judgement that the search for an ethical language that can help in practice to smooth the ruffled feathers of global civil society, to soothe and reconcile its irreconcilable differences and plausibly justify them to the outside world, is nothing but a fool's errand.

The School of Cantankerousness

According to this criticism – let us call it the School of Cantankerousness – global civil society evidently contains a huge *variety* of ethical ways of life that do not cohere into an ethical consensus. That heterogeneity cannot be reduced to one definition, which is unsurprising, according to some writers, because the human condition is riddled with *ethical disagreement* that ensures permanent conflict and power struggles at the heart of global

---

[9] See Manfred Riedel, 'Der Begriff der "Bürgerliche Gesellschaft" und das Problem seines geschichtlichen Ursprungs', in Ernst-Wolfgang Bockenforde (ed.), *Staat und Gesellschaft* (Darmstadt, 1976), pp. 77–108; and my 'Despotism and Democracy: The Origins and Development of the Distinction Between Civil Society and the State 1750–1850', in John Keane (ed.), *Civil Society and the State: New European Perspectives* (London and New York, 1988 [reprinted 1998]).

[10] John Keane, *Civil Society: Old Images, New Visions* (Oxford and Stanford, 1998), pp. 32ff.

[11] S. Gaschke, 'Irgendjemand wird schon helfen', *Die Zeit*, 30 (22 July 1999), p. 8; cf. the diatribe against the concept of civil society as 'overused, overrated, and analytically insubstantial', in Katherine Fierlbeck, *Globalizing Democracy. Power, Legitimacy and the Interpretation of Democratic Ideas* (Manchester and New York, 1998), chapter 6.

civil society. This society 'is a geographically and socially uneven landscape, reflecting inequalities in society at large: landlords and landless
labourers, financiers and slumdwellers, people of different religions or
ethnic origins. It is and always will be contested terrain.'[12]

Chantal Mouffe's recent work on the ethics of 'antagonism' and
'agonism' exploits this point, twisting it against the very ideal of a global
civil society.[13] In effect, her argument is this: social relations are shot
through with power and difference, and difference breeds antagonisms,
which are resolvable, if they are resolvable at all, through the development
of political strategies – the stabilisation of a system of differences through
processes of '*mise-en-forme*' – that rely upon tactical calculations, especially definitions of friends and opponents, who are sometimes outright
enemies. The reasoning (as we shall see) has a suspiciously ontological
ring to it, despite its avowed opposition to all forms of 'essentialism'. It
supposes that civil society is full of potential or actual scoundrels. Stripped
down to its premises, the argument is that the normative ideal of global
civil society is thoroughly incoherent, as one would expect in a world
filled with cantankerousness: 'there is no true meaning of civil society',
comments Mouffe, adding that that is fortunate, since 'it is important
that a confrontation exists between different understandings of the good
society'. The normative ideal of a civil society is also unfeasible. Not only
are its various usages bound together by 'a common distrust of the state'
(an exaggeration that contradicts the prior claim that the language of civil
society has no semantic centre). That vision of a world with less government is utterly naïve, says Mouffe, since much more probable, unless
strictly regulated, is a world in which the principle of *homo homini lupus*
(man a wolf to men) operates to draw everybody into a state of nature.

The view owes much to Thomas Hobbes and, more recently, to the
work of Carl Schmitt, whose classic essay on the concept of the political
supposed the world to be a dangerous place pushed and pulled –
sometimes torn apart – by struggles among allies and opponents to decide who gets what, when and how in the name of some or other ethical
principle.[14] The world is a pluriverse, a dangerous jungle of self-interested
partnerships, venomous tongues, open disagreements, shifting tactical alliances, even outbreaks of violent conflict. These phenomena reflect the

---

[12] Jamie Swift, *Civil Society in Question* (Toronto, 1999), p. 148.
[13] Chantal Mouffe, 'Civil Society Beyond Liberalism and Communitarianism', typescript
of a public lecture delivered in Vienna (30 November 2001).
[14] Here I am drawing on a previous study, 'Dictatorship and the Decline of Parliament. Carl
Schmitt's Theory of Political Sovereignty', in John Keane, *Democracy and Civil Society.
On the Predicaments of European Socialism, the Prospects for Democracy, and the Problem of
Controlling Social and Political Power* (London 1998 [1988]), pp. 153–89.

fact that human beings – here Schmitt acknowledges an insight drawn from Machiavelli – are dynamic and often dangerous creatures who are prone, by force of circumstances, to commit sly and devilish acts. Life constantly involves confrontations with alien others, by strangers with whom conflict, even violent conflict, is both possible and probable. On this view, those who take seriously, at face value, talk of ethical principles, such as rational debate, pluralism, acceptance of differences, understanding and compassion for others, are foolish. Ethics are always and everywhere the convenient masks of power and power conflicts. It follows that considerations of ethical questions are not only (as Mouffe says) naïve; they are also exercises in useless abstraction unless they recognise that *ought* is the concrete refuge of the *is* of power.

The critique of global civil society launched by the School of Cantankerousness has three merits. First, it warns of the need to be on the lookout for *maquillage* – for particular interests dressed up in the fine cloth and jewellery of universal principles. Second, it rightly points as well to the omnipresent possibility of conflict within and among cross-border civil society organisations, networks and movements. It is redolent of Hegel's insight that civil society is a restless battlefield on which interest meets interest. That insight remains important: global civil society, including its more local domains, contains no 'natural' tendency towards equilibrium. It is rather the contingent outcome, the resultant, of its various interacting elements. Finally, the critique launched by the School of Cantankerousness implies the need for legal and political regulation of global civil society. This follows from its rough and tumble quality: for if there is a constant possibility of uncivil deception, cunning and violent opposition from opponents, then global civil society stands in need of measures, enacted and enforced by governing institutions, that maximise its *civility*.

These points are valuable. The friends of global civil society nevertheless need to be suspicious of the way in which the School of Cantankerousness gives short shrift to talk of ethics. It does so because it secretly adheres to an ontology of conflict, thereby contradicting its own disavowal of ontology. It correctly emphasises the contingency of identities and, correspondingly, deigns to heap doubt upon all normatively inclined ontologies – upon all species of normative claims that suppose that there is an underlying reality that exists in itself and has determinate effects upon everybody and everything within the world. The trouble is that the School of Cantankerousness pursues its claims on the basis of an *obsession* with antagonism. 'The same movement that brings human beings together in their common desire for the same objects', writes Mouffe, 'is also at the origin of their antagonisms. Far from being the exterior of exchange, rivalry and violence are therefore its ever-present possibility . . . violence is ineradicable.'[15] This secret attraction to an ontology of conflict – ironically – wins it honorary membership of the Club of Believers in First Principles, a motley philosophical circle that contains other, competing ontologies, each of which vies or cries out for attention as the supposedly best way to live life on this planet called Earth.

The School of Cantankerousness alludes to the importance of democracy – understood as 'agonistic pluralism' – but given its aesthetic attraction to power conflicts and violence (Mouffe describes her political thinking as that of a 'democratic Hobbesian') this seems to rest upon purely tactical considerations. The best institutional conditions of possibility of democracy are left unexamined. The whole approach prematurely calls into question the normative ideal of global civil society – or hastily judges and condemns it to death as an unrealisable, hopelessly naïve utopia. In so doing, the School of Cantankerousness turns a blind eye to the theoretical problem of *alterity*, especially to the need to think against common sense views of clashes and conflicts among groups, to see instead that the self and other, the internal and the external, may well not be opposites, but that they are often enough *always inside one another*. I shall return to this point, and for the moment merely make the more limited empirical observation that the School of Cantankerousness wilfully neglects the (history of) actually existing ethical *agreements* and patterns of *ethical solidarity* that abound within global civil society. The School of Cantankerousness is curmudgeonly: it is less than interested, or downright uninterested, in loyalties and agreements, which are dismissed or devalued as mere tactical moves by otherwise antagonistic combatants. The obsession with antagonism of the School of Cantankerousness leads it to ignore or denigrate the various attempts, made during the past decade, to launch an ethical defence of global civil society. It is important to address and critically assess these attempts, not merely as an exercise in limbering up our thoughts about global civil society, but as a way of enriching our appreciation of its ethical advantages and unresolved ethical problems. Naturally, the topic is large and complex and space does not permit fastidious attention to detail. So let us think for a moment in the simplifying terms of a continuum of possible positions.

A Western ideal?

Standing at one end of the continuum are observers, especially those who are sensitive to time–space variations among ethical views, who insist that

---

[15] 'Foreword' to Pierre Saint-Amand, *The Laws of Hostility. Politics, Violence, and the Enlightenment* (Minneapolis and London, 1996), pp. ix, x.

global civil society is one particular – historically specific – ideal among others. Let us call this approach Particularism. Its various proponents are agreed that global civil society is not a principle that has universal validity. It is unmistakably a child of 'the West', or 'the Atlantic region', despite all grand claims to the contrary. The principle of global civil society – and its corresponding emphasis on non-violence, pluralism, self-organisation, individuality, equality, mutual assistance and self-reflexiveness – may be appealing, but it is nonetheless a *pseudo-universal*. It is the practice of ethical parochialism behind the mask of universal ethics.

Particularists disagree about whether or not the ethic itself should be rejected. There are certainly those who shun talk of global civil society, or who express outright hostility towards it. They say that the fancy ethic of global civil society is reducible to core 'Western' or 'American' values – principally, to the shabby ideology of liberal or market individualism. Various commentators on the Left, supporters of some brand of Marxism included, are certain that the institutional structures and moral standards of the emerging global society are essentially organised by the power relations radiating from 'liberalism' and its corresponding system of private property, market competition, and commodity production and exchange. Global civil society is a new phase of Western *bourgeois* society lubricated by a particular set of historically specific *bourgeois* values. Common sense thinks of global civil society as the silver bullet that is capable of 'opening' repressive regimes and guaranteeing or deepening democratic liberties. It is considered good because it is by definition separated from and opposed to (bad) governmental power. But the sober truth, so the argument of Particularism runs, is that global civil society is 'part of the dominant ideology of the post-cold war period: liberal market capitalism'. The language of global civil society gravely misdescribes the world, and its speakers, whether they know it or not, are 'the useful idiots of . . . the privatization of the world, commonly known as globalisation'.[16]

Such perceptions attract strange bedfellows, including religious opponents of 'globalisation', who agree that talk of global civil society is a stalking horse for 'Western values' and American-led turbocapitalism. There are other Particularists who acknowledge that the principle of global civil society is historically specific, but who at the same time insist on its ethical importance, even superiority, when compared to its rivals on the world scene. 'Most people – especially people relatively untouched by European Enlightenment – simply do not think of themselves as, first and foremost,

---

[16] The quotations are drawn from David Rieff, 'The False Dawn of Civil Society', *The Nation*, February 22, 1999, pp. 11–16. See also my earlier critical account of nineteenth- and twentieth-century socialist mis-representations of the state – civil society distinction in *Democracy and Civil Society*.

a human being', writes Richard Rorty.[17] That some part of the world's population does so is a mark not only of the 'peculiarity' of the 'North Atlantic culture' in which liberal humanism hatched. In spite of its historical contingency, this culture should be understood as 'morally superior' because it is 'a culture of hope – hope of a better world as attainable here below by social effort – as opposed to the cultures of resignation characteristic of the East.'[18]

Rorty does not speak of civil society, only of its morals, which he regards as superior (and hence of global relevance) for reasons that seem rather arbitrary. The West gave birth to the impressive principle of human improvement through social effort – 'a culture of secular humanism' – but even though that principle is only one among many others it is evidently superior. 'There is much still to be achieved', he says at one point, 'but basically the West is on the right path. I don't believe it has much to learn from other cultures. We should aim to expand, to westernise the planet.'[19] Why support this process of Westernisation, others will quickly ask? Rorty does not clearly say, for he wants deliberately to avoid any form of universal reasoning and to stay within the modest confines of Particularism. So too does another species of Particularism, which sets aside the problem by putting forward the bold empirical claim that the global civil society that originated in the West has become a *de facto universal*. An exemplar of this line of reasoning is presented by Buzan and Segal.[20] During the course of the twentieth century, they observe, everwider networks of human contact and organisation were built up, culminating in the creation, for the first time, of 'a single global space for humankind'. Buzan and Segal hesitate in giving this space a name, but it is clear from their account that it consists of various dynamics that elsewhere parade under such names as 'the global economy', 'the international system' of territorial states, and the least familiar term of 'world society', which refers to the growth of shared experiences and identities cultivated by the spread of world-wide communications.[21] The combined effect of these dynamics, Buzan and Segal argue, is that human beings, especially the wealthy, cannot now avoid knowing about each other because their actions intersect in ever more complicated *Western* ways. A coming global 'clash of civilisations' is unlikely, principally because during the

---

[17] Richard Rorty, 'Human Rights, Rationality, and Sentimentality', in *Truth and Progress* (Cambridge, 1998), p. 178.

[18] Richard Rorty, 'Rationality and Cultural Difference', in *Truth and Progress* (Cambridge, 1998), p. 197.

[19] From an interview with Mathias Greffrath and others, 'Den Planeten verwestlichen!', *Süddeutsche Zeitung* (München), 20 November 2001 (translation mine).

[20] Barry Buzan and Gerald Segal, *Anticipating the Future* (London, 1998), p. 74.

[21] Buzan and Segal, *Anticipating the Future*, p. 183.

past four centuries or so there has been an accelerating planetary diffusion of the key factors that gave the West a huge power advantage over rival systems: empirical–analytic science, political liberalism, market-driven industrialisation and the territorial nation-state equipped with modern weapons.

Buzan and Segal compare this triumph of Western ways to the vast penumbra of peoples and cultures influenced by classical Greece and Rome. Just as that 500-year period was followed by nearly 2,000 years of Hellenistic civilisation, from Alexander's conquests to the fall of Byzantium, so too can the 500-year period of 'classical' Western civilisation be distinguished from the multi-centred period of 'Westernistic civilisation' that has now begun. The analogy is stretched further, because during the twentieth century, they claim, the global grip of the West was weakened by several world wars and decolonisation, which signalled the end of its direct political and military control of the planet's peoples and territories. The upshot is ironic: although the power of the West (understood as the core OECD states and economies) has declined, there is much evidence, symbolised by the rise of East Asia, of the triumph of *Westernisation* around the world.[22] The West may have succeeded in conquering the world in the most subtle way possible: through the inculcation of a cluster of Western norms and techniques. Yet that has had the unintended effect of encouraging the world's peoples to think of themselves as equals and even rivals of the old Western core, as actors who are capable of operating at arm's length from it, who have certain entitlements in relation to it and who, on the basis of their new-found power position in the world, feel that they have the authority to act upon it in *Western* ways.

This species of Particularism avoids the concept of a global civil society, even though, when referring to the development of a 'world society' and 'world economy', it clearly has something similar in mind, however vaguely. A price is paid for the absence of the term civil society: the rather one-sided impression is created that the 'single global space' is now framed by 'settled' norms clustered around scientific–technical progress, the market and the system of territorial states and interstate laws and customs (or what is called, following Hedley Bull and others, 'international society'). The analysis rather understates the global turbulence that

---

[22] See Buzan and Segal, *Anticipating the Future*, pp. 185–6: 'The continuing success of East Asia seems to depend on it retaining the fundamental features taught by the Atlantic world. Every successful economy in East Asia has accepted the logic of a market economy. Every society that has done so has also moved down the road to a variation of political liberalism and primary stress on the rights of individuals. The trend is lumpy but no state goes backward in any of these key respects of westernisation and still remains an economic success (Singapore is perhaps the exception that proves the rule).'

arises within the older cores of non-Western civilisations, most notably those centred in Muslim societies and East Asia, which are increasingly able and willing not only to defend themselves, and to project power into their own regions, but to insist on the legitimacy of their own cultural values. The analysis also ignores the conflict potential generated by the (potential) incompatibility within Western norms. The tense and often contradictory relationship between market and state is among the best-known,[23] but perhaps the more striking fact is that because the category of global civil society is neglected so too are the forces within it that generate normative conflicts. The disregard of public spheres of non-violent controversy about who gets what, when and how – one of the defining organising principles of the West – is a case in point. So too is the neglect of religion, which (intended or not) creates the secularist impression that religion is 'withering away'. Most definitely it is not, which is among the reasons why ethical standards are currently alive and well within civil society at the global level, why global civil society itself is normatively contested – and why various attempts are currently underway to elicit its First Principles and, thus, to defend and justify it as a normatively superior form of life.

First Principles?

The Club of Believers in First Principles has a wide range of different members. While they have in common one basic characteristic – their commitment to specifying a set of *universal* ethical principles that in some way could serve as both inspirational motive and a guide to practice – each pursues (as we shall see) quite different strategies of ethically justifying global civil society. It is important to be aware of their approaches – if only to assess their respective degrees of plausibility.

Natural law

The history of modern ethics, beginning with *The Rights of War and Peace* by Hugo de Groot,[24] has seen many attempts to establish universal standards of ethics that are said to be objective because they conform deductively to the tenets of *natural law*. Such attempts have their antecedents in the search within Roman law for a body of first principles – the *jus gentium* – that could be applied to all the peoples governed by that law. This body of principles subsequently was often described and analysed

---

[23] See Claus Offe, *Contradictions of the Welfare State*, ed. John Keane (London, 1984).
[24] Hugo de Groot, *De Jure Belli ac Pacis*, 3 vols. (London, 1715).

as *jus naturale* – as a body of natural law that served as an incontestable standard for deciding how all human beings should live together under the laws. Natural law reasoning undoubtedly has had 'secular' intentions, outlined in the famous (originally theological) formulation that natural laws are valid even if God does not exist or human affairs are not in his care (*etiamsi daremus non esse Deum aut non curari ab eo negotia humana*). The natural law approach also implies that ethics should not depend upon convention, but only on 'nature', usually understood as 'human nature' itself. This criterion functions in effect as *the* standard for reasoning about ethical standards – as the criterion of validity that is logically prior to, and independent of, actually existing or 'positive' laws or customs. Natural law is a system of ethics that is binding upon all individuals; it calls upon them to recognise and respect its rules, by means of such 'natural' faculties as the capacity for reason.

Today, the most common and influential version of this approach is the doctrine of universal human rights. Among its earliest statements is J. G. Fichte's *Grundlage des Naturrechts nach Principien der Wissenschaftslehre* (1795–6), which vigorously defends 'cosmopolitan right' as the 'original human right which precedes all rightful contracts and which alone makes them possible . . . the one true human right that belongs to the human being as such: the right to be able to acquire rights'.[25] Fichte of course stipulated that these rights be made strongly conditional upon the foreigner's 'unavoidable' acknowledgement of and respect for the powers of sovereign territorial states. He did not spot the (potentially) tense relationship between these states and universal human rights, but exactly that tension has come to dog discussions of human rights. One way forward – the move has been a source of inspiration to two generations of supporters of the growth of global civil society – is to posit the *universal primacy* of human rights, such as the freedom from torture and arbitrary government and, more positively, the entitlement of citizens to healthcare and education that is provided collectively.

The ethic of human rights – the claim that global civil society is its outcome and guarantor – has been criticised on several grounds. There are certainly deep ambiguities within the definition of what counts as 'human' or 'human nature'; the book of human nature, when opened, is not easily read and in any case gives rise to competing and sometimes hostile interpretations. Talk of human rights and human rights abuses is also vulnerable to the objection that it rests on the hidden presumption

---

[25] J. G. Fichte, *Grundlage des Naturrechts nach Principien der Wissenschaftslehre* (1795–6), in *Johann Gottlieb Fichtes sämmtliche Werke*, ed. I. H. Fichte (Berlin, 1845–6), vol. 3, p. 384.

that being human is a good thing, or that humans are good, or at least that humans are 'essentially' capable of goodwill. Such objections are telling and in practice they fuel the search for different, more secure ethical arguments in support of global civil society.

A human consensus?

Standards of ethical behaviour based on natural law theories are derived deductively from First Principles like 'all human beings are equal, and are therefore entitled to live within a global civil society and to exercise their rights equally'. By contrast, there is a second type of ethical justification of global civil society that is reached inductively. Persuaded by Hume's thought that 'mankind [*sic*] is much the same in all times and places',[26] this approach argues that there are certain First Principles of global civil society, and that these can be divined from the historical and/or actual observation that certain ethical standards, or some version of these standards, have come to be common to all of humanity, in all times and places. Hume observed that human cooperation – two men rowing a boat, for instance – results not from rational promising and contracting among individuals, but from trial-and-error recognition of the advantages of rubbing along together – of jointly learning to taste 'the sweets of society and mutual assistance'.[27] Neo-Humean approaches to ethics emphasise that basic agreements among all human beings (*consensus humani generis*) can and do encompass such matters as respect for life, freedom from fear, and adequate food, clothing and shelter. Proponents of this human consensus approach are notably shy of being too specific on these matters. They typically adopt a dynamic standpoint, in that they argue for the *possibility* of developing a transcultural consensus about 'common human values' through intercultural exchanges.

Parekh's defence of a species of non-ethnocentric 'minimum universalism' falls into this category.[28] He supposes that there are some definable universal values that can and should function as a basic ethical

---

[26] David Hume, *Essays Moral and Political*, eds. T. H. Green and T. H. Grose, 4 vols. (London 1875), vol. 2, p. 68.

[27] David Hume, *A Treatise of Human Nature: Being an Attempt to Introduce the Experimental Method of Reasoning into Moral Subjects* (London, 1739), book 3, section 7.

[28] Bhikhu Parekh, 'Non-Ethnocentric Universalism', in Tim Dunne and Nicholas J. Wheeler (eds.), *Human Rights in Global Politics* (Cambridge and New York, 1999), pp. 128–59. Parekh refines the details of his argument in *Rethinking Multiculturalism* (London, 2000) and 'Cosmopolitanism and Global Citizenship', a revised typescript first delivered as the E. H. Carr Memorial Lecture (University of Wales at Aberystwyth, 2002).

threshold, as a kind of 'floor' of values that no individual, group or whole society can undermine without losing its entitlement to be accepted as 'good', or as worthy of toleration by others. Thanks to the great technological advances of our age, global interdependence is promoting 'a vague but unmistakable sense of global moral community'. So what are these common human values? Parekh speaks of certain 'universal human constants' that both distinguish human beings as superior to the animals and enable human beings to see eye-to-eye with others. These constants include 'human unity, human dignity, human worth, promotion of human well-being or fundamental human interests, and equality'. Parekh denies that these universals are ontological in any simple sense, that they are somehow immune from the vagaries of time and space; they are rather the products of phylogenesis in that human societies 'have decided for good reasons to live by them and confer on them the status of values'. And he admits – echoing Michael Walzer's well-known distinction between the 'thick' lumps of morality of particular human societies and the 'thin' strips of morality that stretch between otherwise different societies[29] – that these universals are stretched and 'thin' compared to the densely bundled or 'thick' moral structures or 'special ties' that give a distinctive shape to different societies and political communities. These human constants nevertheless imply two fundamental duties: not to inflict evils like poverty or torture on others by damaging their ability to pursue their self-defined well-being; and the duty to alleviate their suffering and render them such help as they need, within the limits of the resources that are available. These duties are expressions of our common humanity. They also function as supports in a bridge that enables a 'cross-cultural deliberation on moral values'. Such deliberation is necessary and desirable because although universal human constants are 'universally valid' they are by their nature quite general and in need of interpretation; they need as well to be prioritised and applied to the particular circumstances of each society. Parekh says that any particular society (note the abstract use of the term) cannot presume that others will agree automatically with its own interpretation of any one constant like 'human life'. Respect for human dignity, for instance, can imply the ethic of individualism within a turbocapitalist system or instead an ethic of citizenship bolstered by social security provision; human dignity may be seen, minimally, as the prohibition of enslavement, torture, rape and genocide or, maximally, as the satisfaction of all the desirable conditions of the

---

[29] Michael Walzer, *Thick and Thin: Moral Argument at Home and Abroad* (Notre Dame, 1994).

good life. How to decide among these various options, it might be asked? Parekh's answer: 'an open-minded cross-cultural dialogue in which participants rationally decide what values are worthy of their allegiance and respect'.[30]

This approach suffers from certain weaknesses. Its understanding of 'the human' is rather vague and arguably understates, to say the least, the incurable ethical ambivalence that lies at the heart of 'being human'. And quite aside from the fact that it begs many questions about exactly how an open-minded, robust, uninhibited, cross-cultural dialogue is institutionally possible – the category of public spheres is obviously needed, but goes unmentioned – its avowed attachment to 'rational' decisionmaking and 'dialogue' arouses the suspicion that it *presumes* what needs to be demonstrated: that there is an already-existing will at the planetary level to engage in a cross-cultural dialogue founded upon a prior consensus about being human. No doubt, in certain circles, within ecumenical religious groups, for instance, such a will already exists. But where it does not, and where there is profound disagreement about what being 'human' means, the presumption that rational dialogue is a good thing cannot operate as a life jacket in stormy seas. The case for 'minimum universalism' goes under, dragged down by a presumption that needs to be demonstrated.

Neo-Kantian approaches

Another strategy for rebutting ethical particularism denies that ethical principles of universal scope are uselessly abstract as well as insensitive to ethical differences. It supposes that a set of ethical First Principles can be described and justified through rational procedures. These First Principles, it is said, must take account of empirical conditions and consequences of action without however deferring to either empiricism or consequentialism. The starting point, according to this neo-Kantian strategy, is to explore the possibility that ethical principles that cannot serve for a plurality of different actors should be rejected; and, conversely, that ethical principles must be *universally* applicable. This categorical imperative or Moral Law runs something like: 'Act in all situations and at all times only in accordance with the maxim that your will is at the same time a universal law.' This approach emphasises that ethical worthiness is measured by acting 'out of duty' to universalisable principles. It naturally

[30] Parekh, 'Non-Ethnocentric Universalism', pp. 149–50, 150, 140, 158; cf. 'Cosmopolitanism and Global Citizenship', p. 27: 'What we need . . . is openness to the other, an appreciation of the immense range and variety of human existence, an imaginative grasp of what both distinguishes and unites human beings, and the willingness to enter into a non-hegemonic dialogue.'

questions the view that ethics are bounded by territorial state boundaries and the national and cultural differences they contain. Kant's view that a fully adequate account of ethics must be cosmopolitan is the essential starting point.

Cosmopolitans like to point to the fact that our world is one in which action and interaction at a distance are probable. 'Huge numbers of distant strangers may be benefited or harmed, even sustained or destroyed, by our action, and especially by our institutionally embodied action, or inaction – as we may be by theirs', observes O'Neill.[31] She goes on to ask whether or not that means that we have *obligations* to others who are distant from us. Her reply is that if there is no *general* reason to suppose that distance obstructs action, or that action must affect or respect only a few people, then there is no *general* reason to conclude that justice or other ethical obligations between vast numbers of distant strangers are impossible. She observes that in everyday action actors commonly assume that distant strangers both within and *without* our societies are both agents and subjects. 'Importers and exporters rely on complex assumptions about the capacities of distant trading partners. Broadcasters make complex assumptions about distant audiences; airlines about distant customers; both make assumptions about distant regulators. Banks borrow and lend on complex assumptions about a widely dispersed, possibly global, range of savers and borrowers and about their propensities to deposit and borrow given certain rates of interest.' O'Neill's reasoning, rather like the later Kant's historicised understanding of our status as free beings, depends upon what she calls a 'practical, contextual approach'. Implicitly – though she does not use the phrase – she supposes the existence of a global civil society. She wants to emphasise that in our daily lives 'we' hang on a 'vast web of assumptions'; 'we' constantly assume that countless others whom we will never meet can and do produce and consume, trade and negotiate, translate and settle payments, pollute or protect the environment. It does not follow that we *should* show kindness and beneficence towards them, or that we have the normative resources to discharge our duties towards *all* people. Ethical virtues and duties have to be discharged selectively. That being so, cosmopolitanism today can be only 'approximate moral cosmopolitanism'. Yet since at least some strangers deserve our current solidarity that implies the possibility that 'we' could work towards *institutional cosmopolitanism* – not necessarily towards a stateless world, but towards a world in which certain global institutional forms ensure that ethical boundaries between people become ever more porous.

[31] Onora O'Neill, *Bounds of Justice* (Cambridge and New York, 2000), pp. 187, 183, 201.

God and global civil society

The neo-Kantian perspective on ethics has been criticised for its fetish of reason at the expense of the passions, its empty formalism, its rigid and context-insensitive rules that are blind to the need for 'trade-offs' among conflicting universal rules, and its dependence upon the distinction between the *phenomenal* (natural, causally determined) and the *noumenal* (non-natural, self-determining). These criticisms need not detain us here, because it is easy to see that each of the proposed ethical justifications of global civil society outlined above is marked by scratches and faults. The simple juxtaposition of these various justifications – following the well-known method employed in Abu Hamid Al-Ghazali's *The Incoherence of the Philosophers* (*Tahafut al-falasifah*)[32] – is revealing of their theoretical and practical incompatibility. Much can of course be learned positively from their comparison, including the imperative to *acknowledge* each of them in any revised account of a global ethic. Yet logical flaws and slips of reasoning abound; the vitality of each is hampered by blind eyes or dulled senses about important matters; and when considered together, it is clear that they have not all been cut from the same cloth and that therefore the problem they set out to solve – to settle once and for all questions about the ethical status of global civil society – is compounded by their incommensurability. None of this should be surprising, since elsewhere in the field of philosophy all attempts to provide a rational foundation for ethical principles seem to have failed. One does not have to accept the melancholy conclusion of Wittgenstein – that 'the tendency of all men who ever tried to write or talk Ethics or religion was to run against the boundaries of language. This running against the walls of our cage is perfectly, absolutely hopeless'[33] – to see the initial problem. Since Wittgenstein, techniques of rational argumentation and logical reasoning have become ever more subtle, but the outcome remains the same: confusion and disagreement that resembles the tower of Babel, tempered only by temporary trends in favour of this or that approach – yesterday universal pragmatics and liberal theories of justice, today communitarianism and deconstruction – whose persuasiveness is mainly determined by rhetorical charm, institutional support, charisma, the art of timing and luck.

Given these limitations and outright failures of ethical rationalism, it should not be surprising that there are signs of the rebirth and renewed

---

[32] Abu Hamid Muhammad Bin Al-Ghazali, *The Incoherence of the Philosophers/Tahafut al-falasifah*, trans., introd. and annot. by M. E. Marmura (Provo, UT, 2000).

[33] Ludwig Wittgenstein, 'A Lecture on Ethics', in Peter Singer (ed.), *Ethics* (Oxford, 1994), pp. 146–7.

popularity of religious justifications of ethics. Moral discomfort with ethical confusion is the humus in which the plant of religious ethics grows; it is fed by the sense that although humans cannot avoid reasoning, reason alone is not enough.[34] It is true that the historical and intellectual relationship between religiosity and civil society in its various forms is close, yet tense and complex. The religious origins of civil society are a matter of some dispute. There are for instance Muslim clerics and scholars, Rashid al-Ghannouchi among them, who point out that the basic elements of a civil society were introduced by Islam well before it made its appearance in western Europe.[35] Within Christian Europe, from the sixteenth century onwards, there were contrasting efforts to rescue and defend the ideal of *societas civilis* as an antidote to religious fanaticism.[36] This paved the way, intellectually speaking, for several ironic effects, including arguments for the toleration of (some) religious differences within the Earthly City of actually existing civil society, as well as claims that it is precisely this space for religious toleration, founded on the separation of church from state, that marks off the West as historically unique – and better than other civilisations.

These complex points need not detain us here. They merely serve as something of a backdrop for understanding contemporary efforts to bring the world's religions and their ethics back into the world – to give them a voice in defining the contemporary globalisation of civil society. Religious justifications of global civil society are certainly in abundance. One version is well illustrated in the steely reasoning of the leading theologian, Hans Küng. 'No survival without a world ethic. No world peace without peace between the religions. No peace between the religions without dialogue between the religions', he writes.[37] While acknowledging the ways in which the world's religions have failed to live up to their own prescribed norms, Küng emphasises their surprising degree of consensus about important ethical matters. Each emphasises, for instance, the need for consciousness of a responsibility – towards oneself and the world. Examples of this world-defining ethics include Buddhist 'composure' in

---

[34] See my 'Secularism?', in David Marquand and Ronald L. Nettler (eds.), *Religion and Democracy* (Oxford, 2000); the text of the German Publishers' Peace Prize address by Jürgen Habermas, 'Glauben und Wissen', *Der Tagesspiegel* (Berlin), 15 October 2001; and Wolfgang Kraus, *Nihilismus heute oder die Geduld der Weltgeschichte* (Frankfurt am Main, 1985), p. 138: 'The frustration, the embitterment, the hatred of history, of the illusions of the past and the reality of today are the origin of that nihilism which is inundating us. Nihilism is the other side of the hope for a man-made paradise.'

[35] See my *Civil Society: Old Images, New Visions* (Oxford and Stanford, 1998), pp. 28–31.

[36] Dominique Colas, *Le Glaive et le fléau: Généalogie du fanatisme et de la société civile* (Paris, 1992), esp. chapters 1–3.

[37] Hans Küng, *Projekt Weltethos* (München, 1990), p. xv ff.

dealings with the world; the commandments of the Torah and Talmud; the social duties which structure the whole life of a Hindu; the teachings of Confucius aimed at wisdom; the instructions related to everyday life in the *Qur'ān*; and the preachings of Jesus Christ. All religions, says Küng, require individuals to observe and embrace certain categorical rules and virtues that can guide their worldly actions, from within. Among these 'golden rules' is the importance of working for human well-being. Hence the demand of the *Qur'ān* for justice, truth and good works, the Buddhist doctrine of overcoming human suffering, the Hindu striving to fulfil 'dharma', the Confucian requirement to preserve the cosmic order, including the *humanum*, the Jewish commandment to love God and one's neighbour, and its radicalisation (to the point of loving one's enemy) in Jesus' mountain sermon.

These various ethical strategies – despite their categorical prohibition of such acts as lying, stealing and murder – obviously contain different rules. Some Catholic Christians oppose artificial contraception; some Muslims favour amputation as a punishment for theft; some Hindus defend the caste system; and so on. Yet Küng insists that they are equally united in their opposition to 'unprincipled libertinism' and in their active belief in an unconditioned Absolute. Their commitment to a First Principle is particularly important, for religion brings certainty to the sphere of ethics. It follows, in the face of uncertainty and spiritual emptiness, that religions can bring strength to individuals. They can 'credibly demonstrate with a unique power of conviction a horizon of meaning on this earth – and also a final goal'. Religion puts a sting in the tail of ethical entitlements and obligations; it blesses them with *deep meaning*, with 'absoluteness and universality'.

Global civil society – without foundations

From Capetown to Cairo, and from Fairbanks to Fremantle, such claims usually stir up passionate public controversies about the 'truth' of religion versus the 'truth' of secular views. These disputes are not easily resolved, and often become violently heated, which is why elsewhere I have pointed to the need in ethical matters to call a truce by respecting the Law of Unending Controversy.[38] This practical rule – it is not a 'law' in any received sense other than playfulness – underlines the implausibility of practical attempts to generate ethical consensus through communication (along

---

[38] An illuminating example is Umberto Eco and Cardinal Carlo Maria Martini, *Belief or Nonbelief? A Confrontation* (New York, 2000). See also my essay on the historical origins and contemporary limits of secularism, 'Secularism?', in Marquand and Nettler (eds.), *Religion and Democracy*, pp. 5–19.

the lines of Habermas' well-known formula). It points as well to the improbability of efforts at harmonising competing ethical claims, let alone of crafting something like a meta-language which could satisfy all disputants, reconcile all opposites, and make lions lie down meekly with lambs.

In matters of religion, this Law certainly applies. It helps us to see that human beings can't be absolutely sure that God exists, or does not exist; that when we talk about God we don't know for certain who or what we are talking about; and that, conversely, we don't know how best to summarise, using the language of immanence, the true nature of Humanity and the World. The Law of Unending Controversy begs us to see more clearly that the nineteenth-century secularist view that religion is a man-made whopping tale, and that religious believers are therefore like Ixion copulating with clouds and breeding monsters, applies just as well to secularists themselves, who have fared no better in the search for compelling reasons why religion is daft, why we should believe only in ourselves, and why human beings are as we are. Given this stalemate, the Law of Unending Controversy prods us to see that we are left with no other intellectual and political option – if we want to avoid social entropy and political violence – but to seek ways of maximising the freedom and equality and mutual respect of non-believers and believers alike.

The Law of Unending Controversy most definitely applies to religious and non-religious justifications of global civil society. Theological approaches rest upon bold assertions about, and a faithful trust in, the existence of a transcendental First Principle that seeks to explain and make sense of the world. These religious assertions can easily be countered with equally bold 'secular' or this-worldly (immanent) claims, for instance by some species or another of the view that all ethical systems are thoroughly human inventions, more or less elaborate human stories that help to make sense of the vast world in which we are fated to dwell. Much the same dynamic of unending dispute about global civil society applies potentially or actually to all other ethical claims that compete for our attention and favour. All of them are contestable. None of them is immortal. Each one is vulnerable to being picked on and picked open – to expose the fact that they are language games operating according to contingent rules that are often enough incommensurable.

Some might be tempted to draw pessimistic conclusions from this Law of Unending Controversy, for the improbability of permanently settling ethical disputes seems to fling us back into the ranks of the Cantankerous School of ethics. Do not these conclusions imply the permanence of bickering, tension, hot disputation, and potentially violent conflict? Those kinds of outcomes are indeed anathema to the positive spirit of compromise and mutual recognition and acceptance of differences that is so vital to any vibrant civil society. Yet to conclude that the improbability of ethical consensus makes global civil society an impossible ideal is a faint-hearted *non sequitur*. True, the practical adjudication of such claims and counter-claims is not easy, but there is one way in which these normative disputes can be openly handled and reach a compromise, with a maximum of fairness and openness, without igniting violence. It is called – paradoxically – global civil society.

Moralities

In what way can global civil society be understood as a normative ideal? There are at least two overlapping or interdependent ways of responding effectively to this question. Both are necessary ingredients of a new theory of ethics beyond borders. One possible answer to the question is to understand global civil society, in both a theoretical and practical sense, as a condition of possibility of *multiple moralities* – in other words, as a universe of freedom *from* a singular Universal Ethic. The members of every past and present civil society – and, by definition, every imaginable civil society of the future – are tangled in self-spun webs of normative meanings. Civil society so conceived contains many and varied, often competing sets of values and valued ways of living that exist side by side, or pass through, each other. Moral harmony does not come naturally to a civil society. Within its spaces of interaction, instances of what Kant called 'asocial sociability' are commonplace. This follows from the fact that individuals' moral identities are the product of functional differentiation: people participate in various groups and associations, and they therefore do so only with part of themselves. In this way, common ethical bonds are snapped and broken into many separate links of morality. Civil society makes possible, in principle at least, an infinite variety of different morals. This of course sharpens the knives of cynics and critics alike, especially those who highlight its moral incoherence (Etzioni) and unflagging inner capacities for criticising its own power relations.

The objections of these cynics and critics – to put it politely – are to be expected and welcomed within any civil society, precisely because the tendencies towards moral pluralism ('moral incoherence') and self-criticism that they highlight are in fact the normative stuff of which any properly functioning civil society is made. A civil society is full of moral fibres. It comprises many social spaces within which morals of many different varieties can and do seek refuge. Derrida's recent appeal for establishing 'cities of refuge' may be re-interpreted more broadly as a metaphor for imagining what a civil society is and does best: it provides worldly protection for the right and duty of hospitality for refugees from every part of the globe.[39] Within a world otherwise riddled by violence, great imbalances of wealth, and nasty prejudice, global civil society is a safe haven that guarantees the right to asylum for many different and potentially or actually conflicting morals. It provides *permanent* sanctuary for those who do not necessarily agree. In respect of this permanency, it goes beyond what Kant had in mind when he spoke of civil society – using the classical rather than the modern understanding of this term – as a place where universal peace can reign because strangers, exercising their natural right of *visitation* (*Besuchsrecht*), can enter and reside there *temporarily*.[40] Civil society rather guarantees the right of *permanent residence* (*Gastrecht*) for moralities of all kinds. This is why those who live within its bounds are duty-bound to enjoy and protect some of its moral ground rules.

These rules are today most often summarised, rather too glibly, in the phrase 'social capital'. 'By the term "social capital" ', one of its best analysts writes succinctly, 'we refer to a syndrome of cognitive and moral dispositions of citizens that lead them to extend trust to anonymous fellow citizens (as well as the political authorities that, after all, one's fellow citizens have endowed with political power), to practise the "art of association", and to be attentive to public (as opposed to their own narrowly circumscribed group-specific) affairs and problems'.[41] If a civil society is rich in social capital in this sense, then what are its moral attributes, we might ask? To begin with, a civil society is equipped with what might be called '-ism-shields'. Its members cultivate the understanding – traceable to eighteenth-century figures like Thomas Paine, the inventor of the modern term 'civilised society' – that few things have brought greater harm to the world than the belief on the part of individuals or groups or parties, states, churches or whole nations that they are in *sole* possession of 'the truth', and that therefore those who differ from them must be not merely wrong-headed, but depraved, mad or wicked. The morals of a civil society stand guard against presumption and arrogance and hatred. Its morals are *humble* morals. They embrace the ancient dictum of Al-Shafi'i: 'my opinion is correct but capable of error, and the opinion of the other is erroneous but capable of being correct'. Thereby these morals

[39] Jacques Derrida, *Cosmopolites de tous les pays, encore un effort!* (Paris, 1997). See also the meditation on refuge and hospitality in Emmanuel Levinas, 'Les Villes-refuges', in *L'Au-delà du verset* (Paris, 1982).

[40] Immanuel Kant, *Zum ewigen Frieden. Ein philosophischer Entwurf* (Königsberg, 1795), third article.

[41] Claus Offe, 'Civil Society and Social Order: Demarcating and Combining Market, State and Community', *Archives européennes de sociologie*, 41:1 (2000), p. 94.

ensure as well deep suspicion of stereotypes – unfounded rumours and claims that others are stupid, or inferior, or downright evil.[42] Civil societies undoubtedly nurture stereotypes. The public freedoms they cultivate enable individuals and groups to clown around (send the old out into snowstorms, send all men to the moon, especially since they've already been there) but also to say serious things with greater consequence, like: blacks are all brawn and no brain, the Irish are romantic drunks, the Jews are calculating money grubbers, and Muslim men are religious fundamentalists who maltreat women. But the fact that civil societies harbour many moralities means that they also enable the heaping of profound public suspicion upon such stereotypes – and resistance to social complacency as well. Civil society can cultivate social mediocrity, a general lack of adventurousness about life. Its members can smugly come to believe in their own good-natured tolerance and acceptance of the 'other': the 'good' other, of course, the citizen who favours all the things we favour, like parliamentary democracy, free markets, caring for the environment, feminism, and freedom of opinion, of course. Philosophers of ethics sometimes reinforce such smugness by giving the impression that 'being good' is natural.[43] Not only is that conclusion historically naïve. It also understates the *dynamics* of civil societies, their tendency to stimulate their members' sensitivity to the language in which differences are described. They institute a learning process that by definition cannot come to an end: a process of recognising that it is possible to lead lives very different than our own, and that coming to understand that accepting or compromising with others whom we know little about, or do not understand, or for whom we have little or no sympathy, is the mark of civility.

Civility

To say that civil societies are havens of moral pluralism is to force a rethinking of the concept of civility. The moral language of civility has an ambiguous history with ambiguous effects. During the early modern period in Europe, and especially in the Atlantic region between the time of

---

[42] See Isaiah Berlin, 'Notes on Prejudice', *The New York Review of Books* (October 18 2001), p. 12.

[43] An example is found in Simon Blackburn, *Being Good. A Short Introduction to Ethics* (Oxford, 2001), section 21: 'Gratitude to those who have done us good, sympathy with those in pain or in trouble, and dislike of those who delight in causing pain and trouble, are natural to us, and are good things. Almost any ethic will encourage them . . . these are just features of how most of us are, and how all of us are at our best'. Note the hesitation – rather characteristic of life in a civil society – about whether to speak of 'us' or 'most of us' (and one should add 'some of us') in matters of morals.

the American and French Revolutions, 'civility' and 'civilised' typically
referred to bodily manners and speech that gave others the positive impression of being 'polite', 'polished', 'cultivated' – in contradistinction
to the 'rude', 'uncivill', 'impolite', 'bellicose', 'savage' and 'barbarian'
habits of the great unwashed majority of the population living at home
and abroad.[44] The famous late seventeenth-century epistolary conversation between the philosopher John Locke and the Dublin gentleman-
politician William Molyneux is a slow-motion exemplar of such attitudes:
their extended conversation is oiled by gentle appeals to informality, the
avoidance of inherited prejudice and febrile zeal, the celebration of en-
lightened 'politeness', talk of the love of 'experimental knowledge' and
'truth', and it is marked at one point by Locke's good-mannered evasion
of his partner's question concerning why Ireland – and by implication
any colony – should be subservient to England given the Lockean claim
that a people cannot be bound to government, except through their own
consent.[45] The particular example reveals the more general point that
civility was a privileged discourse of the privileged; it supposed and required the exclusion of whole categories of the world's population because
of such 'inferior' characteristics as skin colour, gender, religion or lack of
upbringing.

Most of these old meanings of civility – with the exception of 'bellicose'
or 'violent' – understandably grate on the conscience of today's friends
of civil society. For them, 'civility' has quite different connotations: it
means not only 'non-violent', but also 'respectful of others', 'polite towards strangers', 'tolerant', even 'generous'. The connotative change is
immense. It dovetails with these reflections on the morals of civil society,
and could be summarised in the following formula: civil are those individuals and groups who use such techniques as indirection, face-saving
and self-restraint to demonstrate their commitment, in tactful speech and
action and bodily manners, to the worldly principle of a peaceful plurality
of morals.

Civility in this sense implies that civil society is marked permanently
by moral ambivalence. 'Morality is incurably *aporetic*', observes Bauman.
'Few choices (and only those which are relatively trivial and of minor

---

[44] See Jean Starobinski, 'Le mot civilisation', *Le temps de la réflexion* (Paris, 1983), part 4,
pp. 13 ff.; Jörg Fisch, 'Zivilisation, Kultur', in Otto Brunner *et al.* (eds.), *Geschichtliche
Grundbegriffe. Historisches Lexikon zur politisch-sozialen Sprache in Deutschland* (Stuttgart,
1992), vol. 7, pp. 679–774; and Robert Hefner (ed.), *Democratic Civility: The History and
Cross-Cultural Possibility of a Modern Political Ideal* (New Brunswick, NJ, 1998). Compare
the revised philosophical account of civility in Mark Kingwell, *A Civil Tongue. Justice,
Dialogue, and the Politics of Pluralism* (University Park, PA, 1995).
[45] First published in rather inaccurate form in *Some Familiar Letters Between Mr Locke and
Several of his Friends* (London, 1708).

existential importance) are unambiguously good. The majority of moral choices are made between contradictory impulses...The moral self moves, feels and acts in the context of ambivalence and is shot through with uncertainty.'[46] Seen from inside this society, moral purity is an existential impossibility. Living a morality is always an ambiguous and trying saga, in that it involves the visceral recognition that the morals of some are an affront to others, or that they simply leave them cold. That is why it entails as well the recognition that the price of sticking to one's morals through thick and thin (vividly highlighted in Nick Hornby's novel *How To Be Good*) is the loss of a sense of humour, and of what is called common sense. Naturally, morals require moral *judgements*. Navigating through daily life and social relations more generally requires constant efforts at explaining differences, forging agreements, pretending that we tolerate differences, criticising excesses, telling others off, being diplomatic, making compromises, avoiding clashes, patching up differences, saying nothing, turning a blind eye. None of this adds up to moral consistency. It certainly has nothing to do with moral universals, which do not and cannot exist so long as a civil society remains a civil society. Moral algebra – trying like Procrustes to fling morals onto a rack and to stretch and reshape them so that they fit a regularised grid of certainties, so that life can be lived 'according to proper morals' – is anathema to civility.

Towards an ethic of civil society

So much for a brief summary of why global civil society should comprise a wide variety of morals. Naturally a new question arises: should anything

---

[46] From the stimulating reflections on morality of Zygmunt Bauman, *Postmodern Ethics* (Oxford and Cambridge, MA, 1994), p. 11. The following paragraph draws upon Bauman, but it strongly rejects, by way of an immanent critique, what elsewhere I have called his dogmatic pessimism in matters of politics and (in this work) his moral melancholia. It is significant that Bauman's account of 'modernity' is silent about either civil society or public spheres or representative-legal-democratic norms and institutions. The silence leads him to equate modernity with the essentially genocidal search for 'an ethics that is universal and "objectively founded"'. Post-modernism is then linked with the struggle to recognise a plurality of *morals* and the *moral ambivalence* of meaning-creating, self-responsible subjects. Bauman does not see that this universalising prescription contradicts itself. Nor does he ask after the *tu quoque* institutional preconditions – civil societies, public spheres, representative-legal-democratic institutions – of moral ambivalence. He leaves us only with a species of existentialism that could be said to resemble either the former 'dissident' stance in central–eastern Europe (the anti-political 'living in the truth') or a version of Michel Foucault's morality of 'souci de soi', 'self-concern', the self-realisation of the individual *against* any generally valid ethics. The genealogy and limits of the former are discussed in my *Václav Havel: A Political Tragedy in Six Acts* (London and New York, 1999), pp. 268–86. My previous comments on Bauman's dogmatic pessimism are found in *Civil Society: Old Images, New Visions* (Oxford and Stanford, 1998), pp. 127–9.

go within this society? Given that actually existing global civil society is pushed and pulled internally by a large variety of morals, some of which (like global terrorist networks) are morally dubious to say the least, can and must we conclude that each and every one of these morals be understood as 'valid' or 'legitimate'? The answer is a resounding 'no', and not only because – *pace* the School of Cantankerousness – letting hundreds of flowers bloom will lead sooner or later to the tyranny of weeds. The negative answer is driven by counterfactual reasoning to ask after the positive conditions of possibility of a plurality of morals. Here we come to ask after the *universalisable* Ethic of global civil society.

This society can be seen as the ethical *conditio sine qua non* of moral pluralism. Insofar as global civil society has to do with an *ethos* in the strict original meaning of the word, that is, with the home, the residence, the familiar place of dwelling, the manner in which we relate to ourselves in re-lation to others, this society and its institutional structures enable morals to survive and thrive. Considered as an ethical ideal, global civil society parts company with all versions of the old-fashioned, originally Platonic ideal of gathering together and subsuming all differences within a single Universal Ideal. It has no truck with *Gleichschaltung* in any form. It assid-uously resists all political campaigns to asphyxiate differences and above all eliminate all obstreperous and 'wild' sources of moral judgement. In this respect, the ethic of global civil society rejects the new-fangled post-modernist glorification of singularity – the dogmatic emphasis on the variety of different contexts and ideals. The ethic of global civil society steers a course through Plato and post-modernism, and in doing so it goes beyond each of these two extreme ways of thinking about ethics. Like post-modernism and other species of pluralism, the ethic of global civil society celebrates social diversity, but it does so by asking after the universal preconditions of dynamic social diversity. It takes a fresh look at what was earlier described as the problem of *alterity*. It points espe-cially to the need to think against common sense views of clashes and conflicts among morals, to see instead that in all situations except those in which violence has erupted, 'our' morals and 'their' morals, self and other, the internal and the external, are not in fact opposites, but are *always inside one another*. Which is to say, to put it most simply, that the durable co-existence of many moral ways of life requires each to accept unconditionally the need for the institutions of a civil society.

So understood, global civil society is not only (to use the words of Hannah Arendt) a space within which 'the infinite plurality and differ-entiation of human beings'[47] can appeal and flourish. It is also an ethical

---

[47] Hannah Arendt, *The Origins of Totalitarianism* (London, 1973), p. 438.

ideal that is universally applicable – in China no less than in Chile, in Afghanistan as well as Andorra – precisely because it is the only ethic capable of recognising and respecting a genuine plurality of social differences. Of course, in practice, this universal ethic can be rejected. A gun may even be waved about, or electrodes applied to someone's genitals, to make the point painfully clear. The structures of a global civil society can be mocked, cunningly avoided, killed off. But those who so reject those structures perforce suppose that they themselves are above and beyond all idle chatter about morals – that the way they live, or intend to live, is the way everybody else should live. Like all Robespierres of the world, they get on with the job of ushering in the bright dawn of universal satisfaction – their *own* satisfaction – sealing their work if necessary with fear and blood. They pursue their First Principle and in so doing exterminate morals.

Global civil society is not an ethical First Principle in this sense. It cannot and should not be compared to the belief in Universal Satisfaction, or a God, or to any other species of other-worldly or this-worldly Universal Principle that subordinates and stifles all particularities. Global civil society is rather to be interpreted as an implied logical and institutional precondition of the survival and flourishing of a genuine plurality of different ideals and forms of life. This precondition is anchored within the actually existing global civil society, whose functioning relies upon the more or less unuttered inference that it is a space of many ideals and ways of life, and that civil society for that reason is a good thing. It is as if global civil society requires each of its participants or potential members to sign a contract: to acknowledge and to respect the principle of global civil society as a *universal* ethical principle that guarantees respect for their moral differences.

The ethic of global civil society is of course not 'timeless'. It has a past history and an uncertain future. It could be that it will perish, the victim of force of arms or accumulations of arrogant power. It is not a transhistorical or supra-historical ideal in any conventional sense. Yet in spite of its mutability, global civil society is not just one moral norm among others. Like a large and elaborate table that serves as the structure that facilitates a round-table meeting – or like the network of air traffic control systems that span the globe – global civil society is a 'categorical' – not a 'hypothetical' – requirement in the sense of Kant. Everyone who likes participating within global civil society, or who wants to, must observe its normative rules. It is categorical, without any ifs and buts, in that it is the condition of possibility of the dynamic interactions among its manifold social participants. Global civil society promotes awareness of differences, but it also implies and requires awareness of connections.

In order for its differences to be recognised and contested as such, global civil society must be present as a common framework of intelligibility that encompasses the principles, means, modes and substance of disagreement. Understood in this way, global civil society is a universal ethical ideal. But it is a universal principle with a difference. It is the universal precondition of the open acceptance of difference. In the absence of its institutional structures, different individuals, groups, movements and organisations cannot otherwise co-exist peacefully. So, those who support it should not be embarrassed by questions about its 'founding' philosophic or ethical principles. The fact is that it does not have need of any such First Principles.

Bassam Tibi has correctly observed that the ethic of a civil society serves as something of a bridge linking differences among widely different societies equipped with different morals.[48] This is so, but the non-foundationalist understanding of global civil society sketched here is nonetheless vulnerable to those forces – individuals, groups, movements, organisations – that want nothing of social pluralism and everything of their own particular way of life. Bombers with a bee in their bonnet determined to level a concrete shopping mall onto the heads of shoppers, angry artillery men pounding civilian life into the ground, fat cats selfishly preoccupied with adding to their wealth and income at the expense of others: what does the ethic of global civil society have to say to such figures? Quite a lot. In principle, the ethic of global civil society does not tolerate its intolerant opponents. It cannot do so because that would be to contradict and weaken its own spirit of generosity. The friends of global society must always be on the look-out for its opponents, who cannot be allowed to experiment on others with their own winner-take-all obsessions. Monism is always and everywhere a threat to the pluralism of civil society. There are of course no hard-and-fast rules for spotting and dealing with monist opponents of global civil society. There is simply no substitute for the task of making difficult judgements in particular contexts, which is why the friends of global civil society must always keep an open mind about the different forms of monism that spring up within its spaces, or threaten it from outside. Some forms of monism – like fascist cells – have monistic effects from start to finish. Other forms have unintended mixed effects – defences of 'the nation' are a case in point – while sometimes there are cases – think of the protest of Romantic artists and their supporters against modernity – that end up having pluralising

---

[48] Bassam Tibi, 'The Cultural Underpinning of Civil Society in Islamic Civilization', in Elisabeth Özdalga and Sune Persson, *Civil Society, Democracy and the Muslim World* (Istanbul, 1997), pp. 23–31.

effects on actually existing civil societies by adding to their repertoire of diversity.

Defensive means

Sensitivity to ambiguity and awareness of irony are important components of the ethic of global civil society, as is the concern for developing a variety of sensible techniques for handling its opponents. The arsenals of global civil society can be stocked with various defensive means. Broadly speaking, they are of two types. Political, legal and police–military means emanate from within governmental institutions and they are by definition 'external' to the institutions of global civil society. They can powerfully function as enabling devices for the non-governmental sphere, for instance by providing military and police protection; casting nets of legal contracts over individuals and whole social groups; enabling the legal representation of social grievances through the courts; and disbursing of financial resources in support of the infrastructures of global civil society. These *governmental* sources of protection of pluralism – treated in the previous section – can in principle be supplemented by *non-governmental* means that arise from within global civil society itself.

With the clear exception of money-mediated market relations, these social mechanisms have in general been poorly researched and for reasons of space can be only mentioned here. They include lots of different and interesting practices with enigmatic effects. Many living within a civil society sense in their own way the truth of Oscar Wilde's one-liner: 'Any preoccupation with ideas of what is right or wrong in conduct shows an arrested intellectual development.'[49] That is to say, a well-developed sense of humour, especially of the kind that pricks the pride of the pompous, is an important social lubricant, if only because it encourages a healthy appreciation of the ironies of life. Then there are other non-governmental weapons in defence of civility: the learned art of

---

[49] Oscar Wilde, *The Complete Works of Oscar Wilde* (Leicester, 1987), p. 1113. The 'democratisation' of humour, a specifically modern development, contrasts with the treatment of humour as bad taste among the early modern European upper classes. 'Jesters, satyrs, peasants, drunks, bagpipe-players', comments Johan Verberckmoes, 'were all presumed to be the opposite of what a civilized person was supposed to be' ([*Schertsen, schimpen en schateren: Geschiedenis van het lachen in de zuidelijke Nederlanden, zestiende en zeventiende eeuw*], Nijmegen, 1998, p. 47, cited in Benjamin Roberts, 'Humor', in Peter N. Stearns (ed.), *Encyclopedia of European Social History. From 1350 to 2000*, Detroit, 2001, vol. 5, p. 132). Only later, roughly around the time of the eighteenth-century modernisation of the old language of civil society, did 'civilised' people come to value humour as a substitute for fighting duels, as a technique for resolving differences with the witty tongue rather than the sword. The role of humour in this civilising process deserves much greater attention from researchers.

learning through exposure to otherness – 'imparative' reasoning[50] – and of negotiating and striking compromises that are mutually agreeable, for instance through conferences and parallel summits; the persuasion of others through the force of better arguments, or what Jürgen Habermas has famously called 'communicative action orientated to reaching consensus' (*Verständigungsorientierten Handelns*); the exercise of civil virtues like charity, meekness, and humility[51]; the ostracism of uncivil offenders through shame campaigns; and cultivating the ability to live according to the standard that there can be no future for global civil society unless there is forgiveness of others who have wronged.

Long-distance responsibilities

These are just some examples of the governmental and non-governmental mechanisms that can be used to combat the various forms of dogmatism and hostility that can tear apart the delicate tissues of global civil society. These mechanisms may not always be effective and at certain times and places they may well have contradictory effects. The only thing that is certain is that those who suppose that global civil society can do without them are naïve. This civil society is a shaky order. It contains forces of stability and forces of entropy; its universal potential is constantly thwarted; its vision of a unification of worlds is bogged down in misunderstandings and confusions. Global civil society has no 'natural' tendency towards harmony. From within and without it is subject to perennial threats, above all those from power groups that want nothing of its pluralism. That is why the ethic of global civil society – an ethic without foundations – cannot and should not be a soft touch. In the face of a challenge, it is not squeamish. In the absence of a challenge, it is not mopish, a willing victim of ennui. Global civil society is a militant ethic. It is unrelenting in its quest to secure freedom and equality and solidarity through non-governmental links that stretch peacefully to all four corners of the planet. It feels discomfort in the presence of signs like *Linea de policia por favor no cruzar*. Borders are bricked-up windows, armed force, guard dogs, crows'-nests, passports, barbed wire, walls sprayed with graffiti and gang-signs. The ethic of global civil society is certainly not soft-witted about violent threats to its ethos. It knows that there are

---

[50] From *imparare* (Lat.: learning through interaction with others who are different). See Raimundo Panikkar, 'What is Comparative Philosophy Comparing?', in Gerald J. Larson and Eliot Deutsch (eds.), *Interpreting Across Cultures: New Essays in Comparative Philosophy* (Princeton, 1988), pp. 116–36.

[51] See my remarks on Norberto Bobbio's *In Praise of Meekness. Essays on Ethics and Politics* (Cambridge and London, 2000), in *CSD Bulletin*, 9:1 (Winter 2001–2), pp. 15–16.

times when violence must be used as a last line of defence to counter such threats.[52] But – the qualification is unconditional – there is one striking exception to this rule: it concerns instruments of violence that have the technical potential to wipe civil society off the face of the earth.

The unavoidable subject of ethics is made all the more unavoidable because a momentous ethical question now overshadows global civil society. No previous world view has had to cope with it: it is the issue of whether and why human life on earth should continue. Hans Jonas has pointed out that before modern times this issue did not arise. Matters of good and evil were typically local affairs. There was concern with ultimate matters, like the creation of the world and gods and God, certainly. And rulers of empires were required to practise the art of long-distance thinking and planning. Yet the fact is that before modern times the ethical universe of most people, rulers and ruled alike, was neighbourly. Actions had mainly local effects and normative judgements about those actions were correspondingly local matters; since action with long-distance effects was unlikely or impossible for technical reasons – there were no ocean-going warships, jet engines, telegraph systems or an Internet – matters of right and wrong were restricted to the here and now. Ethics were rooted in geographic proximity. 'All this has decisively changed', Jonas writes. 'Modern technology has introduced actions of such novel scale, objects, and consequences that the framework of former ethics can no longer contain them.'[53] Under modern conditions, doers and their deeds have long-distance effects, and the consequence is that the stocks of ethical questions and answers that we have inherited from the past are far too parochial to address these *global* developments. The globalisation of human power, including the technological power to destroy life on earth, reveals that ethical judgements rooted in immediate neighbourhoods and those near and dear to us, while of continuing personal relevance and necessity, are wholly inadequate to the problems now confronting every person living on the planet. These problems are distinguished not only by their implications for the species as a whole, rather than for just a few, but also by their *invisibility*. For instance, parents and grandparents normally know that they have moral obligations to feed, clothe, teach and love their children – and normally they are inventive in finding ways of satisfying these obligations. They can see, and judge, the effects of their own actions. Trouble sets in when human actions, or non-actions, begin

---

[52] This point is developed at length in John Keane, 'Judging Violence', in *Reflections on Violence* (London and New York, 1995), pp. 61–104.

[53] Hans Jonas, *Philosophical Essays: From Ancient Creed to Technological Man* (Englewood Cliffs, 1974), pp. 7–8; see also his *Das Prinzip Verantwortung. Versuch einer Ethik für die technologische Zivilisation* (Frankfurt am Main, 1979), pp. 36, 80, 86, 91, 94.

to have far-away effects. Parents and grandparents may not know of these effects, and so remain blissfully unworried about them. If they do know about them, then they may be told, or come to believe, that others – in far-away institutions – are taking care of those problems. In either case, these parents and grandparents feel little or no interest in, let alone the capacity or obligation to do anything about, those problems.

Enter, stage centre, a global problem like nuclear weapons. The story is told that when the scientist Niels Bohr arrived at Los Alamos in 1943, his first serious question was: 'Is it really big enough?'[54] He was of course referring to the nuclear bomb and whether it would be powerful enough to both end a world war and big enough to challenge humanity to reach beyond man-made death to a world that was peaceful and open unto itself. Bohr's question can be answered retrospectively in a variety of ways. Whether the bomb dropped on Hiroshima subsequently 'kept the peace' is deeply questionable (Peace for whom? How can the claim be verified? What about the present-day nuclear build-up?). It certainly turned the screw, to make the prospect of future war unendurable, if only because it signalled a gigantic increase in the technical capacity to kill and maim people and their environment – and to do so in a frighteningly easy manner. The invention and deployment of nuclear weapons throws into question the huge gap between human omnipotence and human emptiness in matters of ethics. Nuclear weapons have *visible* implications for all people in all local milieux, including households. The global circulation of the first images and eye-witness accounts of the grisly effects of atomic weapons dropped on human beings marked the beginning of this global recognition of a profound ethical problem concerning what some human beings do to others.[55] Since that time, the same problem has not gone away, thanks to the chemical and political fall-out and long-term radiating effects of the splitting of the atom. Untold numbers of households around the world – including my own, in the Australia of my childhood – have suffered death, confusion and disruption at the hands of nuclear testing programmes. The bomb has had globalising effects, among which is the circulation around the world of a chilling clutch of questions: Are some human beings entitled to play with the lives of others, or all others, on a world scale? Would a major nuclear war or nuclear accident be such a bad thing? Why should there continue to be life on earth? Perhaps humanity, like miserable individuals, has the right to suicide? If not, why not?

54 From the third of the unpublished lectures of Robert Oppenheimer, 'Niels Bohr and his Times' (1963), cited in Richard Rhodes, *The Making of the Atomic Bomb* (New York and London, 1988), p. 778.
55 Robert Jay Lifton, *Death in Life* (New York, 1967).

These questions are disturbing, but most definitely warranted, for there are plausible reasons for expecting that human life may well not or cannot survive. Think just for a few seconds of the nuclear weapons stockpiled around the world, or the possibility of a chemical or biological weapons strike by apocalyptic terrorists, or the current radical alteration of the earth's ecosystem by *homo sapiens*. Under pressure from these facts alone, there is some probability that the collective suicide of humanity will happen because of design, or negligence, or unintended consequence. Hans Jonas thought that the long-range effects of technological inventions like nuclear weapons had to be met with a new 'first duty' of a new ethics: the urgent duty of all people to visualise and then ponder the long-range effects of modern technologies. If taken to heart, and acted upon, this duty would lead to a heightened appreciation of just how powerful and successful and *potentially destructive* at least some of these technologies are. The first duty of ethics is to be afraid of the uncertainty that these technologies bring. 'The prophecy of doom is to be given greater heed than the prophecy of bliss', he concludes. The first priority in matters of global ethics is the public cultivation of 'an ethics of preservation and prevention, not of progress and perfection'.[56]

Jonas is right, but the matter of global ethics cannot and should not be left hanging on that soberly apocalyptic note. Reaching for the emergency brake is in some spheres, like the nuclear problem, undoubtedly necessary, but it is not very inspiring. A global ethics needs to open its eyes and stretch out its hands, to embrace something wholly more positive. A start could be made by giving recognition to something new that has been born: the sense among many millions of the world's population that they are living as citizens within a civil society that stretches to all four corners of this planet. This global civil society is a haven of difference and identity – a space of many different, overlapping and conflicting moralities. Those who dwell within it have at least one basic thing in common: they have an ethical aversion to grandiose, pompous, power-hungry actions of those who suppose, falsely, that they are God, and try to act like God. This ethics of pluralism is not negotiable, and it is why civil society, the space of multiple moralities, responds in a thousand different ways to the question, posed by Jonas, as to why the human species should not terminate its own existence: my family, my children; I love my work; I believe in God; life's too much fun. Others would respond by playing music, or drawing and painting, or rolling backgammon dice with others, or hopping on their mountain bikes, or by preparing their fishing nets.

---

[56] Jonas, *Das Prinzip Verantwortung*, p. 70.

Meanwhile, sustained by such responses, an *ethic* of global civil society puts pressure on any and all actors – within the governmental or non-governmental domains – who are tempted to play dangerous games with humankind and its biosphere. This universal ethic heaps doubt on their arrogance. It calls upon them to restrain themselves – and if they fail to do that, the ethic of global civil society, in the name of the supreme ethical obligation to respect humanity in all its diversity, calls for tough action, in the form of practical moratoria on the playing of suicidal power games in any form. Naturally, the ethic of global civil society will still have its opponents. They will table their objections, their ifs and buts. They will grimace and snarl, or prepare their strategies. It would be interesting to know why these opponents are indifferent to questions about why human life on earth should survive. Perhaps the faceless figures of contemporary power – and well-known power experts like Henry Kissinger, Ariel Sharon, Saddam Hussein, Slobodan Milosevic, Osama bin Laden, George Bush, or Jiang Zemin – have more definitive and more compelling answers than that posed by the civil society ethic? Perhaps they should be asked to explain their indifference, or their cynicism? What might they say?

Further reading

Readers interested in deepening their understanding of the subject may wish to consult the following additional literature on global civil society, written at different moments during the twentieth century by specialists in various academic disciplines. The publisher has used its best endeavours to ensure that the URLs for external websites referred to in this book are correct and active at the time of going to press. However, the publisher has no responsibility for the websites and can make no guarantee that a site will remain live or that the content is or will remain appropriate.

For generous and competent research assistance in the preparation of this and other parts of the book, and for the expert preparation of the index, I should like to thank Martyn Oliver.

Jeffrey C. Alexander (ed.), *Real Civil Societies. Dilemmas of Institutionalization* (London, 1998)
Helmut Anheier *et al.* (eds.), *Global Civil Society 2001* (Oxford, 2001)
Raymond Aron, 'The Dawn of Universal History', in Miriam Conant (ed.), *Politics and History. Selected Essays by Raymond Aron* (New York and London, 1978)
Roland Axtmann, 'Kulturelle Globalisierung, kollektive Identität und demokratischer Nationalstaat', in *Leviathan*, 23:1(1995), pp. 87–101
Bertrand Badie, *L'état importé: L'occidentalisation de l'ordre politique* (Paris, 1992)
Gideon Baker, 'The Taming of the Idea of Civil Society', *Democratization*, 6:3 (Autumn 1999), pp. 1–29
Benjamin Barber, *Jihad vs. McWorld: How Globalism and Tribalism are Reshaping the World* (New York, 1995)
Gary J. Bass, *Stay the Hand of Vengeance. The Politics of War Crimes Tribunals* (Princeton and Oxford, 2000)
Ulrich Beck, *What is Globalization?* (Cambridge, 2000)
John Boli and George N. Thomas (eds.), *Constructing World Culture: International Non-Governmental Organizations Since 1875* (Stanford, 1999)
Fernand Braudel, *Civilization and Capitalism. 15th–18th Century*, vol. 1 (London, 1984)
Hedley Bull and Adam Watson (eds.), *The Expansion of International Society* (Oxford, 1984)

John Burbidge (ed.), *Beyond Prince and Merchant: Citizen Participation and the Rise of Civil Society* (New York, 1997)

David Callahan, 'What is Global Civil Society?' www.civnet/org/journal/vol3no1/ftdcall.htm

Simone Chambers and Will Kymlicka (eds.), *Alternative Conceptions of Civil Society* (Princeton, 2000)

Neera Chandhoke, *State and Civil Society. Explorations in Political Theory* (Delhi, 1995)

Neera Chandhoke 'The "Civil" and the "Political" in Civil Society', *Democratization*, 8:2 (2001), pp. 1–24

Steve Charnovitz, 'Two Centuries of Participation: NGOs and International Governance', *Michigan Journal of International Law*, 18:2 (Winter 1997), pp. 183–286

Dominique Colas, *Le Glaive et le fléau: Généalogie du fanatisme et de la société civile* (Paris, 1992)

Fred R. Dallmayr, 'Globalization from Below', *International Politics*, 36 (September 1999)

Jacques Derrida, *Cosmopolites de tous les pays, encore un effort!* (Paris, 1997)

John Dewey, 'Civil Society and the Political State', in Jo Ann Boydston (ed.), *John Dewey. The Middle Works, 1899–1924* (Carbondale and Edwardsville, 1978)

Peter Dicken, *Global Shift. Transforming the World Economy*, 3rd edn., (London, 2000)

Nigel Dower, *World Ethics: The New Agenda* (Edinburgh, 1998)

Tim Dunne and Nicholas J. Wheeler (eds.), *Human Rights in Global Politics* (Cambridge, 1999)

Michael Edwards, *Future Positive. International Co-Operation in the 21st Century* (London, 2000)

Michael Edwards and John Gaventa (eds.), *Global Citizen Action* (Boulder, 2001)

Richard Falk, 'The World Order Between Inter-State Law and the Law of Humanity: The Role of Civil Society Institutions', in *Explorations at the Edge of Time: The Prospects for World Order* (Philadelphia, 1992)

Richard Falk, *Predatory Globalization. A Critique* (Oxford, 1999)

Felipe Fernández-Armesto, *Civilizations* (London, 2000)

A. M. Florini (ed.), *The Third Force. The Rise of Transnational Civil Society* (Tokyo and Washington, DC, 2000)

Ernst Gellner, *Conditions of Liberty. Civil Society and Its Rivals* (London, 1994)

Gary Gereffi and Miguel Korzeniewicz (eds.), *Commodity Chains and Global Capitalism* (Westport, CT, 1994)

Jürgen Habermas, 'Civil Society and the Political Public Sphere', in *Between Facts and Norms* (Cambridge, MA, 1996)

Michael Hardt and Antonio Negri, *Empire* (Cambridge, MA and London, 2000)

Pierre Hassner, *La violence et la paix: de la bombe atomique au nettoyage ethnique* (Paris, 1995)

Robert Hefner (ed.), *Democratic Civility: The History and Cross-Cultural Possibility of a Modern Political Ideal* (New Brunswick, NJ, 1998)

David Held and Anthony McGrew (eds.), *The Global Transformations Reader* (Oxford, 2000)

Eric Hobsbawn, *The Age of Empire 1875–1914* (New York, 1989)

Peter J. Hugill, *Global Communications Since 1844. Geopolitics and Technology* (Baltimore and London, 1999)

Michael Ignatieff, *Virtual War* (London, 2000)

Harold James, *The End of Globalization: Lessons from the Great Depression* (Cambridge, MA, 2001)

Sudipta Kaviraj and Sunil Khilnani (eds.), *Civil Society: History and Possibilities* (Cambridge and New York, 2001)

John Keane, 'Structural Transformations of the Public Sphere', *The Communication Review*, 1:1 (1995)

John Keane, *Civil Society: Old Images, New Visions* (Oxford and Stanford, 1998)

John Keane (ed.), *Civil Society and the State: New European Perspectives* (London, 1998)

Margaret E. Keck and Kathryn Sikkink, *Activists Beyond Borders: Advocacy Networks in International Politics* (Ithica, 1998)

Samir Khalaf, *Cultural Resistance. Global and Local Encounters in the Middle East* (London, 2001)

David C. Korten, *Globalizing Civil Society. Reclaiming our Right to Power* (New York, 1998)

Ira M. Lapidus, *History of Islamic Societies* (Cambridge, 1998)

Emmanuel Levinas, *On Thinking-of-the-Other* (London, 1998)

Ronnie D. Lipschutz and Judith Mayer, *Global Civil Society and Global Environmental Governance. The Politics of Nature from Place to Planet* (Albany, 1996)

Edward Luttwak, *Turbo-Capitalism. Winners and Losers in the Global Economy* (New York, 1999)

William H. McNeill, *The Rise of the West. A History of the Human Community* (Chicago and London, 1963)

Célestin Monga, *The Anthropology of Anger. Civil Society and Democracy in Africa* (Boulder and London, 1996)

Joseph S. Nye and John D. Donahue (eds.), *Governance in a Globalizing World* (Washington, DC, 2000)

Aihwa Ong, *Flexible Citizenship: The Cultural Logics of Transnationality* (Durham, 1999)

Dianne Otto, 'Nongovernmental Organizations in the United Nations System: The Emerging Role of International Civil Society', *Human Rights Quarterly*, 18 (1996), pp. 107–41

Anthony Pagden, *Lords of All the World. Ideologies of Empire in Spain, Britain and France c. 1500–c.1800* (New Haven and London, 1995)

Victor M. Peréz-Diaz, *The Return of Civil Society. The Emergence of Democratic Spain* (Cambridge, MA and London, 1993)

Victor M. Pérez-Diaz, 'La formación de Europa: nacionalismos civiles e inciviles', *Claves* (Madrid), 97 (November 1999)

Kenneth Pomeranz and Steven Topik, *The World That Trade Created. Society, Culture, and the World Economy, 1400 to the Present* (London, 2002)

John Rawls, *The Law of Peoples* (Cambridge, MA, 1999)

David Reynolds, *One World Divisible. A Global History Since 1945* (London, 2000)

T. Risse-Kappen (ed.), *Bringing Transnational Relations Back In. Non-State Actors, Domestic Structures and International Institutions* (Cambridge, 1995)

James N. Rosenau and Ernst-Otto Czempiel (eds.), *Governance Without Government: Order and Change in World Politics* (Cambridge and New York, 1992)

Yoshikazu Sakamoto, 'An Alternative to Global Marketization', in Jan Nederveen Pieterse (ed.), *Global Futures: Shaping Globalization* (London and New York, 2000)

Martin Shaw, *Theory of the Global State. Globality as an Unfinished Revolution* (Cambridge, 2000)

Hernando de Soto, *The Mystery of Capital: Why Capitalism Triumphs in the West and Fails Everywhere Else* (London, 2000)

Ignatius Swart, 'Toward a Normative Politics of Global Transformation: Synthesizing Alternative Perspectives', www.uai.org/uiata/swart1.htm

Charles Taylor, 'Civil Society in the Western Tradition', in E. Groffier and M. Paradis (eds.), *The Notion of Tolerance and Human Rights: Essays in Honour of Raymond Kilbanksy* (Ottawa, 1991)

Bryan S. Turner, 'Orientalism and the Problem of Civil Society in Islam', in Asaf Hussain *et al.* (eds.), *Orientalism, Islam and Islamists* (Brattleboro', VT, 1984)

Robert B. J. Walker, 'Social Movements/World Politics', *Millennium*, 23:3 (1994), pp. 669–700

Paul Wapner, 'The Normative Promise of Nonstate Actors: A Theoretical Account of Global Civil Society', in Paul Wapner and Lester Edwin J. Ruiz (eds.), *Principled World Politics. The Challenge of Normative International Relations* (Lanham, MD, 2000)

Tadashi Yamamoto (ed.), *Emerging Civil Society in the Asia Pacific Community* (Singapore, 1995)

Danilo Zolo, *Cosmopolis: Prospects for World Government* (Cambridge, 1997)

Michael Zürn, 'Democratic Governance Beyond the Nation-State', *European Journal of International Relations*, 6:2 (2000), pp. 183–222

Index